WITHDRAWN

10/94

THE BILL OF RIGHTS

OPPOSING VIEWPOINTS®

Other Books in the American History Series:

The American Frontier
The American Revolution
The Cold War
The Great Depression
Immigration
Puritanism
Slavery

THE BILL OF RIGHTS

OPPOSING VIEWPOINTS®

David L. Bender, *Publisher*
Bruno Leone, *Executive Editor*

Teresa O'Neill, *Series Editor*
John C. Chalberg, Ph.D., professor of history,
  Normandale Community College,
  Consulting Editor

William Dudley, *Book Editor*

AMERICAN HISTORY SERIES

No part of this book may be reproduced or used in any form or by any means, electrical, mechanical, or otherwise, including, but not limited to, photocopy, recording, or any information storage and retrieval system, without prior written permission from the publisher.

Cover photos: (top and middle) Library of Congress, (bottom both) AP/Wide World

Library of Congress Cataloging-in-Publication Data

The Bill of Rights : opposing viewpoints / William Dudley, book editor.
    p.   cm. — (American history series)
  Includes bibliographical references (p.) and index.
  ISBN 1-56510-088-3 (lib : acid-free paper) — ISBN 1-56510-087-5 (pbk. : acid-free paper)
  1. Civil rights—United States. 2. United States—Constitutional law—Amendments—1st-10th I. Dudley, William, 1964-   . II. Series: American history series (San Diego, Calif.)
KF4750.B49   1994
342.73'085—dc20
[347.30285]   93-4575
                                                              CIP

© 1994 by Greenhaven Press, Inc., PO Box 289009,
San Diego, CA 92198-9009
Printed in the U.S.A.

"America was born of revolt, flourished in dissent, became great through experimentation."

Henry Steele Commager, American Historian, 1902-1984

Contents

Foreword

Aboard the *Arbella* as it lurched across the cold, gray Atlantic, John Winthrop was as calm as the waters surrounding him were wild. With the confidence of a leader, Winthrop gathered his Puritan companions around him. It was time to offer a sermon. England lay behind them, and years of strife and persecution for their religious beliefs were over, he said. But the Puritan abandonment of England, he reminded his followers, did not mean that England was beyond redemption. Winthrop wanted his followers to remember England even as they were leaving it behind. Their goal should be to create a new England, one far removed from the authority of the Anglican church and King Charles I. In Winthrop's words, their settlement in the New World ought to be "a city upon a hill," a just society for corrupt England to emulate.

A Chance to Start Over

One June 8, 1630, John Winthrop and his company of refugees had their first glimpse of what they came to call New England. High on the surrounding hills stood a welcoming band of fir trees whose fragrance drifted to the *Arbella* on a morning breeze. To Winthrop, the "smell off the shore [was] like the smell of a garden." This new world would, in fact, often be compared to the Garden of Eden. Here, John Winthrop would have his opportunity to start life over again. So would his family and his shipmates. So would all those who came after them. These victims of conflict in old England hoped to find peace in New England.

Winthrop, for one, had experienced much conflict in his life. As a Puritan, he was opposed to Catholicism and Anglicanism, both of which, he believed, were burdened by distracting rituals and distant hierarchies. A parliamentarian by conviction, he despised Charles I, who had spurned Parliament and created a private army to do his bidding. Winthrop believed in individual responsibility and fought against the loss of religious and political freedom. A gentleman landowner, he feared the rising economic power of a merchant class that seemed to value only money. Once Winthrop stepped aboard the *Arbella*, he hoped, these conflicts would not be a part of his American future.

Yet his Puritan religion told Winthrop that human beings are fallen creatures and that perfection, whether communal or individual, is unachievable on this earth. Therefore, he faced a paradox: On the one hand, his religion demanded that he attempt to live a perfect life in an imperfect world. On the other hand, it told him that he was destined to fail.

Soon after Winthrop disembarked from the *Arbella*, he came face-to-face with this maddening dilemma. He found himself presiding not over a utopia but over a colony caught up in disputes as troubling as any he had confronted in his English past. John Winthrop, it seems, was not the only Puritan with a dream of a heaven on earth. But others in the community saw the dream differently. They wanted greater political and religious freedom than their leader was prepared to grant. Often, Winthrop was able to handle this conflict diplomatically. For example, he expanded, participation in elections and allowed the voters of Massachusetts Bay greater power.

But religious conflict was another matter because it was grounded in competing visions of the Puritan utopia. In Roger Williams and Anne Hutchinson, two of his fellow colonists, John Winthrop faced rivals unprepared to accept his definition of the perfect community. To Williams, perfection demanded that he separate himself from the Puritan institutions in his community and create an even "purer" church. Winthrop, however, disagreed and exiled Williams to Rhode Island. Hutchinson presumed that she could interpret God's will without a minister. Again, Winthrop did not agree. Hutchinson was tried on charges of heresy, convicted, and banished from Massachusetts.

John Winthrop's Massachusetts colony was the first but far from the last American attempt to build a unified, peaceful community that, in the end, only provoked a discord. This glimpse at its history reveals what Winthrop confronted: the unavoidable presence of conflict in American life.

American Assumptions

From America's origins in the early seventeenth century, Americans have often held several interrelated assumptions about their country. First, people believe that to be American is to be free. Second, because Americans did not have to free themselves from feudal lords or an entrenched aristocracy, America has been seen as a perpetual haven from the troubles and disputes that are found in the Old World.

John Winthrop lived his life as though these assumptions were true. But the opposing viewpoints presented in the American History Series should reveal that for many Americans, these assumptions were and are myths. Indeed, for numerous Americans, liberty has not always been guaranteed, and disputes have been an integral, sometimes welcome part of their life.

The American landscape has been torn apart again and again by a great variety of clashes—theological, ideological, political, economic, geographical, and social. But such a landscape is not necessarily a hopelessly divided country. If the editors hope to prove anything during the course of this series, it is not that the United States has been destroyed by conflict but rather that it has been enlivened, enriched, and even strengthened by Americans who have disagreed with one another.

Thomas Jefferson was one of the least confrontational of Americans, but he boldly and irrevocably enriched American life with his individualistic views. Like John Winthrop before him, he had a notion of an American Eden. Like Winthrop, he offered a vision of a harmonious society. And like Winthrop, he not only became enmeshed in conflict but eventually presided over a people beset by it. But unlike Winthrop, Jefferson believed this Eden was not located in a specific community but in each individual American. His Declaration of Independence from Great Britain could also be read as a declaration of independence for each individual in American society.

Jefferson's Ideal

Jefferson's ideal world was composed of "yeoman farmers," each of whom was roughly equal to the others in society's eyes, each of whom was free from the restrictions of both government and fellow citizens. Throughout his life, Jefferson offered a continuing challenge to Americans: Advance individualism and equality or see the death of the American experiment. Jefferson believed that the strength of this experiment depended upon a society of autonomous individuals and a society without great gaps between rich and poor. His challenge to his fellow Americans to create—and sustain—such a society has itself produced both economic and political conflict.

A society whose guiding document is the Declaration of Independence is a society assured of the freedom to dream—and to disagree. We know that Jefferson hated conflict, both personal and political. His tendency was to avoid confrontations of any sort, to squirrel himself away and write rather than to stand up and speak his mind. It is only through his written words that we can grasp Jefferson's utopian dream of a society of independent farmers, all pursuing their private dreams and all leading lives of middling prosperity.

Jefferson, this man of wealth and intellect, lived an essentially happy private life. But his public life was much more troublesome. From the first rumblings of the American Revolution in the 1760s to the North-South skirmishes of the 1820s that ultimately produced the Civil War, Jefferson was at or near the center of American political history. The issues were almost too many—and too crucial—for one lifetime: Jefferson had to choose

11

between supporting or rejecting the path of revolution. During and after the ensuing war, he was at the forefront of the battle for religious liberty. After endorsing the Constitution, he opposed the economic plans of Alexander Hamilton. At the end of the century, he fought the infamous Alien and Sedition Acts, which limited civil liberties. As president, he opposed the Federalist court, conspiracies to divide the union, and calls for a new war against England. Throughout his life, Thomas Jefferson, slaveholder, pondered the conflict between American freedom and American slavery. And from retirement at his Monticello retreat, he frowned at the rising spirit of commercialism he feared was dividing Americans and destroying his dream of American harmony.

No matter the issue, however, Thomas Jefferson invariably supported the rights of the individual. Worried as he was about the excesses of commercialism, he accepted them because his main concern was to live in a society where liberty and individualism could flourish. To Jefferson, Americans had to be free to worship as they desired. They also deserved to be free from an over-reaching government. To Jefferson, Americans should also be free to possess slaves.

Harmony, an Elusive Goal

Before reading the articles in this anthology, the editors ask readers to ponder the lives of John Winthrop and Thomas Jefferson. Each held a utopian vision, one based upon the demands of community and the other on the autonomy of the individual. Each dreamed of a country of perpetual new beginnings. Each found himself thrust into a position of leadership and found that conflict could not be avoided. Harmony, whether communal or individual, was a forever elusive goal.

The opposing visions of Winthrop and Jefferson have been at the heart of many differences among Americans from many backgrounds through the whole of American history. Moreover, their visions have provoked important responses that have helped shape American society, the American character, and many an American battle.

The editors of the American History Series have done extensive research to find representative opinions on the issues included in these volumes. They have found numerous outstanding opposing viewpoints from people of all times, classes, and genders in American history. From those, they have selected commentaries that best fit the nature and flavor of the period and topic under consideration. Every attempt was made to include the most important and relevant viewpoints in each chapter. Obviously, not every notable viewpoint could be included. Therefore, a selective, annotated bibliography has been provided at the end of each book to aid readers in seeking additional information.

The editors are confident that as this series reveals past conflicts, it will help revitalize the reader's views of the American present. In that spirit, the American History Series is dedicated to the proposition that American history is more complicated, more fascinating, and more troubling than John Winthrop or Thomas Jefferson ever dared to imagine.

John C. Chalberg
Consulting Editor

Introduction

"Americans may not always agree on the precise meaning of the Bill of Rights. . . . But the Bill of Rights and civil liberties are a real and vital part of the American political landscape. So are debates over just what these rights are."

On the evening of August 22, 1918, it rained in New York City. Confined to an area near Second Avenue and Eighth Street, this "rain" had a curious meteorological pedigree. The "drops" were large, mostly white, and not at all wet. What exactly was it that fell on the streets of the city on a summer evening near the end of World War I? The raindrops were thousands of leaflets.

Written in English and Yiddish, these leaflets had been thrown from the roofs of buildings along Second Avenue. A surprised store owner picked one up, hurriedly scanned its contents, and instantly became angry enough to race up the nearest set of stairs to find the rainmaker. But he found no one. Disappointed but determined, the merchant delivered the document to the police, who promptly began their own futile search.

The next morning three men appeared at the police station with more copies of the pamphlet. There a captain of the U.S. Army's Military Intelligence Division read the document and declared it to be "of a decidedly seditious character." So dangerously treasonous did he judge its contents that he immediately assigned two detectives to the task of hunting down its phantom distributors.

Methodical searches and neighborhood stakeouts soon netted a number of alleged leafleteers. Within two days Jacob Abrams, Hyman Lachowsky, Samuel Lipman, and Mollie Steimer had been arrested, arraigned, and charged with violating the Sedition Act of 1918. Pending their trial or the appearance of a monied angel of mercy, the four would be confined to the city prison, bail having been set at the then unreachable figure of ten thousand dollars for each of them.

The United States in Wartime

Why the anger and the flurry of police activity? Why the harsh bail terms? And just what was a military intelligence officer do-

14

ing in that New York City police station?

These were not ordinary times. The United States had been at war against Germany and Austria-Hungary since April 1917. For the first time in United States history, an American army had been dispatched to Europe. For nearly three centuries the United States had been a haven for draft evaders as well as ideological and political dissenters from various European countries. Now the United States was drafting an army of its own for service against the kaiser. In addition, the federal government and various state governments were attempting to suppress domestic dissent, no matter what form it might take, because they feared the large and lively opposition to President Woodrow Wilson's decision to join the war.

The United States was far from a united country in the spring of 1917. Many Americans were strongly opposed to going to war on the side of Great Britain. Irish-Americans with long memories of English oppression and German-Americans with more recent memories of the British blockade of their homeland were not eager to come to the rescue of Great Britain. Others, especially midwestern Americans, perceived no danger from the kaiser's army or his vaunted U-boats. Still others, many of them progressive reformers, looked upon Germany as the model welfare state and, consequently, wanted to learn from it, not fight it. In addition, debt-ridden American farmers, especially cotton and wheat farmers, who saw themselves as victims of international finance and the international price of their produce, viewed Wall Street, not Germany, as their enemy. Wall Street, after all, had been quick to come to the financial rescue of England but had never favored cheap money for rural America. Finally, American radicals of many varieties regarded this terrible war as yet another manifestation of the evils of nationalism, capitalism, and imperialism.

On April 6, 1917, fifty representatives and six senators demonstrated how divided America was by voting against President Wilson's request for a declaration of war. And proponents and opponents of American military involvement in the Great War remained at loggerheads throughout that difficult year and right up to Armistice Day, November 11, 1918.

Russian Triumph Inspired American Radicals

In November 1917 many radicals were buoyed by the apparent triumph of bolshevism in Russia. For a good forty years occasional voices for radicalism—socialist, anarchist, and communist—had spoken out in the United States. Many of these radicals were immigrants, a good number of them of Russian-Jewish origin. They came to America fleeing oppression and seeking the equality promised by the Declaration of Independence. During their years in America many of these immigrant radicals became disillusioned. Capitalist America was not an America committed to equality. In fact, as World War I approached, few of them dared any longer to dream that their egalitarian utopia would be realized anywhere on earth.

Then Lenin, Trotsky, and Stalin overthrew the Russian czar and established their own regime, a regime that promised equality to all peoples. The radical spirit, even in America, once again dared to hope.

By the following spring, however, the Bolshevik regime stood in great danger of being swept away. Anticommunist White Russian forces were in open rebellion against Bolshevik rule, and land-hungry German armies were streaming into Russia. To save his teetering regime, Lenin decided that he had no choice but to negotiate with Germany. The subsequent agreement, to which Russia's erstwhile allies in the fight against the kaiser—the United States, Great Britain, and France—were not party, gave Germany the luxury of fighting only a one-front war.

To aid their new White Russian anti-Bolshevik friends, and to make amends for Lenin's act of betrayal, Great Britain and France dispatched troops to the Russian front to prevent Allied supplies from falling into German hands—and to block the spread of bolshevism.

As spring gave way to summer, British and French diplomats increased their pressure on a reluctant Wilson administration to join this Allied anti-Bolshevik effort. The president had advertised himself as a champion of self-determination for people everywhere. Now he was being asked to violate his own standard by sending an army to Russia to help tip the scales against one side in what was essentially an internal conflict.

But by July the president finally relented. Wilson the anticommunist democrat proved stronger than Wilson the proponent of international self-determination. American troops would soon be on their way to both Europe and Siberian Russia.

That military decision prompted the leaflets that descended on the streets of New York City a month later. Those leaflets, in turn, prompted the dragnet that led to the arrest and conviction of their authors and distributors. And those convictions ultimately led to a historic Supreme Court case that produced a landmark dissenting opinion in the unfolding history of freedom of speech in the United States.

Inflammatory Leaflets

What was on those thin sheets of paper? And why were the words so inflammatory? The pamphlet's headline blared: "The Hypocrisy of the United States and Her Allies." In a spare four

16

hundred words, written largely by Samuel Lipman, the pamphlet accused President Wilson of "shameful, cowardly silence" about the real reasons for the American decision to intervene in a civil war against the regime that had withdrawn Russia from the war against Germany.

Afraid of the consequences, Lipman wrote, the president refused to state openly that "we capitalistic nations cannot afford to have a proletarian republic in Russia." But honesty was impossible under any circumstances, he continued, because Wilson was simply an "agent of the plutocratic gang in Washington." To combat that gang of politicians, who he claimed were little more than agents of big capitalism, Lipman called on American workers to come to the support of their brethren in Russia: "Workers of the world! Awake! Rise! Put down your enemy and mine! Yes friends, there is only one enemy of the workers of the world and that is capitalism."

There is no doubt that Lipman and his cohorts were angry. In their view Wilson had lied to the American people when he defended his decision to send troops to Russia as a humanitarian act and as being consistent with the aims of the larger fight against Germany. Wilson claimed that he had to act to save a legion of Czech troops that were trapped on the Russian front when peace had suddenly broken out between Germany and Russia. These Czechs, no longer on a war front, had to be rescued. Or so Wilson rationalized. To Lipman and his compatriots this official explanation was sheer hypocrisy.

Although the pamphlet attacked the evils of the American government, it did distinguish between that institutional hypocrisy and the innocence of the American people. Furthermore, the pamphlet did not call for violence against the hypocrites in Washington, and it did not so much as hint at sympathy for the kaiser or German militarism.

Nonetheless, U.S. attorney Francis Caffey immediately pressed for indictments under the Sedition Act of 1918. Passed to criminalize written and spoken efforts to obstruct the war effort, this legislation was ready-made for an aggressive prosecutor. Caffey had no doubt that he would obtain an easy conviction: Logic said that those who opposed American military intervention in Russia must be supporters of the Bolsheviks; those who sided with the Bolsheviks must be pro-German; and those who were pro-German ought to be tried, convicted, sentenced, and jailed.

In 1917 Harry Weinberger, the lawyer for the defendants, had established a name for himself by defending American radicals who had tried to block implementation of the military draft of 1917. To Weinberger the draft was unconstitutional because it violated the Thirteenth Amendment, which banned not only slavery but all involuntary servitude. In 1918 Weinberger, who called the Bolsheviks the "hope of the world," refused to invoke the writings of Marx or Lenin or Trotsky to defend his anticapitalist idealists. Instead, he turned to the handiwork of James Madison—specifically, to the First Amendment in the Bill of Rights. He charged that the Sedition Act was unconstitutional because it violated the First Amendment provision that "Congress shall make no law . . . abridging the freedom of speech."

The Trial

The presiding judge at the New York trial was one Harry Clayton of Alabama. A longtime Wilson supporter, Clayton had already made it clear that even naturalized citizens who "unfairly" criticized the American government ought to "go back to the country they left." He was also a not-so-silent supporter of the strident patriotism frequently displayed in the streets of New York City. One more bit of evidence that hinted at Clayton's possible attitude toward antiwar dissenters was this: the judge had a younger brother, a colonel in the American army, who was the highest ranking American officer to die in combat during World War I.

Harry Clayton did not merely sit in judgment over the proceedings. He actively participated in the trial. For example, he cross-examined Jacob Abrams, taking exception to the defendant's insistence that he and his compatriots held views similar to "our forefathers of the American Revolution." The judge was not impressed. The gentlemanly revolutionaries of 1776 could not be compared to the scruffy crew who sat in his courtroom. The revolution of 1776 had given the American people freedom and a chance at prosperity. The quartet before him had threatened to overturn the revolution of 1776 and wipe out American prosperity. The judge adamantly asserted, "If we have got to meet anarchy, let us meet it right now." He was all for suppressing any action that threatened the American political system and the war effort of the Wilson administration.

But defense counsel Weinberger was not about to surrender. Yes, his clients were sympathetic to Bolshevik principles and to Lenin's revolution. But they had had no intention of interfering with the Allied war against Germany. Therefore, what was contained in their pamphlet was not seditious. A key feature of the trial was the focus on legal definitions. Just what constituted intent? According to Weinberger, *intent* meant what the defendants *wanted* to happen when they drafted their leaflet. However, the prosecution argued that *intent* ought to include what reasonable people should have known would happen as a result of their behavior. The prosecution contended that the defendants should have known that their leaflet was likely to incite some citizens to obstruct the Allied war against Germany.

On the stand Mollie Steimer conceded that she had wanted to call to the attention of American workers the fact that international capitalism was attempting to crush bolshevism. She also testified that she favored a general work strike in order to block American military intervention in Russia. Clayton interrupted to ask whether such a strike would include workers in munitions factories. Yes, replied Steimer matter-of-factly. Then it was Weinberger's turn to break in: His client sought only to prevent American military intervention in Russia, not to block American prosecution of the war against Germany.

Weinberger went on to defend anarchism generally and his anarchist defendants specifically, all of whom were entitled "to their dreams." They were "liberty-loving" Russian immigrants, not pro-German militarists.

The Verdict

In the end the jury disagreed with Weinberger. After little more than an hour's deliberation, they found all of the defendants guilty of violating the Sedition Act. Each of the three men was fined one thousand dollars and sentenced to twenty years on each of four counts, to run concurrently. Steimer was given a five-hundred-dollar fine and a single fifteen-year sentence.

Weinberger moved immediately to appeal the verdict. Though he was not optimistic about a reversal, he was prepared to take his case all the way to the Supreme Court. In November 1919 the four radicals' appeal was heard by Chief Justice Edward D. White and his eight colleagues. White was a Confederate Civil War veteran who had been appointed to the Court by President Grover Cleveland. Elevated to chief justice by President William Howard Taft, White presided over a Court whose commitment to private property rights was matched only by its fear and hatred of any radical, socialist, anarchist, or other person whose philosophy challenged those rights.

But on this Court were two justices to whom Weinberger expressly hoped to pitch his appeal. One was relatively new to the Court, having been appointed in 1915 by President Wilson. He was also the first Jewish-American to be confirmed to a Supreme Court seat. His name was Louis Brandeis. The other justice was the first Court appointment made by President Theodore Roosevelt. Appointed in 1902 and now better than halfway through an illustrious thirty-year career on the high Court, he was just beginning to take a serious interest in the rights of dissenting minorities. His name was Oliver Wendell Holmes.

Earlier in his career Holmes had invariably supported the state when its interests clashed with the rights of an individual. Order, in other words, came before individual liberty in Holmes's hierarchy of values. For example, on the issue of the constitutionality of the military draft, Holmes was clear and concise. He said, "If conscripts are necessary for [a nation's] army, it seizes them, and marches them with bayonets in their rear, to death."

In another draft-related case Holmes first enunciated his momentous "clear and present danger" test. Charles Schenck, the general secretary of the Socialist party of Philadelphia, had mailed letters to those who had passed draft physicals. In this form letter he attacked conscription as a violation of the Constitution. In all, he sent fifteen thousand such letters. Each contained the following line: "A conscript is little better than a convict." For these words and this use of the mails Schenck was charged with "obstructing the recruiting and enlistment services of the United States." His subsequent conviction resulted in a six-month jail term and a case that wound its way to the Supreme Court.

Holmes voted with the majority to uphold the original conviction of Schenck. In his concurring opinion the justice argued that the "most stringent protection of free speech would not protect a man in falsely shouting fire in a theater and causing a panic." This was the heart of Holmes's clear and present danger doctrine. Schenck, he contended, had presented a clear and present danger to the security of the United States by urging people to ignore the draft.

In 1919 Holmes also voted to uphold the conviction and ten-year sentence of socialist leader Eugene V. Debs, who had admitted that he had tried to obstruct the American war effort. But later that same year the justice began to regret his role in keeping Debs behind bars. The sentence, he concluded, was too long. And Debs, he decided, was not a threat to the United States. True, he was a socialist, but as such, he believed in the ballot box, not bullets.

Such second thoughts led Holmes to enter into a dialogue with more libertarian-minded judges and scholars. The justice had long argued that the law was malleable, that it could change as society's values changed. And as the tumultuous year of 1919 unfolded, Holmes decided it was an appropriate time to rethink his own values.

As anarchist bombs rocked American cities and violent strikes shut down industry after industry, Holmes read and studied the arguments of civil libertarians in the quiet of his study. Some form of his clear and present danger test still made sense to him. But the question was where to draw the line—when did an act actually become a clear and present danger and when was it merely a nuisance?

Holmes slowly came to the conclusion that wartime speech

should be subject to criminal prosecution only if it could be clearly demonstrated to have a directly negative bearing on the conduct of the war. Any government, the justice still maintained, had to be concerned about the preservation of order in the name of the successful prosecution of a legally declared war. But at the same time a compassionate government ought to be concerned about creating an atmosphere of open dialogue. As he learned from his study, "Truth can be sifted out from falsehood only if the government is open to vigorous and constant cross-examination."

In the Highest Court

Holmes may have been moving in a libertarian direction, but he was not moving far enough or fast enough to suit Harry Weinberger. In the defense counsel's view, his clients had confined themselves to peaceful criticism of government policy. He did concede that the controversial leaflet could be construed as "inflammatory," but he asserted that it was still within the legitimate domain of "public discussion of a public policy." Furthermore, that policy concerned the decision to send American troops into a country with which the United States was not formally at war.

In addition, Weinberger continued to assert, the Sedition Act was an unconstitutional interference with the natural right of all citizens to debate all public issues. According to Weinberger only overt acts were punishable. Speech, however inflammatory or otherwise mischievous, must be left perfectly unrestrained.

The Supreme Court, however, was unmoved. By a vote of seven to two the Court ruled that the defendants "must be held to have intended, and to be accountable for, the effects which their acts were likely to produce."

The two dissenters among the nine justices were Oliver Wendell Holmes and Louis Brandeis. In his dissent Holmes drew a precariously fine line when he stipulated that the leaflet had called for a general strike, which, had it been successful, would certainly have curtailed military production. But such a declaration was not a criminal act, he concluded, because there was no "intent . . . to cripple or hinder the United States in the prosecution of the war." Moreover, the purpose of the document was primarily to aid Russia and only secondarily to block American military intervention in the Russian civil war.

Justice Holmes had drawn his line. It was not quite the line Weinberger would have drawn, but it was much closer to the defense counsel's constitutional point of view than it was to that of seven of his brethren on the high Court. To Holmes, and to Weinberger, there had to be a clear and present danger before the government should even think about getting into the nasty business of prosecuting speech, however controversial.

A Compelling Precedent Is Established

While Holmes's dissent did not rewrite the Constitution as of 1919, his reassertion of the clear and present danger formula did gain a constitutional foothold in the Supreme Court even before Holmes retired in 1932. In subsequent Supreme Court cases his formula achieved majority status. This is not to say that the meaning of the First Amendment is now sacrosanct and undebatable. Striking the proper balance between order and liberty is a never-ending task and the source of perpetual conflict, both within the Court and within the country at large.

Meanwhile, two of the defendants, Abrams and Lipman, decided to jump bail and flee to Russia by way of New Orleans and Mexico. Steimer and Lachowsky objected to their compatriots' attempt to escape the legal consequences of their actions. But soon the point was moot. Abrams and Lipman were captured while still on American soil. Instead of finding freedom in the new Soviet Union they were taken to the Atlanta federal penitentiary, temporary home of another dissenter, Eugene Debs.

Ultimately three of the four defendants ended up in that same prison. Steimer was the exception. In 1919 no federal prisons existed for women, so she was sent to the Missouri state penitentiary for women, where she met two other notorious radicals, the anarchist Emma Goldman and the socialist Kate Richards O'Hare.

If Woodrow Wilson had been willing to countermand his attorney general, these four pamphleteers would not have gone to jail at all. Progressive reformers petitioned the president to issue immediate pardons for "our political prisoners." Wilson, who was still recuperating from a stroke he had suffered in September, considered their request. But Attorney General Thomas Gregory persuaded Wilson that there were no political prisoners in American federal prisons. These people, he argued, had violated the law. As such, they were convicted felons, not political prisoners.

Weinberger continued to disagree with Gregory's categorization and to work for the release of his clients. In November 1921 he finally succeeded in obtaining their release, with the proviso that all four accept deportation to the Soviet Union. Abrams and Lipman readily agreed to this condition, which had been negotiated with the new administration of President Warren Harding. Mollie Steimer and Hyman Lachowsky tried to take a different course. Steimer refused the deal out of her love for the United States. Lachowsky did so because, he said, "I think that I have a right to live where I want."

Ultimately, however, all four radicals were deported to the Soviet Union, as a result of a decision by President Harding to shorten their sentences if they could obtain permission to live there. Sadly, it did not take some of these anarchists long to discover that they were as unwelcome in Soviet Russia as they had been in the United States. Within a few years Abrams left his new home, first for western Europe, and finally for Mexico. Lachowsky and Lipman chose to remain in Russia, the latter eventually applying for membership in the Communist party. Both eventually died violent deaths, Lipman at the hands of Stalinists during the purges of the 1930s, and Lachowsky as a result of the German offensive against Russia in 1941.

And Molly Steimer? A dedicated anarchist to the end of her days, she spent two years in "administrative exile" in Siberia before being officially deported from Lenin's paradise in 1923. In 1941 she and her husband joined Abrams in Mexico, where they lived until their deaths.

Ongoing American Story

The case of Abrams, Steimer, Lipman, and Lachowsky did not end when the Court handed down its decision in the fall of 1919. It did not end when Congress repealed the Sedition Act in 1921. It did not end when the four dissenters left the United States. And it did not end when a majority on the Court began to apply the Holmesian clear and present danger criterion.

The case of Abrams, Steimer, Lipman, and Lachowsky is a piece of American history that is also a piece of the ongoing American story. Ironically—and sadly—in a land established to assure the right of every citizen to pursue happiness in his or her own way, and in a land that claims to live under the Bill of Rights, civil liberties have not always been protected. Molly Steimer and her three comrades, many people would say, are testimony to that. But neither are American civil liberties a myth. Americans may not always agree on the precise meaning of the Bill of Rights. They may not even agree on what constitutes a civil liberty. But the Bill of Rights and civil liberties are a real and vital part of the American political landscape. So are debates over just what these rights are.

In 1788 the nation's founders hotly debated whether a bill of rights ought to be included as a part of the Constitution. Patrick Henry and many of his anti-Federalist supporters certainly thought so. In their view the new, more centralized Constitution of 1787 required the specific protections afforded by a bill of rights. To James Madison such bills of rights were already imbedded in most state constitutions, which is just where he thought they belonged. To add a national bill of rights was simply redundant. Worse than that, it would delay adoption of the Constitution itself.

Madison won that debate of 1788. He was instrumental in securing ratification of the new constitution without prolonged debate over a bill of rights. But as a first-term representative he did work to gain passage of the Bill of Rights in the form of the first ten amendments to the Constitution. With the security of the Constitution's ratification behind him, Madison proved more than willing to accede to the wishes of his rivals of 1788.

However, not until World War I, when the United States experienced what Patrick Henry had feared, namely the overreaching power of a central government bent on suppressing dissent, did the Bill of Rights reclaim its place in American history. Granted, the Alien and Sedition Acts of the late 1790s and the demands of the Civil War did occasion the use of federal muscle, which in turn produced a flurry of controversy and concern. But with World War I and a Wilson administration insistent on suppressing dissent came a rebirth of interest in the Bill of Rights. In fact, more than one historian has argued that the efforts of the Wilson administration to squelch wartime dissent led first to the discovery of civil liberties—and ultimately to the rediscovery of the Bill of Rights.

No brief collection of primary sources and opposing viewpoints could possibly provide a comprehensive historical treatment of all ten amendments. What follows is a series of chapters on various aspects of American civil liberties—criminal rights, due process, church-state relations, and freedom of speech. Here is constitutional law with a human dimension. Here are compelling controversies that originated far from the courtroom. Here are intriguing debates and decisions whose ramifications go well beyond the range of any thudding Supreme Court gavel.

But it is not thudding gavels that ensure greater freedom. In a free society there can be no guarantee that freedom will necessarily grow firmer with each new court decision. In a truly free society the only guarantee is that there will be controversy and that such controversy will be resolved by open, spirited, and reasoned debate such as that exemplified in the viewpoints to be found in this volume.

John C. Chalberg
Consulting Editor

CHAPTER 1

Does the Constitution Need a Bill of Rights?

Chapter Preface

The U.S. Constitution as it was originally drafted in 1787 and submitted for ratification to the original thirteen states did not include what we now call the Bill of Rights. This omission was the cause of much debate and controversy as Americans had to decide whether to accept the new Constitution and the federal government it created. The existence of the Bill of Rights today is in large part due to this controversy and especially to the actions and objections of people who opposed the whole Constitution.

In 1787 the United States consisted of thirteen former British colonies loosely bound since 1781 by the Articles of Confederation. Most of the states had fashioned their own constitutions and their own state bills of rights—lists of fundamental freedoms that the government could not infringe. The sources and predecessors of these bills of rights included English law traditions dating back to the 1215 Magna Carta and the 1689 English Bill of Rights, the colonies' original charters, and the ideas concerning natural rights developed by such political philosophers as John Locke and cited in the Declaration of Independence to justify the American Revolution.

The first of the colonies to establish a bill of rights was Virginia, in 1776. George Mason, a Virginia planter and legislator, was the principal author of Virginia's Declaration of Rights. The seventeen-point document combined philosophical declarations of natural rights with specific limitations on government actions. It was a model for other states when they made their own bills of rights for their constitutions.

The Articles of Confederation, which served as the national constitution from 1781 to 1788, lacked a bill of rights. In part this was because the national government it created had little authority by design and was believed by most to pose little threat to civil liberties. Unfortunately, the very weakness of the national government was criticized by many influential leaders for creating its own problems, including failures in conducting a coherent foreign policy, settling disputes between states, printing money, and coping with internal revolts such as the 1786 Shays's Rebellion. A growing number of Americans called for reforming and strengthening America's national government.

It was against this backdrop that American political leaders convened in Philadelphia in May 1787. The stated intent was to amend the Articles of Confederation. Four months later the Philadelphia Constitutional Convention, going beyond its original mandate, had created a whole new Constitution with a stronger national government. But the new Constitution, while it contained some civil liberties measures, still lacked a bill of rights. George Mason was one of several delegates in Philadelphia who argued that a federal bill of rights should be included. His arguments were rejected, and Mason refused to sign the document. His reasons for his refusal to sign, which he wrote in September 1787 while he was still at the convention, were widely published and distributed in the following months. Mason began:

> There is no Declaration of Rights, and the Laws of the general government being paramount to the laws and constitution of the several States, the Declaration of Rights in the separate States are no security.

Mason's essay was one of hundreds of pamphlets, newspaper editorials, and other writings produced between September 1787 and July 1788, the period during which the American states decided whether to ratify the new Constitution. The supporters of the newly drafted Constitution and a stronger national government became known as Federalists, while the loosely organized group of political leaders who opposed the Constitution were called anti-Federalists. The anti-Federalists opposed the new document on several grounds. Among them were the arguments that the presidency it created would result in a new king, that Congress would not be truly representative of the people, and that state and local governments would be jeopardized by the new national government. However, the argument that was most popular and telling with the American people was that the Constitution lacked a bill of rights.

In ratification debates and in pamphlets, the Federalists at first responded to this omission by asserting that the Constitution needed no bill of rights because the new federal government had no power over individual rights and liberties. State governments, and their own bills of rights, were ultimately responsible for protecting people's liberties, according to the Federalists.

Anti-Federalists responded to such arguments by stating that the new Constitution created a stronger government. Such a concentration of power further removed from the people than the state governments, they argued, placed the people's rights in jeopardy if they were not explicitly provided for in a bill of rights.

As popular sentiment for a bill of rights increased and the Constitution consequently seemed in jeopardy of being rejected in the key states of Virginia and New York, a compromise was reached. Anti-Federalists agreed to ratify the Constitution if Federalists pledged to amend it providing a bill of rights. Of the eleven states that voted to ratify the Constitution, six appended to their approval a total of two hundred suggested amendments. It was from these amendments and the debates that created them that the first Congress fashioned what eventually became the first ten amendments to the Constitution, the Bill of Rights.

VIEWPOINT 1

"In forming a government on its true principles, the foundation should be laid . . . by expressly reserving to the people . . . their essential natural rights."

The Constitution Needs a Bill of Rights

Brutus

In the months following the 1787 Philadelphia Convention the states convened special conventions for the sole purpose of ratifying or rejecting the proposed Constitution. One of the most intense debates occurred within the state of New York. Although by the time its ratifying convention assembled on June 17, 1788, most of the states had already approved the Constitution, New York's vote was crucial if the Constitution was to have a practical chance of working. Among the prominent participants in the debate were John Jay, Alexander Hamilton, and Robert Livingston on the Federalist side supporting the Constitution, and Governor George Clinton, Melancton Smith, and John Lansing on the Antifederalist side. One of the main objections of the Antifederalists to the Constitution was that it lacked a bill of rights.

The debates at the convention were mirrored in numerous pamphlet and newspaper debates. The following viewpoint is taken from an influential Antifederalist essay, one of several written under the pseudonym of Brutus. In it the author argues that the absence of a written bill of rights is a fatal flaw of the proposed Constitution. He asserts that the liberties enjoyed by Americans

Brutus, "To the Citizens of the State of New York," *New York Journal*, November 1, 1787.

would be in jeopardy without a written guarantee that they would be preserved, and he rejects arguments that the bills of rights found in state constitutions provided adequate protection.

Some historians have attributed the essays of Brutus to Robert Yates (1738-1801), an attorney and justice of the New York Supreme Court following the American Revolution. A New York delegate at the Constitutional Convention, Yates refused to sign the finished product because he believed it granted too much power to the states.

To the citizens of the state of New-York.

I flatter myself that my last address established this position, that to reduce the Thirteen States into one government, would prove the destruction of your liberties.

But lest this truth should be doubted by some, I will now proceed to consider its merits.

Though it should be admitted, that the argument against reducing all the states into one consolidated government, are not sufficient fully to establish this point; yet they will, at least, justify this conclusion, that in forming a constitution for such a country, great care should be taken to limit and define its powers, adjust its parts, and guard against an abuse of authority. How far attention has been paid to these objects, shall be the subject of future enquiry. When a building is to be erected which is intended to stand for ages, the foundation should be firmly laid. The constitution proposed to your acceptance, is designed not for yourselves alone, but for generations yet unborn. The principles, therefore, upon which the social compact is founded, ought to have been clearly and precisely stated, and the most express and full declaration of rights to have been made—But on this subject there is almost an entire silence.

Natural Rights

If we may collect the sentiments of the people of America, from their own most solemn declarations, they hold this truth as self evident, that all men are by nature free. No one man, therefore, or any class of men, have a right, by the law of nature, or of God, to assume or exercise authority over their fellows. The origin of society then is to be sought, not in any natural right which one man has to exercise authority over another, but in the united consent of those who associate. The mutual wants of men, at first dictated the propriety of forming societies; and when they were estab-

29

lished, protection and defence pointed out the necessity of instituting government. In a state of nature every individual pursues his own interest; in this pursuit it frequently happened, that the possessions or enjoyments of one were sacrificed to the views and designs of another; thus the weak were a prey to the strong, the simple and unwary were subject to impositions from those who were more crafty and designing. In this state of things, every individual was insecure; common interest therefore directed, that government should be established, in which the force of the whole community should be collected, and under such directions, as to protect and defend every one who composed it. The common good, therefore, is the end of civil government, and common consent, the foundation on which it is established. To effect this end, it was necessary that a certain portion of natural liberty should be surrendered, in order, that what remained should be preserved: how great a proportion of natural freedom is necessary to be yielded by individuals, when they submit to government, I shall not now enquire. So much, however, must be given

A Permanent Landmark

Robert Whitehill was a member of the Pennsylvania state assembly and helped write Pennsylvania's 1776 state constitution. In 1787, Pennsylvania held a convention to decide whether to ratify the proposed federal Constitution. On November 28, at the convention, Whitehill attacked the absence of a written bill of rights.

If indeed the constitution itself so well defined the powers of the government that no mistake could arise, and we were well assured that our governors, would always act right, then we might be satisfied without an explicit reservation of those rights with which the people ought not, and mean not to part. But, Sir, we know that it is the nature of power to seek its own augmentation, and thus the loss of liberty is the necessary consequence of a loose or extravagant delegation of authority. National freedom has been, and will be the sacrifice of ambition and power, and it is our duty to employ the present opportunity in stipulating such restrictions as are best calculated to protect us from oppression and slavery. Let us then, Mr. President, if other countries cannot supply an adequate example, let us proceed upon our own principles, and with the great end of government in view, the happiness of the people, it will be strange if we err. Government we have been told, sir, is yet in its infancy, we ought not therefore to submit to the shackles of foreign schools and opinions. In entering into the social compact, men ought not to leave their rulers at large, but erect a permanent land mark by which they may learn the extent of their authority, and the people be able to discover the first encroachments on their liberties.

up, as will be sufficient to enable those, to whom the administration of the government is committed, to establish laws for promoting the happiness of the community, and to carry those laws into effect. But it is not necessary, for this purpose, that individuals should relinquish all their natural rights. Some are of such a nature that they cannot be surrendered. Of this kind are the rights of conscience, the right of enjoying and defending life, &c. Others are not necessary to be resigned, in order to attain the end for which government is instituted, these therefore ought not to be given up. To surrender them, would counteract the very end of government, to wit, the common good. From these observations it appears, that in forming a government on its true principles, the foundation should be laid in the manner I before stated, by expressly reserving to the people such of their essential natural rights, as are not necessary to be parted with. The same reasons which at first induced mankind to associate and institute government, will operate to influence them to observe this precaution. If they had been disposed to conform themselves to the rule of immutable righteousness, government would not have been requisite. It was because one part exercised fraud, oppression, and violence on the other, that men came together, and agreed that certain rules should be formed, to regulate the conduct of all, and the power of the whole community lodged in the hands of rulers to enforce an obedience to them. But rulers have the same propensities as other men; they are as likely to use the power with which they are vested for private purposes, and to the injury and oppression of those over whom they are placed, as individuals in a state of nature are to injure and oppress one another. It is therefore as proper that bounds should be set to their authority, as that government should have at first been instituted to restrain private injuries.

This principle, which seems so evidently founded in the reason and nature of things, is confirmed by universal experience. Those who have governed, have been found in all ages ever active to enlarge their powers and abridge the public liberty. This has induced the people in all countries, where any sense of freedom remained, to fix barriers against the encroachments of their rulers. The country from which we have derived our origin, is an eminent example of this. Their magna charta and bill of rights have long been the boast, as well as the security, of that nation. I need say no more, I presume, to an American, than, that this principle is a fundamental one, in all the constitutions of our own states; there is not one of them but what is either founded on a declaration or bill of rights, or has certain express reservation of rights interwoven in the body of them. From this it appears, that at a time when the pulse of liberty beat high and when an appeal was made to the people to form constitutions for the government of themselves, it was their universal sense, that such declarations should make a part of their frames of government. It is therefore the more astonishing, that this grand security, to the rights of the people, is not to be found in this constitution.

It has been said, in answer to this objection, that such declaration of rights, however requisite they might be in the constitutions of the states, are not necessary in the general constitution, because, "in the former case, every thing which is not reserved is given, but in the latter the reverse of the proposition prevails, and every thing which is not given is reserved." It requires but little attention to discover, that this mode of reasoning is rather specious than solid. The powers, rights, and authority, granted to the general government by this constitution, are as complete, with respect to every object to which they extend, as that of any state government—It reaches to every thing which concerns human happiness—Life, liberty, and property, are under its controul. There is the same reason, therefore, that the exercise of power, in this case, should be restrained within proper limits, as in that of the state governments. To set this matter in a clear light, permit me to instance some of the articles of the bills of rights of the individual states, and apply them to the case in question.

Securing Life and Liberty

For the security of life, in criminal prosecutions, the bills of rights of most of the states have declared, that no man shall be held to answer for a crime until he is made fully acquainted with the charge brought against him; he shall not be compelled to accuse, or furnish evidence against himself—The witnesses against him shall be brought face to face, and he shall be fully heard by himself or counsel. That it is essential to the security of life and liberty, that trial of facts be in the vicinity where they happen. Are not provisions of this kind as necessary in the general government, as in that of a particular state? The powers vested in the new Congress extend in many cases to life; they are authorised to provide for the punishment of a variety of capital crimes, and no restraint is laid upon them in its exercise, save only, that "the trial of all crimes, except in cases of impeachment, shall be by jury; and such trial shall be in the state where the said crimes shall have been committed." No man is secure of a trial in the county where he is charged to have committed a crime; he may be brought from Niagara to New-York, or carried from Kentucky to Richmond for trial for an offence, supposed to be committed. What security is there, that a man shall be furnished with a full and plain description of the charges against him? That he shall be allowed to produce all proof he can in his favor? That he shall see the witnesses against him face to face, or that he shall be fully heard in his own defence by himself or counsel?

For the security of liberty it has been declared, "that excessive bail should not be required, nor excessive fines imposed, nor cruel or unusual punishments inflicted—That all warrants, without oath or affirmation, to search suspected places, or seize any person, his papers or property, are grievous and oppressive."

These provisions are as necessary under the general government as under that of the individual states; for the power of the former is as complete to the purpose of requiring bail, imposing fines, inflicting punishments, granting search warrants, and seizing persons, papers, or property, in certain cases, as the other.

Securing Property

For the purpose of securing the property of the citizens, it is declared by all the states, "that in all controversies at law, respecting property, the ancient mode of trial by jury is one of the best securities of the rights of the people, and ought to remain sacred and inviolable."

Does not the same necessity exist of reserving this right, under this national compact, as in that of this state? Yet nothing is said respecting it. In the bills of rights of the states it is declared, that a well regulated militia is the proper and natural defence of a free government—That as standing armies in time of peace are dangerous, they are not to be kept up, and that the military should be kept under strict subordination to, and controuled by the civil power.

The same security is as necessary in this constitution, and much more so; for the general government will have the sole power to raise and to pay armies, and are under no controul in the exercise of it; yet nothing of this is to be found in this new system.

I might proceed to instance a number of other rights, which were as necessary to be reserved, such as, that elections should be free, that the liberty of the press should be held sacred; but the instances adduced, are sufficient to prove, that this argument is without foundation.—Besides, it is evident, that the reason here assigned was not the true one, why the framers of this constitution omitted a bill of rights; if it had been, they would not have made certain reservations, while they totally omitted others of more importance. We find they have, in the 9th section of the 1st article, declared, that the writ of habeas corpus shall not be suspended, unless in cases of rebellion—that no bill of attainder, or expost facto law, shall be passed—that no title of nobility shall be granted by the United States, &c. If every thing which is not given is reserved, what propriety is there in these exceptions? Does this constitution any where grant the power of suspending the habeas corpus, to make ex post facto laws, pass bills of attainder, or grant titles of nobility? It certainly does not in express terms. The only answer that can be given is, that these are implied in the general powers granted. With equal truth it may be said, that all the powers, which the bills of right, guard against the abuse of, are contained or implied in the general ones granted by this constitution.

So far it is from being true, that a bill of rights is less necessary in the general constitution than in those of the states, the contrary is evidently the fact.—This system, if it is possible for the people of America to accede to it, will be an original compact; and being the last, will, in the nature of things, vacate every former agreement inconsistent with it. For it being a plan of government received and ratified by the whole people, all other forms, which are in existence at the time of its adoption, must yield to it. This is expressed in positive and unequivocal terms, in the 6th article, "That this constitution and the laws of the United States, which shall be made in pursuance thereof, and all treaties made, or which shall be made, under the authority of the United States, shall be the supreme law of the land; and the judges in every state shall be bound thereby, any thing in the *constitution*, or laws of any state, *to the contrary* notwithstanding. . . .

It is therefore not only necessarily implied thereby, but positively expressed, that the different state constitutions are repealed and entirely done away, so far as they are inconsistent with this, with the laws which shall be made in pursuance thereof, or with treaties made, or which shall be made, under the authority of the United States; of what avail will the constitutions of the respective states be to preserve the rights of its citizens? should they be plead, the answer would be, the constitution of the United States, and the laws made in pursuance thereof, is the supreme law, and all legislatures and judicial officers, whether of the general or state governments, are bound by oath to support it. No priviledge, reserved by the bills of rights, or secured by the state government, can limit the power granted by this, or restrain any laws made in pursuance of it. It stands therefore on its own bottom, and must receive a construction by itself without any reference to any other—And hence it was of the highest importance, that the most precise and express declarations and reservations of rights should have been made.

VIEWPOINT 2

"Bills of rights . . . are not only unnecessary in the proposed constitution, but would even be dangerous."

The Constitution Needs No Bill of Rights

Alexander Hamilton (1755-1804)

Alexander Hamilton, a past military aide to General George Washington and future secretary of the treasury under Washington's presidency, was one of the main supporters of the new Constitution, and he worked hard for its ratification in New York and other states. Among his efforts in support of the Constitution was a collaboration with James Madison and John Jay in a series of eighty-five letters to newspapers under the pseudonym of Publius. These essays, which supported and defended the proposed Constitution against various criticisms and urged ratification, were published in 1788 in book form as *The Federalist*.

Hamilton wrote the bulk of the essays, including no. 84 from which this viewpoint is taken. He directly takes up the criticism that the Constitution lacks a bill of rights. He summarizes the argument many Federalists used in defending the absence of a bill of rights—that the rights of Americans were protected by state constitutions, and that the new federal government was not given express powers to infringe upon individual rights and liberties. The structure of the new government, he asserted, with its separation of powers and guarantees of the right to elect representatives, among other features, was enough to ensure the people's liberties. Hamilton went on to conclude that a listing of rights might be dangerous, because it could be construed to mean that any rights and freedoms not listed would lack protection.

From *The Federalist*, no. 84, May 1788, written by Alexander Hamilton under the pseudonym Publius.

To the People of the State of New-York.

In the course of the foregoing review of the constitution I have taken notice of, and endeavoured to answer, most of the objections which have appeared against it. There however remain a few which either did not fall naturally under any particular head, or were forgotten in their proper places. These shall now be discussed: but as the subject has been drawn into great length, I shall so far consult brevity as to comprise all my observations on these miscellaneous points in a single paper.

The most considerable of these remaining objections is, that the plan of the convention contains no bill of rights. Among other answers given to this, it has been upon different occasions remarked, that the constitutions of several of the states are in a similar predicament. I add, that New-York is of this number. And yet the opposers of the new system in this state, who profess an unlimited admiration for its constitution, are among the most intemperate partizans of a bill of rights. To justify their zeal in this matter, they alledge two things; one is, that though the constitution of New-York has no bill of rights prefixed to it, yet it contains in the body of it various provisions in favour of particular privileges and rights, which in substance amount to the same thing; the other is, that the constitution adopts in their full extent the common and statute law of Great-Britain, by which many other rights not expressed in it are equally secured.

To the first I answer, that the constitution proposed by the convention contains, as well as the constitution of this state, a number of such provisions.

Independent of those, which relate to the structure of the government, we find the following: Article I. section 3. clause 7. "Judgment in cases of impeachment shall not extend further than to removal from office, and disqualification to hold and enjoy any office of honour, trust or profit under the United States; but the party convicted shall nevertheless be liable and subject to indictment, trial, judgment and punishment, according to law." Section 9. of the same article, clause 2. "The privilege of the writ of habeas corpus shall not be suspended, unless when in cases of rebellion or invasion the public safety may require it." Clause 3. "No bill of attainder or ex post facto law shall be passed." Clause 7. "No title of nobility shall be granted by the United States: And no person holding any office of profit or trust under them, shall, without the consent of congress, accept of any present, emolument, office or title, of any kind whatever, from any king, prince or foreign state." Article III. section 2. clause 3. "The trial of all crimes, except in cases of impeachment, shall be by jury; and such trial shall be held in the state where the said crimes shall have been committed; but when not committed within any state, the trial shall be at such place or places as the congress may by law have directed." Section 3, of the same article, "Treason against the United States shall consist only in levying war against them, or in adhering to their enemies, giving them aid and comfort. No person shall be convicted of treason unless on the testimony of two witnesses to the same overt act, or on confession in open court." And clause 3, of the same section. "The congress shall have power to declare the punishment of treason, but no attainder of treason shall work corruption of blood, or forfeiture, except during the life of the person attainted."

тне

FEDERALIST:

A COLLECTION

о ?

E S S A Y S, .

WRITTEN IN FAVOUR OF THE

NEW CONSTITUTION,

AS AGREED UPON BY THE FEDERAL CONVENTION,
SEPTEMBER 17, 1787.

IN TWO VOLUMES.

VOL. I.

NEW-YORK:

PRINTED AND SOLD BY J. AND A. M'LEAN,
No. 41, HANOVER-SQUARE,
M,DCC,LXXXVIII.

One of the first editions of The Federalist, *a collection of essays by Alexander Hamilton, James Madison, and John Jay. Hamilton's essay no. 84 defended the Constitution as it stood, without a bill of rights.*

It may well be a question whether these are not upon the whole, of equal importance with any which are to be found in the constitution of this state. The establishment of the writ of habeas corpus, the prohibition of ex post facto laws, and of Titles of Nobility, to which we have no corresponding provisions in our constitution, are perhaps greater securities to liberty and republicanism than any it contains. The creation of crimes after the commission of the fact, or in other words, the subjecting of men to punishment for things which, when they were done, were breaches of no law, and the practice of arbitrary imprisonments have been in all ages the favourite and most formidable instruments of tyranny. . . .

To the second, that is, to the pretended establishment of the common and statute law by the constitution, I answer, that they are expressly made subject "to such alterations and provisions as the legislature shall from time to time make concerning the same." They are therefore at any moment liable to repeal by the ordinary legislative power, and of course have no constitutional sanction. The only use of the declaration was to recognize the ancient law, and to remove doubts which might have been occasioned by the revolution. This consequently can be considered as no part of a declaration of rights, which under our constitutions must be intended as limitations of the power of the government itself.

It has been several times truly remarked, that bills of rights are in their origin, stipulations between kings and their subjects, abridgments of prerogative in favor of privilege, reservations of rights not surrendered to the prince. Such was Magna Charta, obtained by the Barons, sword in hand, from king John. . . . Such also was the declaration of right presented by the lords and commons to the prince of Orange in 1688, and afterwards thrown into the form of an act of parliament, called the bill of rights. It is evident, therefore, that according to their primitive signification, they have no application to constitutions professedly founded upon the power of the people, and executed by their immediate representatives and servants. Here, in strictness, the people surrender nothing, and as they retain every thing, they have no need of particular reservations. "We the people of the United States, to secure the blessings of liberty to ourselves and our posterity, do ordain and establish this constitution for the United States of America." Here is a better recognition of popular rights than volumes of those aphorisms which make the principal figure in several of our state bills of rights, and which would sound much better in a treatise of ethics than in a constitution of government.

But a minute detail of particular rights is certainly far less applicable to a constitution like that under consideration, which is merely intended to regulate the general political interests of the nation, than to a constitution which has the regulation of every species of personal and private concerns. If therefore the loud clamours against the plan of the convention on this score, are well founded, no epithets of reprobation will be too strong for the constitution of this state. But the truth is, that both of them contain all, which in relation to their objects, is reasonably to be desired.

A Bill of Rights Would Be Dangerous

James Wilson, a lawyer and political leader from Philadelphia, was an important participant in Pennsylvania's convention held to decide whether to ratify the federal Constitution. Wilson's speeches in support of the Constitution were reprinted in newspapers and pamphlets. In an address to the convention given on November 28, 1787, Wilson defended the absence of a written bill of rights.

In a government, consisting of enumerated powers, such as is proposed for the United States, a bill of rights would not only be unnecessary, but, in my humble judgment, highly imprudent. In all societies, there are many powers and rights, which cannot be particularly enumerated. A bill of rights annexed to a constitution, is an enumeration of the powers reserved. If we attempt an enumeration, every thing that is not enumerated, is presumed to be given. The consequence is, that an imperfect enumeration would throw all implied power into the scale of the government; and the rights of the people would be rendered incomplete. On the other hand; an imperfect enumeration of the powers of government, reserves all implied power to the people; and, by that means the constitution becomes incomplete; but of the two it is much safer to run the risk on the side of the constitution; for an omission in the enumeration of the powers of government, is neither so dangerous, nor important, as an omission in the enumeration of the rights of the people.

I go further, and affirm that bills of rights, in the sense and in the extent in which they are contended for, are not only unnecessary in the proposed constitution, but would even be dangerous. They would contain various exceptions to powers which are not granted; and on this very account, would afford a colourable pretext to claim more than were granted. For why declare that things shall not be done which there is no power to do? Why for instance, should it be said, that the liberty of the press shall not be restrained, when no power is given by which restrictions may be imposed? I will not contend that such a provision would confer a regulating power; but it is evident that it would furnish, to men disposed to usurp, a plausible pretence for claiming that power. They might urge with a semblance of reason, that the constitution ought not to be charged with the absurdity of providing against the abuse of an authority, which was not given, and that the provision against restraining the liberty of the press afforded a clear implication, that a power to prescribe proper regulations concerning it, was intended to be vested in the national government. This may serve as a specimen of the numerous handles which would be given to the doctrine of constructive powers, by the indulgence of an injudicious zeal for bills of rights.

On the subject of the liberty of the press, as much has been said, I cannot forbear adding a remark or two: In the first place, I observe that there is not a syllable concerning it in the constitution of this state, and in the next, I contend that whatever has been said about it in that of any other state, amounts to nothing. What signifies a declaration that "the liberty of the press shall be inviolably preserved?" What is the liberty of the press? Who can give it any definition which would not leave the utmost latitude for evasion? I hold it to be impracticable; and from this, I infer, that its security, whatever fine declarations may be inserted in any constitution respecting it, must altogether depend on public opinion, and on the general spirit of the people and of the government. And here, after all, as intimated upon another occasion, must we seek for the only solid basis of all our rights.

There remains but one other view of this matter to conclude the point. The truth is, after all the declamation we have heard, that the constitution is itself in every rational sense, and to every useful purpose, a Bill of Rights. The several bills of rights, in Great-Britain, form its constitution, and conversely the constitution of each state is its bill of rights. And the proposed constitution, if adopted, will be the bill of rights of the union. Is it one object of a bill of rights to declare and specify the political privileges of the citizens in the structure and administration of the government? This is done in the most ample and precise manner in the plan of the convention, comprehending various precautions for the public security, which are not to be found in any of the state constitutions. Is another object of a bill of rights to define certain immunities and modes of proceeding, which are relative to personal and private concerns? This we have seen has also been attended to, in a variety of cases, in the same plan. Adverting therefore to the substantial meaning of a bill of rights, it is absurd to allege that it is not to be found in the work of the convention. It may be said that it does not go far enough, though it will not be easy to make this appear; but it can with no propriety be contended that there is no such thing. It certainly must be immaterial what mode is observed as to the order of declaring the rights of the citizens, if they are to be found in any part of the instrument which establishes the government. And hence it must be apparent that much of what has been said on this subject rests merely on verbal and nominal distinctions, which are entirely foreign from the substance of the thing.

"In Virginia I have seen the bill of rights violated in every instance where it has been opposed to a popular current."

A Bill of Rights Would Be Ineffectual

James Madison (1751-1836)

James Madison has been called the father of the Bill of Rights. However, he was not always supportive of the concept and the evolution of his views toward a bill of rights is an important and revealing subplot in the story of its creation. Of special interest to many historians is the correspondence between Madison and Thomas Jefferson, author of the Declaration of Independence and Madison's political colleague and friend.

Madison was one of the most important and influential figures at the 1787 Philadelphia Convention and one of the principal authors of the new Constitution created at that gathering. However, when fellow Virginia delegate George Mason proposed late in the convention to add a bill of rights to the nearly finished document, Madison, along with most of the other delegates, voted against considering such a measure. He defended the absence of a bill of rights in the subsequent debate over ratification. Madison wrote of the proposed Constitution to Jefferson, then Minister to France, in an October 24, 1787, letter.

Jefferson replied in a December 20, 1787, letter in which he expressed strong support for a bill of rights. He noted that "a bill of

From a letter of James Madison to Thomas Jefferson, dated October 17, 1788.

rights is what the people are entitled to against every government on earth." He repeated his support of the bill of rights in subsequent letters to Madison and others. Madison did not directly respond to Jefferson concerning this issue until October 17, 1788, when he wrote the letter excerpted below.

By this time the Constitution had been ratified by most of the states, but many of the states had accompanied their approval by voicing their desire for a bill of rights and by proposing amendments to be immediately considered by the new national government. (Madison enclosed a pamphlet describing some of the proposed amendments in his letter to Jefferson.) In addition, Madison's political career was in jeopardy because of the bill of rights issue. Madison's role in supporting the new Constitution without a bill of rights contributed to his defeat in his bid to become one of Virginia's first two United States senators. Madison then tried to run for a seat in the House of Representatives, where again he found his lack of support for a bill of rights unpopular. At the time of his October letter he was engaged in a close political contest with James Monroe for the congressional election, and he had pledged in debates and in writing to work to immediately amend the Constitution and add a bill of rights.

However, as his letter to Jefferson makes clear, Madison's ideas on a bill of rights remained ambivalent. "My own opinion has always been in favor of a bill of rights," he states, but "I have never thought the omission a material defect, nor been anxious to supply it . . . for any other reason than that it is anxiously desired by others." Such a measure would do no harm, he argued. However, he lists four proposed objections to a bill of rights, the last of which was that a "parchment barrier" would simply be ineffective if popular majorities wished to deprive minorities of their rights. He argues that the states' bill of rights had been of little use in the past because they include no mechanism for enforcing their restrictions.

Dear Sir,

I have written a number of letters to you since my return here, and shall add this by another casual opportunity just notified to me by Mr. St. John. . . .

The States which have adopted the New Constitution are all proceeding to the arrangements for putting it into action in March next. . . .

The little pamphlet herewith inclosed will give you a collective view of the alterations which have been proposed for the new

Constitution. Various and numerous as they appear they certainly omit many of the true grounds of opposition. The articles relating to Treaties, to paper money, and to contracts, created more enemies than all the errors in the System positive & negative put together. It is true nevertheless that not a few, particularly in Virginia have contended for the proposed alterations from the most honorable & patriotic motives; and that among the advocates for the Constitution there are some who wish for further guards to public liberty & individual rights. As far as these may consist of a constitutional declaration of the most essential rights, it is probable they will be added; though there are many who think such addition unnecessary, and not a few who think it misplaced in such a Constitution. There is scarce any point on which the party in opposition is so much divided as to its importance and its propriety.

James Madison did not at first support adding a bill of rights to the Constitution. Persuaded in part by letters from his friend Thomas Jefferson, he became the leading congressional advocate of such a measure.

My own opinion has always been in favor of a bill of rights; provided it be so framed as not to imply powers not meant to be included in the enumeration. At the same time I have never thought the omission a material defect, nor been anxious to supply it even by subsequent amendment, for any other reason than that it is anxiously desired by others. I have favored it because I supposed it might be of use, and if properly executed could not be of disservice. I have not viewed it in an important light—

1. because I conceive that in a certain degree, though not in the extent argued by Mr. (James) Wilson, the rights in question are reserved by the manner in which the federal powers are granted.

2. because there is great reason to fear that a positive declaration of some of the most essential rights could not be obtained in the requisite latitude. I am sure that the rights of conscience in particular, if submitted to public definition would be narrowed much more than they are likely ever to be by an assumed power. One of the objections in New England was that the Constitution by prohibiting religious tests, opened a door for Jews, Turks & infidels.

3. because the limited powers of the federal Government and the jealousy of the subordinate Governments, afford a security which has not existed in the case of the State Governments, and exists in no other.

4. because experience proves the inefficacy of a bill of rights on those occasions when its controul is most needed. Repeated violations of these parchment barriers have been committed by overbearing majorities in every State. In Virginia I have seen the bill of rights violated in every instance where it has been opposed to a popular current. Notwithstanding the explicit provision contained in that instrument for the rights of Conscience, it is well known that a religious establishment would have taken place in that State, if the Legislative majority had found as they expected, a majority of the people in favor of the measure; and I am persuaded that if a majority of the people were now of one sect, the measure would still take place and on narrower ground than was then proposed, notwithstanding the additional obstacle which the law has since created.

Wherever the real power in a Government lies, there is the danger of oppression. In our Governments the real power lies in the majority of the Community, and the invasion of private rights is chiefly to be apprehended, not from acts of Government contrary to the sense of its constituents, but from acts in which the Government is the mere instrument of the major number of the Constituents. This is a truth of great importance, but not yet sufficiently attended to; and is probably more strongly impressed on my mind by facts, and reflections suggested by them, than on yours which has contemplated abuses of power issuing from a very different quarter. Wherever there is an interest and power to do wrong, wrong will generally be done, and not less readily by a powerful & interested party than by a powerful and interested prince. The difference so far as it relates to the superiority of republics over monarchies, lies in the less degree of probability that interest may prompt more abuses of power in the former than in the latter; and in the security in the former against an oppression of more than the smaller part of the Society, whereas in the [latter] it may be extended in a manner to the whole. The difference so far as it relates to the point in question—the efficacy of a bill of rights in controuling abuses of power—lies in this: that in a monarchy the latent force of the nation is superior to that of the Sovereign, and a solemn charter of popular rights must have a great effect, as a standard for trying the validity of public acts, and a signal for rousing & uniting the superior force of the community; whereas in a popular Government, the political and physical power may be considered as vested in the same hands, that is in a majority of the people, and, consequently the tyrannical will of the Sovereign is not [to] be controuled by the dread of an appeal to any other force within the community.

Benefits of a Bill of Rights

What use then it may be asked can a bill of rights serve in popular Governments? I answer the two following which, though less essential than in other Governments, sufficiently recommend the precaution: 1. The political truths declared in that solemn manner acquire by degrees the character of fundamental maxims of free Government, and as they become incorporated with the national sentiment, counteract the impulses of interest and passion. 2. Although it be generally true as above stated that the danger of oppression lies in the interested majorities of the people rather than in usurped acts of the Government, yet there may be occasions on which the evil may spring from the latter source; and on such, a bill of rights will be a good ground for an appeal to the sense of the community. Perhaps too there may be a certain degree of danger, that a succession of artful and ambitious rulers may by gradual & well timed advances, finally elect an independent Government on the subversion of liberty. Should this danger exist at all, it is prudent to guard against it, especially when the precaution can do no injury. At the same time I must own that I see no tendency in our Governments to danger on that side. It has been remarked that there is a tendency in all Governments to an augmentation of power at the expence of liberty. But the remark as usually understood does not appear to me well founded. Power when it has attained a certain degree of energy and independence goes on generally to further degrees. But when below that degree, the direct tendency is to further degrees of relaxation, until the abuses of liberty beget a sudden transition to an undue degree of power. With this explanation the remark may be true; and in the latter sense only is it, in my opinion applicable to the

Governments in America. It is a melancholy reflection that liberty should be equally exposed to danger whether the Governments have too much or too little power, and that the line which divides these extremes should be so inaccurately defined by experience.

Supposing a bill of rights to be proper the articles which ought to compose it, admit of much discussion. I am inclined to think that absolute restrictions in cases that are doubtful, or where emergencies may overrule them, ought to be avoided. The restrictions however strongly marked on paper will never be regarded when opposed to the decided sense of the public, and after repeated violations in extraordinary cases they will lose even their ordinary efficacy. Should a Rebellion or insurrection alarm the people as well as the Government, and a suspension of the Habeas Corpus be dictated by the alarm, no written prohibitions on earth would prevent the measure. Should an army in time of peace be gradually established in our neighborhood by Britain or Spain, declarations on paper would have as little effect in preventing a standing force for the public safety. The best security against these evils is to remove the pretext for them. . . .

Where the power is in the few it is natural for them to sacrifice the many to their own partialities and corruptions. Where the power as with us is in the many not in the few the danger cannot be very great that the few will be thus favored. It is much more to be dreaded that the few will be unnecessarily sacrificed to the many. . . .

I am, dear sir with the sincerest esteem & affection.

VIEWPOINT 4

"The Declaration of rights is like all other human blessings alloyed with some inconveniences. . . . But the good in this instance vastly overweighs the evil."

A Bill of Rights Would Be Beneficial

Thomas Jefferson (1743-1826)

Thomas Jefferson, author of the Declaration of Independence and future president of the United States, served in a series of diplomatic posts in France from 1784 to 1789. He thus did not take a direct part in the debates over the framing and ratification of the U.S. Constitution. His views on the issue are known mainly from letters to friends and colleagues, especially his correspondence with James Madison. Of special interest to many historians is his letter dated March 15, 1789, in which he directly responds to Madison's arguments against a bill of rights as expressed in an October 1788 letter.

In response to Madison's argument that a bill of rights would be an ineffectual paper barrier against popular prejudices, Jefferson writes that even a partially successful bill of rights is better than none. Jefferson also argues that a bill of rights would give power to the judicial branch of government to enforce its restrictions on government actions. Jefferson reaffirms his beliefs that the advantages of adopting a bill of rights outweigh all disadvan-

From a letter of Thomas Jefferson to James Madison, dated March 15, 1789.

tages. His arguments are credited by some historians as helping to convince Madison of the worthiness of a Bill of Rights, especially with judicial enforcement. "The Jefferson assertion on the matter," writes historian Bernard Schwartz, "led Madison to emphasize, when he later presented his draft of the Bill of Rights to Congress, that the courts would enforce the limitations imposed in his proposed amendments."

Dear Sir,

I wrote you last on the 12th. of Jan. since which I have received yours of Octob. 17. Dec. 8. and 12. That of Oct. 17. came to hand only Feb. 23. How it happened to be four months on the way, I cannot tell, as I never knew by what hand it came. . . . Your thoughts on the subject of the Declaration of rights in the letter of Oct. 17. I have weighed with great satisfaction. Some of them had not occurred to me before, but were acknoleged just in the moment they were presented to my mind. In the arguments in favor of a declaration of rights, you omit one which has great weight with me, the legal check which it puts into the hands of the judiciary. This is a body, which if rendered independent, and kept strictly to their own department merits great confidence for their learning and integrity. . . .

The Good Outweighs the Bad

I am happy to find that on the whole you are a friend to this amendment. The Declaration of rights is like all other human blessings alloyed with some inconveniences, and not accomplishing fully it's [sic] object. But the good in this instance vastly overweighs the evil. I cannot refrain from making short answers to the objections which your letter states to have been raised.

1. That the rights in question are reserved by the manner in which the federal powers are granted. Answer. A constitutive act may certainly be so formed as to need no declaration of rights. The act itself has the force of a declaration as far as it goes, and if it goes to all material points nothing more is wanting. In the draught of a constitution which I had once a thought of proposing in Virginia, and printed afterwards, I endeavored to reach all the great objects of public liberty, and did not mean to add a declaration of rights. Probably the object was imperfectly executed; but the deficiencies would have been supplied by others in the course of discussion. But in a constitutive act which leaves some precious articles unnoticed, and raises implications against oth-

ers, a declaration of rights becomes necessary by way of supplement. This is the case of our new federal constitution. This instrument forms us into one state as to certain objects, and gives us a legislative and executive body for these objects. It should therefore guard us against their abuses of power within the field submitted to them.

2. A positive declaration of some essential rights could not be obtained in the requisite latitude. Answer. Half a loaf is better

Thomas Jefferson, author of the Declaration of Independence, was a diplomat in France from 1784 to 1789. His influence in the ratification debate was limited to his letters to friends in America, including James Madison.

than no bread. If we cannot secure all our rights, let us secure what we can.

3. The limited powers of the federal government and jealousy of the subordinate governments afford a security which exists in no other instance. Answer. The first member of this seems resolvable into the 1st. objection before stated. The jealousy of the subordinate governments is a precious reliance. But observe that those governments are only agents. They must have principles

furnished them whereon to found their opposition. The declaration of rights will be the text whereby they will try all the acts of the federal government. In this view it is necessary to the federal government also; as by the same text they may try the opposition of the subordinate governments.

4. Experience proves the inefficacy of a bill of rights. True. But tho it is not absolutely efficacious under all circumstances, it is of great potency always and rarely inefficacious. A brace the more will often keep up the building which would have fallen with that brace the less. There is a remarkable difference between the characters of the Inconveniencies which attend a Declaration of rights, and those which attend the want of it. The inconveniences of the Declaration are that it may cramp government in it's useful exertions. But the evil of this is shortlived, moderate, and reparable. The inconveniencies of the want of a Declaration are permanent, afflicting and irreparable; they are in constant progression from bad to worse. The executive in our governments is not the sole, it is scarcely the principal object of my jealousy. The tyranny of the legislatures is the most formidable dread at present, and will be for long years. That of the executive will come in it's turn, but it will be at a remote period. I know there are some among us who would now establish a monarchy. But they are inconsiderable in number and weight of character. The rising race are all republicans. We were educated in royalism; no wonder if some of us retain that idolatry still. Our young people are educated in republicanism. An apostacy from that to royalism is unprecedented and impossible. I am much pleased with the prospect that a declaration of rights will be added; and hope it will be done in that way which will not endanger the whole frame of the government, or any essential part of it. . . .

As you will be in a situation to know when the leave of absence will be granted me which I have asked, will you be so good as to communicate it by a line to Mr. Lewis and Mr. Eppes? I hope to see you in the summer, and that if you are not otherwise engaged, you will encamp with me at Monticello for a while. I am with great and sincere attachment Dear sir Your affectionate friend & servt,

CHAPTER 2

Freedom of Speech

Chapter Preface

The First Amendment of the Bill of Rights clearly states that "Congress shall make no law . . . abridging the freedom of speech, or of the press." This chapter examines the first two instances in which Congress passed laws that did just that. The first instance was in 1798, when the Bill of Rights was less than a decade old. The second was more than a century later, in 1917, when the United States was entering World War I. Historians consider both cases pivotal in the evolution of the role of the Bill of Rights in American life. The two cases have a number of remarkable parallels in their context and situation. They also have a number of key differences, especially in the response of the Supreme Court.

In both time periods the political atmosphere was strained by anxieties about foreign enemies and foreign revolutions, fears of aliens and alien ideas, political divisions over the meaning of equality and justice, and a belief by those in power that political criticism of the government threatened the United States and was equal to treason. The combination of perceived internal and external threats was enough to convince Congress to pass laws restricting speech and press freedoms, regardless of the Bill of Rights.

In the 1790s the external enemy was France, with which the United States engaged in an undeclared war between 1797 and 1800. The French Revolution, which had begun in 1789, though celebrated by some Americans, was viewed with suspicion by many because of its violence, instability, and proclamations of radical equality. Disagreements over France and the French Revolution reflected the growing political divisions in the United States between two political factions: the Federalists and the Jeffersonian Republicans. Political science professor Jack W. Peltason wrote in 1954 in *Foundations of Freedom in the American Constitution:*

> During the first ten years of its existence our national government was in the hands of the Federalist Party. The Federalists did not hide their contempt for the general masses or their belief that only the rich and well-born are competent to determine what is in the national interest. When Thomas Jefferson organized the Republican Party (not to be confused with the present Republican Party, organized in 1854) the Federalists were frightened by the possibility that "the people would be seduced by the malicious and false doctrine of equality" which Jefferson proclaimed.

In 1796 relations between the United States and France, already bad, grew tense. Some Federalists believed the nation to be infiltrated by French agents and they accused the Republicans of being French sympathizers. Stung by the harsh criticism of some Republican newspapers and seeing treachery all around them, these Federalists were tempted to suppress Republican political action. Then in 1798, when actual fighting with France occurred, this temptation became too strong to resist.

The result? Congress in 1798 passed the Alien and Sedition Acts. The Sedition Act, passed on July 14, made it illegal for anyone to "print, utter, or publish . . . any false, scandalous, and malicious writing" against the government. Under this law the Federalists arrested twenty-five people and convicted ten. These ten included prominent Republican journalists and Matthew Lyon, a Republican congressman from Vermont.

The context of the sedition laws passed in 1917 and 1918 was similar in some respects to those of 1798. This time the external enemies were Germany, from World War I, and, to a lesser extent, Russia, whose 1905 and 1917 revolutions were disturbing to many Americans who feared social unrest. The alien ideas and doctrines feared by many Americans included anarchism, Marxism, and communism, which, it was argued, threatened to destroy American society and values. Many of the advocates of these ideas were immigrants from Russia and other countries. The dividing political issues of the day again revolved around questions of social equality, with advocates of socialism, women's suffrage, racial equality, labor unions, and other social reforms arrayed against those who believed such changes threatened America's way of life.

The entry of the United States into World War I in 1917, coupled with these other factors, prompted Congress to pass a series of laws proscribing criticism of the government. The Espionage Act of 1917 made it a crime to, among other things, "willfully obstruct the recruiting or enlistment service of the United States;" in other words, to speak against the military draft. The Sedition Act of 1918 added provisions similar to those of the 1798 law, making it a crime to "willfully utter, print, write, or publish any disloyal . . . or abusive language about the form of government of the United States." Under these laws of 1917 and 1918 federal authorities convicted and imprisoned more than two thousand people, including Socialist party leaders Eugene V. Debs and Victor L. Berger.

While there are many similarities in the content and the background of the sedition laws of the late eighteenth century and those of the early twentieth century, there are also important differences in how they fared in America's political and legal system. Although many Republican opponents of the 1798 sedition law argued that it violated the Bill of Rights, they did not take the case to the Supreme Court. The Supreme Court had not yet been established as the final arbiter over the constitutionality of federal laws (a role most historians date from the 1803 case *Marbury v. Madison*). Perhaps more importantly, all the justices, and indeed all federal judges, had been appointed by the Federalist-dominated government. They were for the most part sympathetic to the Sedition Act and probably would have declared it constitutional.

But the fate of the Sedition Act was sealed in the 1800 elections, when Thomas Jefferson was elected president and members of his party, including Matthew Lyon, who campaigned from his prison cell, won decisive victories in Congress. Many historians credit discontent with the Alien and Sedition Acts with helping Jefferson to victory. The Sedition Act was allowed to expire in 1801, and Jefferson pardoned the people who had been convicted under it. (Jefferson's record on civil liberties is not unblemished: While president, he urged state courts to use state sedition laws against his political opponents.)

The effect of the 1917 and 1918 laws was different. Unlike in 1798, no ground swell of public support urged their repeal, although Congress did repeal the 1918 act in 1920. Debs, the Socialist party presidential candidate in 1920, did not achieve electoral success in his campaign from his prison cell as Matthew Lyon did. Still, the laws are significant because controversy over them involved the U.S. Supreme Court in an unprecedented fashion in debating and determining the meaning of the Bill of Rights and in enforcing its implementation by the government. The ideas developed in the Supreme Court opinions on cases examined in this chapter formed the foundation for future Supreme Court actions and continue to affect the role of the Bill of Rights in American lives to this day.

VIEWPOINT 1

"The freedom of the press . . . means the total exemption of the press from any kind of legislative control."

The Sedition Act Violates the Bill of Rights

George Hay (1765-1830)

The Bill of Rights was put to its first major test in 1798, seven years after its adoption by the United States. At this time the country was sharply divided over growing hostilities with France. At the same time, the new nation's political leadership was becoming increasingly divided into two discernible political parties. One was the Federalist party (not to be confused with the Federalists of the Constitution ratification debate). The Federalists, many of whom supported war with France, had control of Congress and the presidency with John Adams. The Democratic-Republican party, led by Thomas Jefferson, included many French and Irish immigrants in its ranks, who were opposed to hostilities with France and were increasingly critical of the Federalists. In 1798 the Federalist-dominated Congress passed four laws known as the Alien and Sedition Acts. The fourth of these laws, the Sedition Act, made sedition against the federal government a criminal offense.

Sedition, acts or words upsetting to governmental authority, had been viewed as punishable in centuries of English common law. In England at certain times a person could be punished simply for insulting the king. The 1798 law passed by Congress made

From George Hay, *An Essay on the Liberty of the Press*, Philadelphia, 1799.

criminal "any false, scandalous and malicious" writings and mutterings against the government and its officials. It called for fines and jail penalties for anyone speaking, writing, or publishing "with intent to defame . . . or bring into contempt or disrepute" the president or other members of government. Under the law several prominent Democratic-Republican newspaper editors and leaders were jailed.

Many argued that the Sedition Act violated the First Amendment of the Bill of Rights, which stated that "Congress should make no law . . . abridging freedom of speech or of the press." Those who defended the Sedition Act argued that the Bill of Rights prevented Congress only from making laws that created a "prior restraint" on newspaper publications. Congress, they argued, could still punish publishers for newspaper articles they found seditious or otherwise dangerous to the public *after* publication. Others disagreed, and the Sedition Act is credited by some historians as stimulating new theories and defenses of the freedom of speech and of the press.

One important pamphlet published in this time was by George Hay, a member of the Virginia House of Delegates and a future federal judge. In 1799 under the pseudonym of Hortensius he wrote a pamphlet titled *An Essay on the Liberty of the Press*. In it he argues that the Sedition Act violated the Bill of Rights by limiting freedoms of speech and of the press. He argues that such freedoms should be defined broadly, and that people should be free to publish strong criticisms of public figures without being subject to prosecution. The ideas expressed by Hay prefigured many of the debates of freedom of speech and of the press that engulfed America in the twentieth century.

———————

It is the object of the succeeding letters, to demonstrate, that so much of the Sedition Bill, as relates to *printed* libels, is expressly forbidden by the constitution of the United States.

This question, in strictness, ought not to be discussed; because, if Congress have not power, either expressly given or by necessary *implication*, to pass the law under consideration, it is totally immaterial whether they are forbidden to pass it or not. But as the "freedom of the press," has never yet been accurately defined, and as there is no subject in which the welfare of society is more essentially concerned, my original undertaking shall be fully performed.

The words of the constitution, which contain the express prohibition here relied on, are, "Congress shall make no law abridging the freedom of speech or of the press.". . .

The words, "freedom of the press," like most other words, have a meaning, a clear, precise, and definite meaning, which the times require, should be unequivocally ascertained. That this has not been done before, is a wonderful and melancholy evidence of the imbecility of the human mind, and of the slow progress which it makes, in acquiring knowledge even on subjects the most useful and interesting.

It will, I presume, be admitted, that the words in question have a meaning, and that the framers of the amendment containing these words, meant something when they declared, that the freedom of the press should not be abridged.

This 1798 engraving of Matthew Lyon fighting Roger Griswold on the floor of Congress indicates the intensity of political differences at this time. Lyon was later prosecuted and imprisoned under the Sedition Act. He was pardoned by Thomas Jefferson in 1801.

To ascertain what the "freedom of the press" is, we have only to ascertain what freedom itself is. For, surely, it will be conceded, that freedom applied to one subject, means the same, as freedom applied to another subject.

Now freedom is of two kinds, and of two kinds only: one is, that absolute freedom which belongs to man, previous to any social institution; and the other, that qualified or abridged freedom, which he is content to enjoy, for the sake of government and society. I believe there is no other sort of freedom in which man is concerned.

The absolute freedom then, or what is the same thing, the freedom, belonging to man before any social compact, is the power uncontrouled by law, of doing what he pleases, *provided he does no injury to any other individual.* If this definition of freedom be applied to the press, as surely it ought to be, the press, if I may personify it, may do whatever it pleases to do, uncontrouled by any law, *taking care however to do no injury to any individual.* This injury can only be by slander or defamation, and reparation should be made for it in a state of nature as well as in society.

But freedom in society, or what is called civil liberty, is defined to be, natural liberty, so far, restrained by law as the public good requires, and no farther. This is the definition given by a writer, particularly distinguished for the accuracy of his definitions, and which, perhaps, cannot be mended. Now let freedom, under this definition, be applied to the press, and what will the freedom of the press amount to? It will amount precisely to the privilege of publishing, as far as the legislative power shall say, the public good requires: that is to say, the freedom of the press will be regulated by law. If the word freedom was used in this sense, by the framers of the amendment, they meant to say, Congress shall make no law abridging the freedom of the press, which freedom, however, is to be regulated by law. Folly itself does not speak such language.

It has been admitted by the reader, who has advanced thus far, that the framers of the amendment meant something. They knew, no doubt, that the power granted to Congress, did not authorise any controul over the press, but they knew that its freedom could not be too cautiously guarded from invasion. The amendment in question was therefore introduced. Now if they used the word "freedom" under the first definition, they did mean something, and something of infinite importance in all free countries, the total exemption of the press from any kind of legislative controul. But if they used the word freedom under the second definition they meant nothing; for if they supposed that the freedom of the press, was absolute freedom, so far restrained by law as the public good required, and no farther, the amendment left the legislative power of the government on this subject, precisely where it was before. But it has been already admitted that the amendment had a meaning: the construction therefore which allows it no meaning is absurd and must be rejected.

The Meaning of Freedom

This argument may be summed up in a few words. The word "freedom" has meaning. It is either absolute, that is exempt from all law, or it is qualified, that is, regulated by law. If it be exempt from the controul of law, the Sedition Bill which controuls the "freedom of the press" is unconstitutional. But if it is to be regulated by law, the amendment which declares that Congress shall make no law to abridge the freedom of the press, which freedom however may be regulated by law, is the grossest absurdity that ever was conceived by the human mind.

That by the words "freedom of the press," is meant a total exemption of the press from legislative controul, will further appear from the following cases, in which it is manifest, that the word freedom is used with this signification and no other.

It is obvious in itself and it is admitted by all men, that freedom of speech means the power uncontrouled by law, of speaking either truth or falsehood at the discretion of each individual, *provided no other individual be injured*. This power is, *as yet*, in its full extent in the United States. A man may say every thing which his passion can suggest; he may employ all his time, and all his talents, if he is wicked enough to do so, in *speaking* against the government matters that are false, scandalous, and malicious; but he is admitted by the majority of Congress to be sheltered by the article in question, which forbids a law abridging the freedom of speech. If then freedom of speech means, in the construction of the Constitution, the privilege of speaking *any thing* without controul, the words freedom of the press, which form a part of the same sentence, mean the privilege of printing *any thing* without controul.

Freedom of Speech and Religion

Happily for mankind, the word "freedom" begins now to be applied to religion also. In the United States it is applied in its fullest force, and religious freedom is completely understood to mean the power uncontrouled by law of professing and publishing any opinion on religious topics, which any individual may choose to profess or publish, and of supporting these opinions by any statements he may think proper to make. The fool may not only say in his heart, there is no God, but he may announce if he pleases his atheism to the world. He may endeavor to corrupt mankind, not only by opinions that are erroneous, but by facts which are false. Still however he will be safe, because he lives in a country where religious freedom is established. If then freedom of religion, will not permit a man to be punished, for publishing any opinions on religious topics and supporting those opinions by false facts, surely freedom of the press, which is the medium of all publications, will not permit a man to be punished, for publishing any opinion on any subject, and supporting it by any statement whatever. . . .

I contend therefore, that if the words freedom of the press, have any meaning at all they mean a total exemption from any law making any publication whatever criminal. Whether the unequivocal avowal of this doctrine in the United States would produce mischief or not, is a question which perhaps I may have leisure to discuss. I must be content here to observe, that the mischief if any, which might arise from this doctrine could not be remedied or prevented, but by means of a power fatal to the liberty of the people.

The Sedition Bill

That the real meaning of the words "freedom of the press," has been ascertained by the foregoing remarks, will appear still more clearly, if possible, from the absurdity of those constructions, which have been given by the advocates of the Sedition Bill.

The construction clearly held out in the bill itself, is, that it does not extend to the privilege of printing facts, that are false. This construction cannot be correct. It plainly supposes that "freedom," extends only as far as the power of doing what is morally right. If, then, the freedom of the press can be restrained to the publication of facts that are true, it follows inevitably, that it may also be restrained to the publication of opinions which are correct. There is truth in opinion, as well as in fact. Error in opinion may do as much harm, as falsity in fact: it may be as morally wrong, and it may be propagated from motives as malicious. It may do more harm, because the refutation of an opinion which is erroneous, is more difficult than the contradiction of a fact which is false. But the power of controuling opinions has never yet been claimed; yet it is manifest that the same construction, which warrants a controul in matters of fact, does the same as to matters of opinion. In addition to this, it ought to be remarked, that the difficulty of distinguishing in many cases between fact and opinion, is extremely great, and that no kind of criterion is furnished by the law under consideration. Of this more, perhaps will be said hereafter.

Again, if the congressional construction be right, if the freedom of the press consists in the full enjoyment of the privilege of printing facts that are true, it will be fair to read the amendment, without the words really used, after substituting those said by Congress to have the same import. The clause will then stand thus: "Congress shall make no law abridging the right of the press, to publish facts that are true!" If this was the real meaning of Congress, and the several States, when they spoke in the state constitutions, and in the amendment of the "freedom of the press," the very great solicitude on this subject displayed throughout the continent, was most irrational and absurd. . . .

This venerable and enlightened assembly had too much wisdom to avow a meaning, so totally incompatible with the real object of their wishes. They knew that there never was a government in the world, however despotic, that dared to avow a design to suppress the truth: they knew that the most corrupt and profligate administrations, that ever brought wretchedness and oppression on a happy and free people, speak in their public acts the language of patriotism and virtue only, and that, although their real object is to stop enquiry, and to terrify truth into silence, the vengeance of the law *appears* to be directed against falsehood and malice only: in fact, they knew, that there are many truths, important to society, which are not susceptible of that full, direct, and positive evidence, which alone can be exhibited before a court and jury:

That men might be, and often would be deterred from speaking truths, which they could prove, unless they were absolutely protected from the trouble, disgrace, losses, and expense of a prosecution.

That in the violence of party spirit which government knows too well how to produce, and to inflame evidence the most conclusive, might be rejected, and that juries might be packed, "who would find Abel guilty of the murder of Cain."

That nothing tends more to irritate the minds of men, and disturb the peace of society, than prosecutions of a political nature, which like prosecutions in religion, increase the evils, they were, perhaps, intended to remove.

They knew that the licentiousness of the press, though an evil, was a less evil than that resulting from any law to restrain it, upon the same principle, that the most enlightened part of the world is at length convinced, that the evils arising from the toleration of heresy and atheism, are less, infinitely less, than the evils of persecution.

That the spirit of inquiry and discussion, was of the utmost importance in every free country, and could be preserved only by giving it absolute protection, even in its excesses.

That truth was always equal to the task of combating falsehood without the aid of government; because in most instances it has defeated falsehood, backed by all the power of government.

That truth cannot be impressed upon the human mind by power, with which therefore, it disdains an alliance, but by reason and evidence only. . . .

But, it has been said, that the freedom of the press, consists not in the privilege of printing truth; but in an exemption from previous restraint, and as the Sedition Bill imposes no previous restraint, it does not abridge the freedom of the press. This *profound* remark is borrowed from Blackstone and De Lolme, and is gravely repeated, by those who are weak enough to take opinions upon trust.

61

If these writers meant to state what the law was understood to be in England, they are correct. Even if they meant to state what the law ought to be in England, perhaps they are still correct; because it is extremely probable, that a press absolutely free, would in the short course of one year "humble in the dust and ashes" the "stupendous fabric" of the British government. But this definition does not deserve to be transplanted into America. In Britain, a legislative controul over the press, is, perhaps essential to the preservation of the "present order of things;" but it does not follow, that such controul is essential here. In Britain, a vast standing army is necessary to keep the people in peace, and the monarch on his throne; but it does not follow that the tranquillity of America, or the personal safety of the President, would be promoted by a similar institution.

A single remark will be sufficient to expose the extreme fallacy of the idea, when applied to the Constitution of the United States. If the freedom of the press consists in an exemption from previous restraint, Congress may, without injury to the freedom of the press, punish with death, any thing *actually* published, which a political inquisition may choose to condemn.

This Is America, Not Britain

But on what ground is this British doctrine respecting the freedom of the press introduced here? In Britain, the parliament is acknowledged to be omnipotent. It has exercised this omnipotence, and converted three years into seven years. In Britain there is no constitution, no limitation of legislative power; but in America, there is a constitution, the power of the legislature is limited, and the object of one limitation is to secure the freedom of the press.

If this doctrine is avowed here, under the idea that the common law of England is in force in the United States, even this idea will be of no avail. The common law knows nothing of printing or the liberty of the press. The art of printing was not discovered, until towards the close of the 14th century. It was at first in England a subject of star-chamber jurisdiction, and afterwards put under a licencer by statute. This statute expired just before the commencement of the present century.

Before this event, the rights of the press, were at the mercy of a single individual. There can be no common law, no immemorial usage or custom concerning a thing of so modern a date.

The freedom of the press, therefore, means the total exemption of the press from any kind of legislative controul, and consequently the Sedition Bill, which is an act of legislative controul, is an abridgment of its liberty, and expressly forbidden by the constitution. Which was to be demonstrated.

VIEWPOINT 2

"The liberty of the press consists not in a license for every man to publish what he pleases without being liable to punishment, if he should abuse this license to the injury of others."

The Sedition Act Does Not Violate the Bill of Rights

5th Congress Majority Report (1799)

Congress passed the Sedition Act in 1798. The law made it criminal for anyone to "print, utter, or publish . . . any false, scandalous, and malicious writing" against the government. Those who made the law interpreted "malicious writing" to include criticism of the Federalist party and its programs. Under the law several prominent newspaper editors who had criticized President John Adams or Congress were imprisoned. The law was criticized by many who argued that it violated the Bill of Right's prohibition against laws "abridging freedom of speech or of the press."

In 1799 the House of Representatives debated whether the act was constitutional. The following viewpoint is taken from the Majority Report of the Congress, which was still under Federalist control. The primary author of the majority report was Chauncey Goodrich of Connecticut. The report defends the Sedition Act, arguing that while Congress had no power to engage in prior re-

Annals of Congress, 5th Cong., 3d sess., 2987-90, 3003-14.

straint of newspapers and speeches, it was entitled to pass laws punishing false and seditious writing.

The largely negative public reaction to the Sedition Act was in part responsible for the victory of Thomas Jefferson over John Adams in the 1800 presidential election. Jefferson pardoned the people convicted under the act, and allowed it to expire in 1801. The question of its constitutionality never reached the Supreme Court. The issues raised by the Alien and Sedition Acts remained relatively dormant until Congress passed a new sedition act over a century later, during World War I.

The "Act in addition to an act entitled an act for the punishment of certain crimes against the United States," commonly called the sedition act, contains provisions of a twofold nature: first, against seditious acts, and, second, against libellous and seditious writings. The first have never been complained of, nor has any objection been made to its validity. The objection applies solely to the second; and on the ground, in the first place, that Congress have no power by the Constitution to pass any act for punishing libels, no such power being expressly given, and all powers not given to Congress, being reserved to the States respectively, or the people thereof.

To this objection it is answered, that a law to punish false, scandalous, and malicious writings against the Government, with intent to stir up sedition, is a law necessary for carrying into effect the power vested by the Constitution in the Government of the United States, and in the departments and officers thereof, and, consequently, such a law as Congress may pass; because the direct tendency of such writings is to obstruct the acts of the Government by exciting opposition to them, to endanger its existence by rendering it odious and contemptible in the eyes of the people, and to produce seditious combinations against the laws, the power to punish which has never been questioned; because it would be manifestly absurd to suppose that a Government might punish sedition, and yet be void of power to prevent it by punishing those acts which plainly and necessarily lead to it; and, because, under the general power to make all laws proper and necessary for carrying into effect the powers vested by the Constitution in the Government of the United States, Congress has passed many laws for which no express provision can be found in the Constitution, and the constitutionality of which has never been questioned. . . .

It is objected to this act, in the second place, that it is expressly contrary to that part of the Constitution which declares, that "Congress shall make no law respecting an establishment of religion, or prohibiting the free exercise thereof, or abridging the liberty of the press." The act in question is said to be an "abridgment of the liberty of the press," and therefore unconstitutional.

What True Liberty Consists Of

To this it is answered, in the first place, that the liberty of the press consists not in a license for every man to publish what he pleases without being liable to punishment, if he should abuse this license to the injury of others, but in a permission to publish, without previous restraint, whatever he may think proper, being answerable to the public and individuals, for any abuse of this permission to their prejudice. In like manner, as the liberty of speech does not authorize a man to speak malicious slanders against his neighbor, nor the liberty of action justify him in going, by violence, into another man's house, or in assaulting any person whom he may meet in the streets. In the several States the liberty of the press has always been understood in this manner, and no other; and the Constitution of every State which has been

Freedom of the Press Does Not Include Sedition

"Long John" Allen, a Connecticut representative from 1797-1799, supported the Sedition Act. Addressing the Congress on July 5, 1798, he attacked several publications for abusing their press freedoms.

Gentlemen contend for the liberty of opinions and of the press. Let me ask them whether they seriously think the liberty of the press authorizes such publications? The president of the United States is here called "a person without patriotism, without philosophy, and a mock monarch," and the free election of the people is pronounced "a jostling him into the chief magistracy by the ominous combination of old Tories with old opinions, and old Whigs with new."

If this be not a conspiracy against government and people, I know not what to understand from the "threat of tears, execrations, derision, and contempt." Because the Constitution guarantees the right of expressing our opinions and the freedom of the press, am I at liberty to falsely call you a thief, a murderer, an atheist? Because I have the liberty of locomotion, of going where I please, have I a right to ride over the footman in the path? The freedom of the press and opinions was never understood to give the right of publishing falsehoods and slanders, nor of exciting sedition, insurrection, and slaughter, with impunity. A man was always answerable for the malicious publication of falsehood; and what more does this bill require?

framed and adopted since the Declaration of Independence, asserts "the liberty of the press;" while in several, if not all, their laws provide for the punishment of libellous publications, which would be a manifest absurdity and contradiction, if the liberty of the press meant to publish any and everything, without being amenable to the laws for the abuse of this license. According to this just, legal, and universally admitted definition of "the liberty of the press," a law to restrain its licentiousness, in publishing false, scandalous, and malicious libels against the Government, cannot be considered as "an abridgment" of its "liberty."

It is answered, in the second place, that the liberty of the press did never extend, according to the laws of any State, or of the United States, or of England, from whence our laws are derived, to the publication of false, scandalous, and malicious writings against the Government, written or published with intent to do mischief, such publications being unlawful, and punishable in every State; from whence it follows, undeniably, that a law to punish seditious and malicious publications, is not an abridgment of the liberty of the press, for it would be a manifest absurdity to say, that a man's liberty was abridged by punishing him for doing that which he never had a liberty to do.

It is answered, thirdly, that the act in question cannot be unconstitutional, because it makes nothing penal that was not penal before, and gives no new powers to the court, but is merely declaratory of the common law, and useful for rendering that law more generally known, and more easily understood. This cannot be denied, if it be admitted, as it must be, that false, scandalous, and malicious libels against the Government of the country, published with intent to do mischief, are punishable by the common law; for, by the 2d section of the 3d article of the Constitution, the judicial power of the United States is expressly extended to all offences arising under the Constitution. By the Constitution, the Government of the United States is established, for many important objects, as the Government of the country; and libels against that Government, therefore, are offences arising under the Constitution, and, consequently, are punishable at common law by the courts of the United States. The act, indeed, is so far from having extended the law and the power of the court, that it has abridged both, and has enlarged instead of abridging the liberty of the press; for, at common law, libels against the Government might be punished with fine and imprisonment at the discretion of the court, whereas the act limits the fine to two thousand dollars, and the imprisonment to two years; and it also allows the party accused to give the truth in evidence for his justification, which, by the common law, was expressly forbidden.

And, lastly, it is answered, that had the Constitution intended to prohibit Congress from legislating at all on the subject of the press, which is the construction whereon the objections to this law are founded, it would have used the same expressions as in that part of the clause which relates to religion and religious texts; whereas, the words are wholly different: "Congress," says the Constitution, (amendment 3d.) "shall make no law respecting an establishment of religion, or prohibiting the free exercise thereof, or abridging the freedom of speech of the press." Here it is manifest that the Constitution intended to prohibit Congress from legislating at all on the subject of religious establishments, and the prohibition is made in the most express terms. Had the same intention prevailed respecting the press, the same expressions would have been used, and Congress would have been "prohibited from passing any law respecting the press." They are not, however, "prohibited" from legislating at all on the subject, but merely from abridging the liberty of the press. It is evident they may legislate respecting the press, may pass laws for its regulation, and to punish those who pervert it into an engine of mischief, provided those laws do not abridge its liberty. Its liberty, according to the well known and universally admitted definition, consists in permission to publish, without previous restraint upon the press, but subject to punishment afterwards for improper publications. A law, therefore, to impose previous restraint upon the press, and not one to inflict punishment on wicked and malicious publications, would be a law to abridge the liberty of the press, and, as such, unconstitutional.

VIEWPOINT 3

"The great mass are indifferent to the constitutionally-guaranteed liberties of others, and so allow sordid self-interest and bigotry to add one limitation after another."

Freedom of Speech Must Be Protected

Theodore Schroeder (1864-1953)

After the 1798 Sedition Act expired without renewal in 1801, no federal law was passed impinging on freedom of speech for more than a century. Consequently there was not much debate or controversy over the First Amendment during this time. This did not mean that freedom of speech in America was unrestricted. Speech was often limited by state laws, local police actions, and social customs. The assassination of President William McKinley by a self-proclaimed anarchist in 1901 caused many states to enact laws prohibiting the advocacy of anarchism or other "dangerous" ideas.

Despite their potential for abridging free speech, these laws did not disturb most Americans. The attitude of many Americans was later summarized by University of Minnesota historian Paul L. Murphy in his book *World War I and the Origin of Civil Liberties in the United States*:

> The attitude of a majority of public and private leaders of the late nineteenth and early twentieth centuries toward civil liberties, as well as the attitude of great numbers of rank-and-file Americans who supported those leaders, held that such liberties were only to be protected for those citizens who had demonstrated, both by their attitudes and their behavior, that

From Theodore Schroeder, "Our Vanishing Liberty of the Press," *The Arena*, December 1906.

they were prepared to utilize those freedoms in positive and constructive ways. The decision as to whether a citizen deserved to have his civil liberties formally protected was to be made by those responsible elements within the society that were knowledgeable in the proper use of personal freedom. Liberty, in short, was a condition conferred by the community at its discretion, usually only to "good people" who had earned their prerogatives. Blacks, Indians, Orientals, aliens—particularly those from Eastern Europe—women, or people espousing radical and destructive economic political theories, clearly were not ready for the full utilization of their constitutional liberties. General doctrines guaranteeing freedom to such citizens were suspect and had to be tempered in subtle ways by those in a position to implement those doctrines.

One of the few people to actively challenge this view was Theodore Schroeder. Schroeder was a writer and activist who wrote and lectured widely on behalf of the civil liberties of anarchists, socialists, labor organizers, immigrants, and others whose civil liberties were being abused at the turn of the century.

In the following viewpoint, taken from a magazine article first published in 1906 and reprinted in book form in 1916, Schroeder argues that the Bill of Rights and its free speech and press protections are being ignored by many American communities. He attacks laws forbidding the immigration of professed anarchists and forbidding publication of anarchist views. He argues that the suppression of the civil liberties of immigrants and citizens espousing anarchist views violates the Bill of Rights and ultimately endangers the civil liberties of all Americans. Schroeder exhorts Americans to take more interest and action in defending their First Amendment civil liberties and to not assume that those liberties are safely enshrined in the Bill of Rights.

For over a century it has been believed that we had abolished rule by divine right, and the accompanying infallibility of officialism, and that we have maintained inviolate the liberty of conscience, of speech and of press. However, this belief of ours is fast becoming a matter of illusion. Though a love for such liberty is still verbally avowed, yet in every conflict raising an issue over it, it is denied in practice. There is not a state in the Union to-day, in which the liberty of the press is not abridged upon several legitimate subjects of debate. Here will be discussed but one of these, and that perhaps the most unpopular.

By gradual encroachments and unconscious piling of precedent upon precedent, we are rapidly approaching the stage in which we will enjoy any liberties only by permission, not as a matter of right. In this progressive denial of the freedom of conscience, speech and press, all three branches of government have transgressed, without seriously disturbing the serene, sweet, century-long slumber, into which we are lulled, by the songs of liberty, whose echoes still resound in our ears, but whose meaning we have long since forgotten.

Constitution Not Self-Enforcing

A century ago we thought that we had settled all these problems of liberty. In all our constitutions we placed a verbal guarantee of liberty of speech and press, and then stupidly went to sleep, assuming that the Constitution had some mysterious and adequate potency for self-enforcement. This is the usual mistake, always so fatal to all liberties, and the multitude is too superficial and too much engrossed with a low order of selfish pursuits to discover that constitutions need the support of a public opinion which demands that every doubtful construction shall be resolved against the state and in favor of individual liberty.

In the absence of such construction, constitutions soon become the chains which enslave, rather than the safeguards of liberty. Thus it has come that under the guise of "judicial construction," all constitutions have been judicially amended, until those who, by a dependence upon the Constitution, endeavor to defend themselves in the exercise of a proper liberty, only make themselves ridiculous. Persons finding satisfaction or profit in repudiating constitutional guarantees, and combining therewith sufficient political power to ignore them with impunity, unconsciously develop in themselves a contempt for the fundamental equalities which most founders of republics sought to maintain. This contempt is soon shared by those who find themselves the helpless victims of misplaced confidence in constitutions, and through them is transfused to the general public, until that which we should consider the sacred guarantee of our liberties becomes a joke, and those who rely upon it are looked upon as near to imbecility.

Some years ago a United States Senator (Mr. Cullom) was reported as saying that "in the United States there is no constitution but public opinion.". . . In Idaho, at the time of the official kidnapping of Charles H. Moyer and others in Colorado, the attorney of these men tried to show the court the unconstitutionality of the procedure, when the baffled rage of the judge prompted him to exclaim: "I am tired of these appeals to the Constitution. The Federal Constitution is a defective, out-of-date instrument, anyhow, and it is useless to fetch that document into court. But Constitution or no Constitution, we have got the men we went after; they are here;

they are going to stay here until we have had our final say, and I would like to know what is going to be done about it?" No wonder that the wise Herbert Spencer wrote: "Paper constitutions raise smiles on the faces of those who have observed their results."

What Freedom Means

In a March 26, 1909, article in Central Law Review, *Theodore Schroeder examines further the concept of freedom of speech.*

If the Constitution had said that "legislative bodies shall make no law abridging man's freedom to breathe," no one would have any doubt as to what was meant, and every one would instantly say that of course it precluded government from passing any law which would prohibit breathing according to the mandate of a policeman, before trial and conviction, and that it would equally preclude the passage or enforcement of any law which would punish breathing, merely as such, upon conviction after the fact. No sane man could be found who would say that such a guarantee, to breathe without any statutory abridgment, only precluded the appointment of Commissioners who should determine arbitrarily what persons might be licensed to breathe and who should not be so licensed, and that it would still permit government to penalize all those who do not breathe in the specially prescribed manner, even though such criminal breathing had not injured anyone.

There is not the slightest reason to be given why "freedom" in relation to speech and press should be differently interpreted. The only explanation for having interpreted it differently is that people generally, and petty officials in particular, believe in unabridged freedom to breathe, but emotionally disbelieve in unabridged freedom of speech, and therefore, they lawlessly read into the Constitutions meanings and exceptions which are not represented there by a single syllable or word, simply because they think, or rather feel, that the Constitution ought not to guarantee freedom of speech and of the press, for those ideas which intensely displease them.

All this is true because the great mass are indifferent to the constitutionally-guaranteed liberties of others, and so allow sordid self-interest and bigotry to add one limitation after another, until all freedom will be destroyed by judicial amendments to our charters of liberty. Furthermore, to most persons, the word liberty is only an empty sound, the meaning of which they know not, because they have never learned the reasons underlying it. Thus they are too stupid to be able to differentiate between their disapproval of an opinion and their opponent's right to disagree with them. They love their own power to suppress intellectual differences more than another's liberty of expressing them, and more than the progressive clarification of human conceptions of truth, which can only come through freedom of discussion. Such persons specially owe to themselves, and to those against whom they are encouraging injustice, that they should read the defenses of liberty as made by the master-minds of the past. . . .

Formerly it was our truthful boast that we were the freest people on earth. To-day it is our silent shame that among all the tyrannical governments on the face of the earth ours is probably the only one which makes the right of admission depend upon the abstract political opinions of the applicant. Our people denounce the unspeakable tyranny of a bloody Czar, and pass laws here to protect him in the exercise of his brutalities in Russia. Instead of being "the land of the free and the home of the brave" we exclude from our shores those who are brave and seek freedom here, and punish men for expressing unpopular opinions if they already live here. In vain do the afflicted ones appeal to a "liberty loving" populace for help in maintaining liberty.

Anarchists and Free Speech

In this short essay I can discuss specifically only the denial of liberty of conscience, speech, and press, as it affects one class of citizens, and I choose to defend the most despised.

Under our immigration laws no anarchist, that is, "no person who disbelieves in or who is opposed to all organized governments" is allowed to enter the United States, even though such person be a nonresistant Quaker. In other words, the persons who believe with the signers of the Declaration of Independence that those who create and maintain governments have a right to abolish them, and who also desire to persuade the majority of their fellow-men to exercise this privilege, are denied admission to our national domain. . . .

Surely people who only ask the liberty of trying to persuade their fellow-men to abolish government, through passive resistance, cannot possibly be a menace to any institution worth maintaining, yet such men we deny admission into the United States. If they chance to be Russians, we send them back, perhaps to end their days as Siberian exiles, and all because they have expressed a mere abstract "disbelief in government," though accompanied only by a desire for passive resistance. . . .

But that is not all we do in this "free" country. If a resident of this "land of the free" should "connive or conspire" to induce any of these non-resistants, who "disbelieve in governments," to come to the United States, by sending one of them a printed or written, private or public, invitation to visit here, such "conspirer" would be liable to a fine of five thousand dollars, or three years' imprisonment, or both. And yet we boast of our freedom of conscience, of speech and of press! . . .

In the state of New York, although satisfied with American conditions and officials, and although you believe in democratic government, if you should orally, or in print, advocate the cause of forcible revolution against Russia, or against "any civilized nation having an organized government," you would be liable, under a state statute, to a fine of $5,000 and ten years' imprisonment besides. Have we, then, freedom of conscience, speech and press? Do we love liberty or know its meaning?

Yes, it may be that a dispassionate and enlightened judge must declare such laws unconstitutional, but such judges are as scarce as the seekers after martyrdom who are willing to make a test case. Hence we all submit to this tyranny. Furthermore, the same hysteria which could make legislators believe they had the power to pass such a law, in all probability would also induce courts to confirm such power. A Western jurist, a member of the highest court of his state, once said to me that it must be a very stupid lawyer who could not write a plausible opinion on either side of any case that ever came to an appellate court. Given the mental predisposition induced by popular panic, together with intense emotions, and it is easy, very easy, to formulate verbal "interpretations" by which the constitutional guarantees are explained away, or exceptions interpolated,—a common process for the judicial amendment of laws and constitutions.

If, then, we truly believe in the liberty of conscience, speech and press, we must place ourselves again squarely upon the declaration of rights made by our forefathers, and defend the right of others to disagree with us, even about the beneficence of government.

As when your neighbor's house is on fire your own is in danger, so the protection of your liberty should begin when it is menaced by a precedent which attacks your opponent's equality of opportunity to express his disagreement with you. Let us then unite for the repeal of these iniquitous laws, born of hysteria and popular panic, and maintained in thoughtless disregard of others' intellectual freedom.

VIEWPOINT 4

"The most stringent protection of free speech would not protect a man in falsely shouting fire in a theater and causing a panic."

Freedom of Speech Must Sometimes Be Limited

Oliver Wendell Holmes (1841-1935)

Despite the occasional writings of Theodore Schroeder and others, the Bill of Rights did not play a major role in American lives at the dawn of the twentieth century. The Supreme Court did not rule on any cases concerning free speech for the first 128 years of the Bill of Rights' existence. In part this was because Congress had passed no federal sedition laws or other measures restricting free speech since the 1798 Sedition Act expired in 1801, and the Supreme Court had consistently held that the Bill of Rights had no standing over state or local governments.

During World War I, for the first time since the 1798 Alien and Sedition Acts, Congress passed a series of laws restrictive of speech and press freedoms and designed to punish criticism of America's war effort. In 1919 the Court ruled on several cases deriving from people arrested and convicted under these laws. One of these persons was Charles T. Schenck, the general secretary of the Socialist party. The party had mailed fifteen thousand leaflets to draftees urging them to resist conscription. Schenck was arrested and convicted under the 1917 Espionage Act, which made it a crime to obstruct military recruitment or otherwise aid the enemy. The Supreme Court unanimously upheld Schenck's convic-

From the majority opinion of the U.S. Supreme Court in *Schenck v. United States*, 249 U.S. 47 (1919).

tion and the constitutionality of the Espionage Act.

The majority opinion was written by Oliver Wendell Holmes, who had been appointed to the Supreme Court by Theodore Roosevelt in 1902. Member of an aristocratic Boston family, Civil War veteran, renowned author and lecturer of legal philosophy, and Massachusetts state court judge, Holmes was considered the leading liberal jurist of his time. *Schenck v. United States* was the first of several significant majority and dissenting opinions by Holmes concerning the Bill of Rights. In the *Schenck* ruling, Holmes argued that freedom of speech was not absolute and that Congress had the right to restrict speech if it was used in circumstances that "create a clear and present danger" to the public. Despite that fact that Holmes voted to uphold Schenck's conviction, the "clear and present danger" test became an important judicial milestone in the development of free speech protections in the United States.

This is an indictment in three counts. The first charges a conspiracy to violate the Espionage Act of June 15, 1917 . . . by causing and attempting to cause insubordination, &c., in the military and naval forces of the United States, and to obstruct the recruiting and enlistment service of the United States, when the United States was at war with the German Empire, to-wit, that the defendants wilfully conspired to have printed and circulated to men who had been called and accepted for military service under the Act of May 18, 1917, a document set forth and alleged to be calculated to cause such insubordination and obstruction. The count alleges overt acts in pursuance of the conspiracy, ending in the distribution of the document set forth.

The second count alleges a conspiracy to commit an offense against the United States, to-wit, to use the mails for transmission of matter declared to be non-mailable by Title XII, § 2, of the Act of June 15, 1917, to-wit, the above-mentioned document, with an averment of the same overt acts. The third count charges an unlawful use of the mails for the transmission of the same matter and otherwise as above. The defendants were found guilty on all the counts. They set up the First Amendment to the Constitution forbidding Congress to make any law abridging the freedom of speech, or of the press, and bringing the case here on that ground have argued some other points also of which we must dispose.

It is argued that the evidence, if admissible, was not sufficient to prove that the defendant Schenck was concerned in sending the documents. According to the testimony Schenck said he was general secretary of the Socialist Party and had charge of the Socialist headquarters from which the documents were sent. He identified a book found there as the minutes of the Executive Committee of the party. The book showed a resolution of August 13, 1917, that fifteen thousand leaflets should be printed on the other side of one of them in use, to be mailed to men who had passed exemption boards, and for distribution.

Schenck personally attended to the printing. On August 20 the general secretary's report said, "Obtained new leaflets from printer and started work addressing envelopes," &c.; and there was a resolve that Comrade Schenck be allowed $125 for sending leaflets through the mail. He said that he had about fifteen or sixteen thousand printed. There were files of the circular in question in the inner office which he said were printed on the other side of the one-sided circular and were there for distribution. Other copies were proved to have been sent through the mails to drafted men. Without going into confirmatory details that were proved, no reasonable man could doubt that the defendant Schenck was largely instrumental in sending the circulars about. . . .

The Incriminating Document

The document in question upon its first printed side recited the first section of the Thirteenth Amendment, said that the idea embodied in it was violated by the Conscription Act and that a conscript is little better than a convict. In impassioned language it intimated that conscription was despotism in its worst form and a monstrous wrong against humanity in the interest of Wall Street's chosen few. It said, "Do not submit to intimidation," but in form at least confined itself to peaceful measures such as a petition for the repeal of the Act.

The other and later printed side of the sheet was headed, "Assert Your Rights." It stated reasons for alleging that anyone violated the Constitution when he refused to recognize "your right to assert your Opposition to the draft," and went on, "If you do not assert and support your rights, you are helping to deny or disparage rights which it is the solemn duty of all citizens and residents of the United States to retain." It described the arguments on the other side as coming from cunning politicians and a mercenary capitalist press, and even silent assent to the conscription law as helping to support an infamous conspiracy. It denied the power to send our citizens away to foreign shores to shoot up the people of other lands, and added that words could not express the condemnation such cold-blooded ruthlessness deserves, &c., winding up, "You must do your share to maintain, support and uphold the rights of the people of this country." Of course the document would not have been sent unless it had been intended to have some effect, and we do not see what effect it could be expected to have upon persons subject to the draft except to influence them to obstruct the carrying of it out. The defendants do not deny that the jury might find against them on this point.

Limits of First Amendment

But it is said, suppose that that was the tendency of this circular, it is protected by the First Amendment to the Constitution. Two of the strongest expressions are said to be quoted respectively from well-known public men. It well may be that the prohibition of laws abridging the freedom of speech is not confined to previous restraints, although to prevent them may have been the main purpose, as intimated in *Patterson* v. *Colorado*.

We admit that in many places and in ordinary times the defendants in saying all that was said in the circular would have been within their constitutional rights. But the character of every act depends upon the circumstances in which it is done. . . . The most stringent protection of free speech would not protect a man in falsely shouting fire in a theater and causing a panic. It does not even protect a man from an injunction against uttering words that may have all the effect of force. . . . The question in every case is whether the words used are used in such circumstances and are of such a nature as to create a clear and present danger that they will bring about the substantive evils that Congress has a right to prevent. It is a question of proximity and degree.

When a nation is at war many things that might be said in time of peace are such a hindrance to its effort that their utterance will not be endured so long as men fight and that no court could regard them as protected by any constitutional right. It seems to be admitted that if an actual obstruction of the recruiting service were proved, liability for words that produced that effect might be enforced. The statute of 1917 in § 4 punishes conspiracies to obstruct as well as actual obstruction. If the act (speaking, or circulating a paper), its tendency and the intent with which it is done are the same, we perceive no ground for saying that success alone warrants making the act a crime.

Viewpoint 5

"It is only the present danger of immediate evil or an intent to bring it about that warrants Congress in setting a limit to the expression of opinion. . . . Congress certainly cannot forbid all effort to change the mind of the country."

Political Protesters Should Be Guaranteed Freedom of Speech

Oliver Wendell Holmes (1841-1935)

Oliver Wendell Holmes was an associate justice of the Supreme Court from 1902 to 1932. He was a pivotal figure in a series of cases the Supreme Court decided in 1919 concerning the First Amendment. Congress had passed a series of laws during World War I that some people argued violated the clause prohibiting the abridgment of free speech.

In *Schenck v. United States*, Holmes wrote the unanimous opinion upholding the Schenck conviction and the constitutionality of such laws. He argued that Congress had the right to restrict speech if it caused a "clear and present danger" to the public, such as by directly inciting unlawful acts. The "clear and present danger" reasoning was used to uphold other convictions as well, including the conviction of Socialist and pacifist leader and presidential candidate Eugene Debs, who was sentenced to ten years imprisonment for speaking out against the war.

In a third case, *Abrams v. United States*, the Supreme Court upheld the convictions of Jacob Abrams and three other Russian an-

From Oliver Wendell Holmes's dissenting opinion in the U.S. Supreme Court decision in *Abrams v. United States*, 250 U.S. 616 (1919).

archist immigrants. They had distributed two leaflets in New York criticizing capitalism and President Woodrow Wilson's war policies and urging a general strike by workers making war-related materials. The Supreme Court ruled that Abrams and the other defendants meant to "excite, at the supreme crisis of the war, disaffection, sedition, riots, and . . . revolution." However, for the first time the Court's unanimity was broken: Holmes and fellow associate justice Louis Brandeis dissented.

In his dissenting opinion, excerpted here, Holmes defends his rulings in *Schenck* and other cases, but argues that in this instance the criminal intent of Abrams had not been demonstrated and that the pamphlets did not constitute a "clear and present danger" to the United States. Holmes goes on to argue in favor of a "free trade in ideas," which he says should be preserved by the Bill of Rights. Historian Richard Polenberg writes in his book *Fighting Faiths* that "the Abrams case led Justice Oliver Wendell Holmes to discover more libertarian possibilities in the 'clear and present danger' standard. . . . The Abrams case, therefore, contributed to a process of judicial reconsideration which eventually placed freedom of speech on a firmer constitutional basis."

This indictment is founded wholly upon the publication of two leaflets which I shall describe in a moment. The first count charges a conspiracy pending the war with Germany to publish abusive language about the form of government of the United States, laying the preparation and publishing of the first leaflet as overt acts. The second count charges a conspiracy pending the war to publish language intended to bring the form of government into contempt, laying the preparation and publishing of the two leaflets as overt acts. The third count alleges a conspiracy to encourage resistance to the United States in the same war and to attempt to effectuate the purpose by publishing the same leaflets. The fourth count lays a conspiracy to incite curtailment of production of things necessary to the prosecution of the war and to attempt to accomplish it by publishing the second leaflet to which I have referred.

The Pamphlets in Question

The first of these leaflets says that the President's cowardly silence about the intervention in Russia reveals the hypocrisy of the plutocratic gang in Washington. It intimates that "German militarism combined with Allied capitalism to crush the Russian revolution," goes on that the tyrants of the world fight each other until they see a common enemy—working-class enlightenment—when they combine to crush it; and that now militarism and capitalism combined, though not openly, to crush the Russian revolution. It says that there is only one enemy of the workers of the world and that is capitalism; that it is a crime for workers of America, &c., to fight the workers' republic of Russia, and ends "Awake! Awake, you workers of the world!" Signed "Revolutionists." A note adds, "It is absurd to call us pro-German. We hate and despise German militarism more than do you hypocritical tyrants. We have more reasons for denouncing German militarism than has the coward of the White House."

The 1918 Sedition Act

The federal law under which Abrams was convicted, parts of which are reprinted here, was passed by Congress in 1918 and repealed in 1920.

Whoever, when the United States is at war, shall willfully utter, print, write, or publish any disloyal, profane, scurrilous, or abusive language about the form of government of the United States, or the military or naval forces of the United States, or the flag of the United States, or the uniform of the Army or Navy of the United States, or any language intended to bring the form of government of the United States, or the Constitution of the United States, or the military or naval forces of the United States, into contempt, scorn, contumely or disrepute, or shall willfully utter, print, write, or publish any language intended to incite, provoke, or encourage resistance to the United States, or to promote the cause of its enemies, . . . or shall willfully by utterance, writing, printing, publication, or language spoken, urge, incite, or advocate any curtailment of production in this country of anything or things, product or products, necessary or essential to the prosecution of the war in which the United States may be engaged, with intent by such curtailment to cripple or hinder the United States in the prosecution of the war . . . shall be punished by a fine of not more than $10,000 or imprisonment for not more than twenty years, or both.

The other leaflet, headed "Workers—Wake Up," with abusive language says that America together with the Allies will march for Russia to help the Czecho-Slovaks in their struggle against the Bolsheviki, and that this time the hypocrites shall not fool the Russian emigrants and friends of Russia in America. It tells the Russian emigrants that they now must spit in the face of false military propaganda by which their sympathy and help to the prosecution of the war have been called forth and says that with the money they have lent or are going to lend "they will make bullets not only for the Germans but also for the Workers' Soviets of Russia," and further, "Workers in the ammunition factories, you are producing bullets, bayonets, cannon, to murder not only the Germans but also your dearest, best, who are in Russia fighting for freedom." It then appeals to the same Russian emigrants at some length not to consent to the "inquisitionary expedition to Russia," and says that the destruction of the Russian revolution is "the politics of the march on Russia." The leaflet winds up by saying "Workers, our reply to this barbaric intervention has to be a general strike!" and after a few words on the spirit of revolution, exhortations not to be afraid, and some usual tall talk, ends "Woe unto those who will be in the way of progress. Let solidarity live! The Rebels."

No argument seems to me necessary to show that these pronunciamentos in no way attack the form of government of the United States, or that they do not support either of the first two counts. What little I have to say about the third count may be postponed until I have considered the fourth. With regard to that it seems too plain to be denied that the suggestion to workers in ammunition factories that they are producing bullets to murder their dearest, and the further advocacy of a general strike, both in the second leaflet, do urge curtailment of production of things necessary to the prosecution of the war within the meaning of the Act of May 16, 1918 . . . amending § 3 of the earlier Act of 1917. But to make the conduct criminal that statute requires that it should be "with intent by such curtailment to cripple or hinder the United States in the prosecution of the war." It seems to me that no such intent is proved.

I am aware of course that the word intent as vaguely used in ordinary legal discussion means no more than knowledge at the time of the act that the consequences said to be intended will ensue. Even less than that will satisfy the general principle of civil and criminal liability. A man may have to pay damages, may be sent to prison, at common law might be hanged, if at the time of his act he knew facts from which common experience showed that the consequences would follow, whether he individually could foresee them or not. But, when words are used exactly, a deed is not done with intent to produce a consequence unless that consequence is the aim of the deed. It may be obvious, and obvious to the actor, that the consequence will follow, and he may be liable for it even if he forgets it, but he does not do the act with intent to produce it unless the aim to produce it is the proximate motive of the specific act, although there may be some deeper motive behind.

It seems to me that this statute must be taken to use its words in a strict and accurate sense. They would be absurd in any other. A patriot might think that we were wasting money on aeroplanes, or making more cannon of a certain kind than we needed, and might advocate curtailment with success, yet even if it turned out that the curtailment hindered and was thought by other minds to have been obviously likely to hinder the United States in the prosecution of the war, no one would hold such conduct a crime. I admit that my illustration does not answer all that might be said but it is enough to show what I think and to let me pass to a more important aspect of the case. I refer to the First Amendment to the Constitution that Congress shall make no law abridging the freedom of speech.

First Amendment Concerns

I never have seen any reason to doubt that the questions of law that alone were before this Court in the cases of *Schenck, Frohwerk* and *Debs*, were rightly decided. I do not doubt for a moment that by the same reasoning that would justify punishing persuasion to murder, the United States constitutionally may punish speech that produces or is intended to produce a clear and imminent danger that it will bring about forthwith certain substantive evils that the United States constitutionally may seek to prevent. The power undoubtedly is greater in time of war than in time of peace because war opens dangers that do not exist at other times.

But as against dangers peculiar to war, as against others, the principle of the right to free speech is always the same. It is only the present danger of immediate evil or an intent to bring it about that warrants Congress in setting a limit to the expression of opinion where private rights are not concerned. Congress certainly cannot forbid all effort to change the mind of the country. Now nobody can suppose that the surreptitious publishing of a silly leaflet by an unknown man, without more, would present any immediate danger that its opinions would hinder the success of the Government arms or have any appreciable tendency to do so. Publishing these opinions for the very purpose of obstructing, however, might indicate a greater danger and at any rate would have the quality of an attempt. So I assume that the second leaflet, if published for the purpose alleged in the fourth count, might be punishable. But it seems pretty clear to me that nothing less than that would bring these papers within the scope of this law.

An actual intent in the sense that I have explained is necessary to constitute an attempt, where a further act of the same individual is required to complete the substantive crime, for reasons given in *Swift & Co.* v. *United States*, 196 U. S. 375, 396. It is necessary where the success of the attempt depends upon others, because if that intent is not present the actor's aim may be accomplished without bringing about the evils sought to be checked. An intent to prevent interference with the revolution in Russia might have been satisfied without any hindrance to carrying on the war in which we were engaged.

I do not see how anyone can find the intent required by the statute in any of the defendants' words. The second leaflet is the only one that affords even a foundation for the charge, and there, without invoking the hatred of German militarism expressed in the former one, it is evident from the beginning to the end that the only object of the paper is to help Russia and stop American intervention there against the popular government—not to impede the United States in the war that it was carrying on. To say that two phrases taken literally might import a suggestion of conduct that would have interference with the war as an indirect and probably undesired effect seems to me by no means enough to show an attempt to produce that effect.

I return for a moment to the third count. That charges an intent to provoke resistance to the United States in its war with Germany. Taking the clause in the statute that deals with that in connection with the other elaborate provisions of the Act, I think that resistance to the United States means some forcible act of opposition to some proceeding of the United States in pursuance of the war. I think the intent must be the specific intent that I have described and for the reasons that I have given. I think that no such intent was proved or existed in fact. I also think that there is no hint at resistance to the United States as I construe the phrase.

In this case sentences of twenty years' imprisonment have been imposed for the publishing of two leaflets that I believe the defendants had as much right to publish as the Government has to publish the Constitution of the United States now vainly invoked by them. Even if I am technically wrong and enough can be squeezed from these poor and puny anonymities to turn the color of legal litmus paper—I will add, even if what I think the necessary intent were shown—the most nominal punishment seems to me all that possibly could be inflicted, unless the defendants are to be made to suffer not for what the indictment alleges but for the creed that they avow—a creed that I believe to be the creed of ignorance and immaturity when honestly held, as I see no reason to believe that it was held here, but which, although made the subject of examination at the trial, no one has a right even to consider in dealing with the charges before the Court.

Persecution for the expression of opinions seems to me perfectly logical. If you have no doubt of your premises or your power and want a certain result with all your heart you naturally express your wishes in law and sweep away all opposition. To allow opposition by speech seems to indicate that you think speech impotent, as when a man says that he has squared the circle, or that you do not care wholeheartedly for the result, or that you doubt either your power or your premises.

Free Trade in Ideas

But when men have realized that time has upset many fighting faiths, they may come to believe even more than they believe the very foundations of their own conduct that the ultimate good desired is better reached by free trade in ideas—that the best test of truth is the power of the thought to get itself accepted in the competition of the market, and that truth is the only ground upon which their wishes safely can be carried out. That, at any rate, is the theory of our Constitution. It is an experiment, as all life is an experiment. Every year if not every day we have to wager our salvation upon some prophecy based upon imperfect knowledge. While that experiment is part of our system I think that we should be eternally vigilant against attempts to check the expression of opinions that we loathe and believe to be fraught with death, unless they so imminently threaten immediate interference with the lawful and pressing purposes of the law that an immediate check is required to save the country.

I wholly disagree with the argument of the Government that the First Amendment left the common law as to seditious libel in force. History seems to me against the notion. I had conceived that the United States through many years had shown its repentance for the Sedition Act of 1798 by repaying fines that it imposed. Only the emergency that makes it immediately dangerous to leave the correction of evil counsels to time warrants making any exception to the sweeping command, "Congress shall make no law . . . abridging the freedom of speech." Of course I am speaking only of expressions of opinion and exhortations, which were all that were uttered here, but I regret that I cannot put into more impressive words my belief that in their conviction upon this indictment the defendants were deprived of their rights under the Constitution of the United States.

VIEWPOINT 6

"It will not do to let freedom of speech obscure for us the demands of other elements of liberty and safety."

Political Protest Should Be Restricted

John H. Wigmore (1864-1943)

John H. Wigmore, dean of the Northwestern Law School from 1902 to 1929, was one of America's most prominent and distinguished legal scholars and the author of numerous texts and articles on legal issues. In March 1920 he published in the *Illinois Law Review* a harsh critique of the dissenting opinion written by Supreme Court justice Oliver Wendell Holmes in the case *Abrams v. United States*. Holmes had questioned the conviction of Jacob Abrams and three other Russian immigrants who had distributed anarchist pamphlets, arguing that their freedom of speech had been abridged. Wigmore criticizes Holmes' reasoning on several points. He argues that the defendants' political philosophy and support of the Bolshevik regime in Russia made them dangerous to America in time of war. He asserts that the Bill of Rights is not intended to protect the advocacy of violent rebellion against the government or the advocacy of any violent and lawless act. Wigmore concludes that the ideal of freedom of speech is misplaced and misused when it is cited to defend the actions of people such as Abrams.

Excerpted from John H. Wigmore, "*Abrams v. U.S.*: Freedom of Speech and Freedom of Thuggery in War-Time and Peace-Time," *Illinois Law Review*, vol. 14, no. 8 (March 1920). Reprinted with permission.

The Minority Opinion in *Abrams* v. *United States*, decided on November 10, 1919 (40 Sup. 21), represents poor law and poor policy; and I wish to point out its dangerous implications. . . .

The individuals who combined in printing and distributing the circulars involved in *Abrams* v. *United States* had lived in this country for from five to ten years, without applying for naturalization. Four took the witness stand voluntarily, of whom three avowed that they were "rebels," "revolutionists," "anarchists"— did not believe in government in any form, and had no interest whatever in the government of the United States. . . .

What did these circulars say? . . .

The specific and concrete actions here urged are reducible to these: (1) A concerted general strike, or cessation of work; (2) particularly by workers in war-munitions factories; (3) with such armed violence that the American troops remaining in the United States would be kept at home to oppose this violence and to preserve civic order.

These three things stare out in plain words. Only the wilfully blind could refuse to see them.

What provisions of law would be violated by the action thus urged?

Under the Espionage Act of 1917, it is a crime (1) to "incite, provoke, and encourage resistance to the United States in said war"; (2) to "urge, incite and advocate curtailment of production of things and products, to-wit, ordnance and ammunition necessary and essential to the prosecution of the war." It is also a crime to utter "scurrilous and abusive language about the form of government of the United States, or to bring that form of government into contempt, scorn, contumely, and disrepute." But no stress was laid on this offense in the majority opinion of the Supreme Court.

That the first two unlawful acts were specifically and exactly committed by the publication of these circulars is obvious.

The Supreme Court

What was the attitude of the Supreme Court?

The majority of seven of the Supreme Court held that there was "competent and substantial evidence before the jury, fairly tending to sustain the verdict of guilty in the third and fourth counts" (representing the first and second offenses above described). There is here nothing further to say as to the majority opinion.

The minority of two held that there was no proof of intent to commit such offenses. We are here concerned with the minority opinion.

It is shocking in its obtuse indifference to the vital issues at stake in August, 1918, and it is ominous in its portent of like in-difference to pending and coming issues. That is why it is worth analysis now.

(1) As to the intent to provoke *resistance to the United States in the war*, the Minority Opinion says that "there is no such hint at resis-tance to the United States," because that statutory resistance must be "some forcible act of opposition to some proceeding of the United States in pursuance of the war," and none such is evident.

(2) As to the intent to *curtail production of munitions*, the Minor-ity Opinion admits that "it seems too plain to be denied," but that to make the conduct criminal the statute elsewhere requires an in-tent to "cripple or hinder the United States in the prosecution of the war," and that this additional intent was not proved.

And, as to both the foregoing, the minority (in a passage which is, however, so unclear that its exact point is difficult to gather) further say that a restriction of free speech is warranted only by "the present danger of immediate evil, or an intent to bring it about"; and that "the surreptitious publishing of a silly leaflet by an unknown man, without more," could not involve any "present danger" to the "success of the government armies.". . .

What we are here concerned with is that state of mind. In a pe-riod when the fate of the civilized world hung in the balance, how could the Minority Opinion interpret law and conduct in such a way as to let loose men who were doing their hardest to paralyze the supreme war efforts of our country?

But this attitude of mind, operating subconsciously, must, in consciously and openly justifying itself, invoke some distinct le-gal principle of universally acknowledged soundness. That is the natural process, deep in human nature, for all of us.

What was this saving principle? The constitutional right of Freedom of Speech.

We are reminded in the Minority Opinion that, after all, Truth is the great desideratum, and that Truth can only be expected to emerge through the unpleasant processes of Freedom of Speech. "Free trade in ideas" is recommended as the panacea. Our anx-ious overstrained patriotism is soothingly pointed away from the disagreeable war situation (there was no "present danger"!); and our minds are recommended to dwell upon the civic blessings of Truth—that ultimate Truth which will some day emerge through the leisurely comparison of what now may only be the obvious seeming truths. "Men may come to believe, even more than they believe the very foundations of their conduct, that the *ultimate good* desired is better reached by free trade in ideas—that the best test of Truth is the *power of the thought to get itself accepted* in the competition of the market.". . .

This disquisition on Truth seems sadly out of place. To weigh in juxtaposition the dastardly sentiments of these circulars and the great theme of world-justice for which our armies were sacrificing themselves, and then to assume the sacred cause of Truth as equally involved in both, is to misuse high ideals. This Opinion, if it had made the law as a majority opinion, would have ended by our letting soldiers die helpless in France, through our anxiety to protect the distribution of a leaflet whose sole purpose was to cut off the soldiers' munitions and supplies. How would this have advanced the cause of Truth?

However, the Minority Opinion does go through the forms of reasoning, though in elliptical fashion, and without definite formulation of rule for the principle of freedom of speech; and we must meet this issue raised by the invocation of freedom of speech.

Out of its indefiniteness, the following two points of issue seem tangible:

(a) If restriction of speech is lawful at all (the Minority Opinion implies), it is only when in war-time there is "the present danger of immediate evil, or an intent to bring it about," and no such danger here existed. Here, of course, we come back to the Minority Opinion's blindness to the danger. To argue about seeing that danger is useless; the dangerous thing to the country is that there are responsible persons who did not and do not see the danger.

(b) But (apart from this danger question) the fundamental assumption of the Minority Opinion is that the principle of freedom of speech does apply to protect these particular circulars, because "expressions of opinion and exhortations were *all that were uttered here.*" It is this fundamental assumption that is thoroughly erroneous. And as thousands of well-meaning persons are obsessed by it, an attempt to clear it up is worth while.

The dilemma, or conflict of principles, is this: The United States may (admits the Minority Opinion) constitutionally "punish persuasion to murder," yet it may not punish a mere "expression of opinion or exhortation" concerning an unlawful or deleterious act, as here. This contrast between persuasion to lethal deed and persuasion to mere change of opinions, is inherent in the situation. We have to face it if any workable rule is ever to be formulated.

"Free trade in ideas," says the Minority Opinion, is vital—"the best test of truth is the power of the thought to get itself accepted in the competition of the market." Very well; but does "free trade in ideas" mean that those who desire to gather and set in action a band of thugs and murderers may freely go about publicly circularizing and orating upon the attractions of loot, proposing a plan of action for organized thuggery, and enlisting their converts, yet not be constitutionally interfered with until the gathered band of thugs actually sets the torch and lifts the rifle? Certainly not, they concede. Then where is the dead-line to be drawn at which Freedom of Speech does not become identical with Freedom of Thuggery?

That is where the champions of freedom of speech give us no solution.

What is that solution?

We must distinguish here the *abnormal* and the *normal* situations.

Following their conviction for sedition and failed appeal to the Supreme Court, Samuel Lipman, Hyman Lachowsky, Mollie Steimer, and Jacob Abrams were eventually deported to Russia in 1921.

The *abnormal* situation is presented in time of a foreign war.

Where a nation has definitely committed itself to a foreign war, all principles of normal internal order may be suspended. As property may be taken and corporal service may be conscripted, so liberty of speech may be limited or suppressed, so far as deemed needful for the successful conduct of the war. The normal rights to life, liberty and property are certainly no less important civically than the normal right to expression of opinion; and all rights of the individual, and all internal civic interests, become subordinated to the national right in the struggle for national life. . . .

Furthermore, any other solution, in a national war by a democracy, stultifies itself. The modern war—our latest, and let us hope, our last war—is fought by the nation itself; and a general consensus of citizen-views against the war must mean a failure in the war itself. Whether the forces be filled by enlistment or by conscription, an unwilling citizenry will soon deplete the forces. I was personally near enough to the center of man-power recruitment to realize keenly that the raising of the nearly 5,000,000 men, whose battle-array ultimately gave Germany its quietus, was due to the popular conviction favoring the prosecution of the war. Had the popular conviction disfavored it, the last 3,000,000 or so would never have been got into uniform, and America's part in the war would have ended ignominiously. The conclusion is that when a nation has once decided upon war, it must stop any further hesitation, or it will fail in the very purpose of the decision. This is sound psychology for the individual, and it is equally sound for the nation.

Hence, the *moral right of the majority to enter upon the war imports the moral right to secure success by suppressing public agitation against the completion of the struggle.* If a company of soldiers in war-time on their way to the front were halted for rest in the public highway, and a disaffected citizen, going among them, were to begin thus to harangue: "Boys! this is a bad war! We ought not to be in it! And you ought not to be in it—" the state would have a moral right to step promptly up to that man and smite him on the mouth. So would any well-meaning citizen, for that matter. And that moral right is the basis of the Espionage Act, in its application to these circulars. . . .

So, on all these grounds, when war is once nationally decided upon, public speech against the rightness of the war may justly be limited or suppressed. And it *must* be limited or suppressed in a war like that one which has just brought victorious relief to the civilized world.

Times of Peace

The *normal* situation, in time of peace, is different. Here the "free trade in ideas" may be left to signify unlicensed ventilation of the most extreme views, sane or insane, on any subject whatsoever. The only problem is (as above noted) to draw the dead-line between "persuasion to murder" (in the phrase of the Minority Opinion), and discussion of the theoretic right and wrong of murder.

Where is the line to be drawn?

The Minority Opinion, and its congeners, seem to go upon the assumption that when in any utterance there is an "expression of opinion" as such, that expression of opinion should include and condone and immune an "exhortation" to illegal acts with which the expression of opinion may culminate. For example, in this view, if I circularize my associates thus: "I want and urge you to go to Washington and kill any two of the Supreme Justices," that utterance may constitutionally be made punishable, in spite of "freedom of speech." But if I precede that incitement by a preambular form of reasoning, thus: "The Government of the United States is capitalistic; it was founded on force; it embedded in the Constitution the foul grip of the property holders of 1789, who have never since let go; it provided a Supreme Court which will nullify any statute that attempts to free the people from that tyrannous clutch; those justices have ratified the verdicts of juries (packed by those same capitalists) which sent to jail such heroes as Debs and Goldman, and have upheld the statute which deported our sainted leader, Berkman, and hundreds of other innocent persons; there is no hope of freeing the Nation from the incubus of this constitution until these pusillanimous judges are terrorized and shown what the future portends for them; and the hope of happiness for the down-trodden multitudes of this doomed country can never revive unless these judges are made to feel that the safety of their lives depends upon right decisions; as the only way to give effect to these views, therefore, *I urge you to go to Washington and kill any two of the Supreme Court Justices.*"

If this preamble of opinion and reasoning be employed, it saves and immunes the murderous incitement in which it culminates— an incitement which would by itself have been punishable.

Such seems to be the underlying notion of the Minority Opinion.

If it is not, let some one who supports that Minority Opinion come forward and provide us with some concrete illustration of what it does mean. Judged by the *Abrams* case, it goes the above length and no less. If such horrific and absurd consequences are not meant, it is time that its defenders clarify its meaning with some canon which the friends of law and order can accept. . . .

The problem as a whole includes always two persons and three or four stages of conduct; (a) A's expression of opinion on a subject, (b) ending in A's exhortation or incitement of (c) B to do an act (d) having consequences deemed deleterious. Suppose a law is passed forbidding A to exhort or incite B to a certain act. If this act is per se illegal, there is virtually no difficulty; a statute may concededly forbid exhortation to do an illegal act. But the act may not in itself be illegal; it may merely have deleterious consequences. For example, the munition workers' cessation of work might be in itself legal; it was the consequences that were deleterious, by curtailment in war-time of indispensable war material. The Legislature must be permitted to take measures to prevent such consequences. The problem is how to define the scope of statute which may thus aim to prevent these consequences while leaving sufficient play for the constitutional sanction of freedom of discussion.

The following would do it:

A statute does not abridge constitutional freedom of speech if it *forbids A's exhortation of B to do a specific act which would have consequences deemed by the legislature to be deleterious to the commonwealth*. But a statute does abridge such freedom which forbids A's expression of opinion to B that a specific act and its consequences ought not to be prevented by law, or forbids A's *exhortation to B to join in removing that legal obstacle by the usual legislative methods. . . .*

For example, take the prohibition measures. It is yet lawful for A to drink intoxicating liquor from his domestic stock, and for B to drink from it at A's invitation. Suppose that a statute should forbid A to invite B to his house for the purpose of so drinking; and suppose that an indignant A circularizes his friends arguing for the folly of such a restriction and urging them to come to his house for the purpose. Could this circular be protected by constitutional freedom of speech? Certainly not. It defies the practical enforcement of the law, and invites to action having precisely the disapproved consequences. Let A, however, if he pleases, argue with his friends that the restriction is excessive, and let him persuade them to appeal to the legislature for a repeal of the statute. But, so long as it remains law, let him not be licensed to undermine its operation on the pretext of freedom of speech. The pretext is needless, for he is still at liberty to discuss the wisdom of the law and to seek to change it by usual methods of changing the public opinion to sounder judgment. And that is all that the right of freedom of speech exists for, in the last analysis.

Americans Have True Freedom of Speech

After all, is not this tenderness for the right of freedom of speech an over-anxiety? Is not this sensitive dread of its infringement an anachronism? Has not the struggle for the establishment of that freedom been won, and won permanently, a century ago? Do we not really possess, in the fullest permanent safety, a freedom and a license for the *discussion* of the pros and cons of every subject under the sun? Simply as a matter of "free trade in ideas," is there not in Anglo-America today an irrevocably established free trade in every blasphemous, scurrilous, shocking, iconoclastic, or lunatic idea that any fanatical or unbalanced brain can conceive? And is there any axiom of law, constitution, morals, religion, or decency which you and I cannot today publicly dispute with legal immunity?

I firmly believe that in these days the tender champions of free speech are, like Don Quixote, fighting giants and ogres who have long since been laid in the dust. John Huss, in his day, five centuries ago, was genuinely in need of a freedom-of-speech right. Galileo suffered for lack of it. Through the long centuries its evolution was landmarked by other champions or victims—Martin Luther, Algernon Sidney, Hugh Latimer, Michael Servetus, William Prynne, John Milton, Jeremy Taylor, Voltaire, John Wilkes, Thomas Paine, Thomas Erskine, Charles James Fox, William Hone —some demagogues, some divines; some scholars, some statesmen; and all of them shatterers of orthodoxy. But when the nineteenth century dawned, the struggle had been won. The principle was established. And, in Anglo-America, at least, there never has been a time since the 1820's when it was really in danger. . . .

Time does settle some things. The emotional conditions of religious and political intolerance and persecution out of which emerged a perception of the need for "free trade in ideas" have long since quieted down. It is an anachronism to imagine that they continue, and to argue as though we were still living in the days of Huss and Galileo and Latimer.

And so the danger now is rather that this misplaced reverence for freedom of speech should lead us to minimize or ignore other fundamentals which in today's conditions are far more in need of reverence and protection. Let us show some sense of proportion in weighing the several fundamentals. No single political principle can override all the others. It will not do to let freedom of speech obscure for us the demands of other elements of liberty and safety. . . .

The truth is that the constitutional guarantee of freedom of speech is being invoked more and more in misuse. It represents the unfair protection much desired by impatient and fanatical minorities—fanatically committed to some new revolutionary belief, and impatient of the usual process of rationally converting the majority. The period is one of changing views in multifarious fields. Institutional reconstruction on a wide scale is due in the coming generation—reconstruction on a wider scale than at any time since three generations ago. Certain leaders of thought— some idealists, some materialists—see only red when their own particular doctrines are balked of immediate general acceptance. Impatient of that "free trade in ideas" which the Minority Opinion assures us will exhibit ultimately the "power of the thought to get itself accepted," these fanatical leaders invoke club-law. They call for "direct action" (this cowardly euphemism for brutal mob-violence must now be familiar to all readers of recent periodical literature). And when their urgent propaganda of club-law meets lawful interference, they invoke the sacred constitutional guarantee of "freedom of speech." It is simply a profanation of that term.

VIEWPOINT 7

"Freedom of speech . . . does not protect publications or teachings . . . prompting the overthrow of the government by force."

Freedom of Speech Must Be Curbed for the Public Good

Edward T. Sanford (1865-1930)

The end of World War I did not end the controversies over government actions restricting free speech. Many leaders urged that wartime laws against Germans and critics of World War I now be used against anarchists, labor leaders, and other critics of the social order. The "Red Scare" of 1919-1920 featured massive government raids leading to the detentions and deportations of suspected radicals, with little regard for free speech or due process. In addition, states and localities enforced their own laws against dissent.

New York was one of thirty-three states in 1921 that had criminal anarchy statutes making it a crime to advocate the violent overthrow of the government. In November 1919 New York police arrested Benjamin Gitlow, a member of the left-wing faction of the Socialist party, and charged him with violating the 1902 Criminal Anarchy Act. Gitlow had published a tract called *The Left Wing Manifesto*, in which he argued that the only way to obtain economic justice in America was by Communist revolution. He was convicted in 1920 and sentenced to five to ten years in prison. With the assistance of the newly established American Civil Liberties Union, Gitlow appealed to the Supreme Court.

From the majority opinion of the U.S. Supreme Court in *Gitlow v. New York*, 268 U.S. 652 (1925).

Gitlow's attorney, Walter Pollak of the American Civil Liberties Union, presented two main arguments before the Supreme Court. One was that the state of New York had failed to prove that Gitlow's publications created a "clear and present danger" of immediate unlawful action. The prosecution thus failed to pass the "clear and present danger" test first proposed by Justice Oliver Wendell Holmes in *Schenck v. United States*. Pollak's second argument was that the Fourteenth Amendment to the Constitution, which prohibited states from depriving "any person of life, liberty, or property, without due process of law," meant that the free speech protections of the Bill of Rights should be applied to state as well as federal laws.

The Supreme Court ruled to uphold Gitlow's conviction, with only Justices Oliver Wendell Holmes and Louis Brandeis dissenting. Edward T. Sanford, who served on the Supreme Court from 1923 until his death in 1930, wrote the majority opinion. In it, he conceded that Gitlow's publications did not necessarily create a clear and present danger. However, he argues, the writings produce a "bad tendency" to corrupt the public and incite crime. He asserts that the government had the proper authority to determine whether to prohibit certain writings that advocate or incite dangerous acts, to preserve its "right of self-preservation." The Supreme Court's only decision, he argued, was to determine if the legislative judgment that produced the criminal anarchy statute was an unreasonable one. Sanford concluded that it was not.

Pollak had more success with his second argument, and that is the main reason *Gitlow v. New York* is remembered today. The Supreme Court had until this time resisted Pollak's interpretation of the Fourteenth Amendment, that the Bill of Rights applied to state governments as well as the federal government. But in his majority opinion, Sanford agreed with this point. A single sentence in this judicial opinion opened the door for future challenges to state laws on First and Fourteenth Amendment grounds. Thus, although Gitlow lost his appeal, his case was an ultimate victory for the Bill of Rights. After serving three years of his sentence, Gitlow was pardoned by New York governor Al Smith.

The correctness of the verdict is not questioned, as the case was submitted to the jury. The sole contention here is, essentially, that as there was no evidence of any concrete result flowing from the publication of the Manifesto or of circumstances showing the likelihood of such result, the statute as construed and applied by the trial court penalizes the mere utterance, as such, of "doctrine" having no quality of incitement, without regard either to the circumstances of its utterance or to the likelihood of unlawful sequences; and that, as the exercise of the right of free expression with relation to government is only punishable "in circumstances involving likelihood of substantive evil," the statute contravenes the due process clause of the Fourteenth Amendment.

The Criminal Anarchy Statute

The 1902 Criminal Anarchy Statute under which Benjamin Gitlow was convicted placed explicit restrictions on freedoms of speech and the press.

Section 161. *Advocacy of criminal anarchy*. Any person who:

1. By word of mouth or writing advocates, advises, or teaches the duty, necessity, or propriety of overthrowing or overturning organized government by force or violence, or by assassination of the executive head or of any of the executive officials of government, or by any unlawful means; or,

2. Prints, publishes, edits, issues, or knowingly circulates, sells, distributes, or publicly displays any book, paper, document, or written or printed matter in any form containing or advocating, advising, or teaching the doctrine that organized government should be overthrown by force, violence, or any unlawful means . . . is guilty of a felony and punishable by imprisonment or fine, or both.

The argument in support of this contention rests primarily upon the following propositions: (1) that the "liberty" protected by the Fourteenth Amendment includes the liberty of speech and of the press; and (2) that while liberty of expression "is not absolute," it may be restrained "only in circumstances where its exercise bears a causal relation with some substantive evil, consummated, attempted, or likely," and as the statute "takes no account of circumstances," it unduly restrains this liberty and is therefore unconstitutional.

The precise question presented, and the only question which we can consider under this writ of error, then, is whether the statute, as construed and applied in this case by the state courts, deprived the defendant of his liberty of expression in violation of the due process clause of the Fourteenth Amendment.

The statute does not penalize the utterance or publication of abstract "doctrine" or academic discussion having no quality of incitement to any concrete action. It is not aimed against mere historical or philosophical essays. It does not restrain the advocacy of changes in the form of government by constitutional and lawful means. What it prohibits is language advocating, advising, or teaching the overthrow of organized government by unlawful means. These words imply urging to action. . . .

The Manifesto, plainly, is neither the statement of abstract doctrine nor, as suggested by counsel, mere prediction that industrial disturbances and revolutionary mass strikes will result spontaneously in an inevitable process of evolution in the economic system. It advocates and urges in fervent language mass action which shall progressively foment industrial disturbances, and, through political mass strikes and revolutionary mass action, overthrow and destroy organized parliamentary government. It concludes with a call to action in these words: "The proletariat revolution and the Communist reconstruction of society—*the struggle for these*—is now indispensable. . . . The Communist International calls the proletariat of the world to the final struggle!" This is not the expression of philosophical abstraction, the mere prediction of future events: it is the language of direct incitement.

The means advocated for bringing about destruction of organized parliamentary government, namely, mass industrial revolts usurping the functions of municipal government, political mass strikes directed against the parliamentary state, and revolutionary mass action for its final destruction, necessarily imply the use of force and violence. . . . That the jury were warranted in finding that the Manifesto advocated not merely the abstract doctrine of overwhelming organized government by force, violence, and unlawful means, but action to that end, is clear.

The First Amendment and the States

For present purposes we may and do assume that freedom of speech and of the press—which are protected by the 1st Amendment from abridgment by Congress—are among the fundamental personal rights and "liberties" protected by the due process clause of the 14th Amendment from impairment by the states. . . .

It is a fundamental principle, long established, that the freedom of speech and of the press which is secured by the Constitution does not confer an absolute right to speak or publish, without responsibility, whatever one may choose, or an unrestricted and unbridled license that gives immunity for every possible use of language, and prevents the punishment of those who abuse this freedom. . . .

That a state, in the exercise of its police power, may punish those who abuse this freedom by utterances inimical to the public welfare, tending to corrupt public morals, incite to crime, or disturb the public peace, is not open to question. . . .

Freedom of speech and press . . . does not protect disturbances of the public peace or the attempt to subvert the government. It does not protect publications or teachings which tend to subvert or imperil the government or to impede or hinder it in the performance of its governmental duties. . . . It does not protect publications prompting the overthrow of government by force; the punishment of those who publish articles which tend to destroy organized society being essential to the security of freedom and stability of the state. . . . And a state may penalize utterances which openly advocate the overthrow of the representative and constitutional form of government of the United States and the several states, by violence or other unlawful means. . . . In short, this freedom does not deprive a state of the primary and essential right of self-preservation, which, so long as human governments endure, they cannot be denied. . . .

By enacting the present statute the state had determined, through its legislative body, that utterances advocating the overthrow of organized government by force, violence, and unlawful means, are so inimical to the general welfare, and involve such danger of substantive evil, that they may be penalized in the exercise of its police power. That determination must be given great weight. Every presumption is to be indulged in favor of the validity of the statute. . . . That utterances inciting to the overthrow of organized government by unlawful means present a sufficient danger of substantive evil to bring their punishment within the range of legislative discretion is clear. Such utterances, by their very nature, involve danger to the public peace and to the security of the state. They threaten breaches of the peace and ultimate revolution. And the immediate danger is none the less real and substantial because the effect of a given utterance cannot be accurately foreseen. The state cannot reasonably be required to measure the danger from every such utterance in the nice balance of a jeweler's scale. A single revolutionary spark may kindle a fire that, smoldering for a time, may burst into a sweeping and destructive conflagration. It cannot be said that the state is acting arbitrarily or unreasonably when, in the exercise of its judgment as to the measures necessary to protect the public peace and safety, it seeks to extinguish the spark without waiting until it has enkindled the flame or blazed into the conflagration. It cannot reasonably be required to defer the adoption of measures for its own peace and safety until the revolutionary utterances lead to actual disturbances of the public peace or imminent and immediate danger of its own destruction; but it may, in the exercise of its judgment, suppress the threatened danger in its incipiency. . . .

We cannot hold that the present statute is an arbitrary or unreasonable exercise of the police power of the state, unwarrantably infringing the freedom of speech or press; and we must and do sustain its constitutionality.

Viewpoint 8

"Fear of serious injury cannot alone justify suppression of free speech and assembly."

Freedom of Speech Benefits the Public Good

Louis Brandeis (1856-1941)

Louis Brandeis was an associate justice of the U.S. Supreme Court from 1916 to 1939. A lawyer and political reformer, Brandeis, along with Oliver Wendell Holmes, is noted for a series of dissents he made in defense of civil liberties, and for criticizing the Supreme Court for invalidating economic and social legislation.

Brandeis gave one of his most famous opinions in the 1927 case *Whitney v. California*. The case involved yet another state law which attempted to outlaw all communist and radical political activity. Historian Franklyn S. Haiman writes:

> Anita Whitney, a niece of former Supreme Court Justice Stephen Field, had been convicted of violating the state's Criminal Syndicalism Act under circumstances suggesting that her "crime" was mere attendance at a radical convention. Because, at her trial, Miss Whitney did not make an issue of whether her activities constituted a clear and present danger, Justice Brandeis felt he had to concur in sustaining the judgment of the lower courts. Nevertheless, he proceeded to make clear his views on the substance of the matter.

Although Brandeis is commenting on a case two years subsequent to *Gitlow v. New York*, historian Harry Kalven Jr. writes in his study *A Worthy Tradition*, "*Whitney* is close enough to *Gitlow*

From Louis Brandeis's dissenting opinion in the U.S. Supreme Court decision in *Whitney v. California*, 274 U.S. 357 (1927).

in its statute and on its facts that Brandeis's opinion can properly be read as though he were responding directly to the Sanford opinion in *Gitlow*." In his judicial opinion Brandeis is further developing views on the "clear and present danger" test first expounded by Oliver Wendell Holmes in 1919. He advocates giving broad latitude for free speech and argues that statutes classifying whole areas or types of speech as harmful violate the intentions of the nation's founders. He argues that free speech in itself is integral to the public good.

This court has not yet fixed the standard by which to determine when a danger shall be deemed clear; how remote the danger may be and yet be deemed present; and what degree of evil shall be deemed sufficiently substantial to justify resort to abridgment of free speech and assembly as the means of protection. To reach sound conclusions on these matters, we must bear in mind why a state is, ordinarily, denied the power to prohibit dissemination of social, economic and political doctrine which a vast majority of citizens believes to be false and fraught with evil consequence.

Those who won our independence believed that the final end of the state was to make men free to develop their faculties; and that in its government the deliberative forces should prevail over the arbitrary. They valued liberty both as an end and as a means. They believed liberty to be the secret of happiness and courage to be the secret of liberty. They believed that freedom to think as you will and to speak as you think are means indispensable to the discovery and spread of political truth; that without free speech and assembly discussion would be futile; that with them, discussion affords ordinarily adequate protection against the dissemination of noxious doctrine; that the greatest menace to freedom is an inert people; that public discussion is a political duty; and that this should be a fundamental principle of the American government. They recognized the risks to which all human institutions are subject. But they knew that order cannot be secured merely through fear of punishment for its infraction; that it is hazardous to discourage thought, hope and imagination; that fear breeds repression; that repression breeds hate; that hate menaces stable government; that the path of safety lies in the opportunity to discuss freely supposed grievances and proposed remedies; and that the fitting remedy for evil counsels is good ones. Believing in the power of reason as applied through public discussion, they eschewed silence coerced by law—the argument of force in its worst form. Recognizing the occasional tyrannies of governing majorities, they amended the Constitution so that free speech and assembly should be guaranteed.

What the First Amendment Protects

Alexander Meiklejohn, a president of Amherst College in Massachusetts, wrote numerous books and articles on the philosophy and meaning of freedom. In his 1948 book Political Freedom, *he criticizes the Supreme Court's* Gitlow *decision restricting speech.*

Freedom to engage in "mere academic and harmless discussion"! Is that the freedom which is guarded by the First Amendment? Is that the cause for which the followers of Socrates have fought and died through the ages? As against that intolerant belittling of the practical value of human freedom of mind, Mr. Holmes, in his dissent, entered spirited, if not very coherent, words of protest. . . .

Human discourse, as the First Amendment sees it, is not "a mere academic and harmless discourse." If it were, the advocates of self-government would be as little concerned about it as they would be concerned about the freedom of men playing solitaire or chess. The First Amendment was not written primarily for the protection of those intellectual aristocrats who pursue knowledge solely for the fun of the game. . . . It offers defense to men who plan and advocate and incite toward corporate action for the common good.

Fear of serious injury cannot alone justify suppression of free speech and assembly. Men feared witches and burned women. It is the function of speech to free men from the bondage of irrational fears. To justify suppression of free speech there must be reasonable ground to fear that serious evil will result if free speech is practiced. There must be reasonable ground to believe that the danger apprehended is imminent. There must be reasonable ground to believe that the evil to be prevented is a serious one. Every denunciation of existing law tends in some measure to increase the probability that there will be violation of it. Condonation of a breach enhances the probability. Expressions of approval add to the probability. Propagation of the criminal state of mind by teaching syndicalism increases it. Advocacy of lawbreaking heightens it still further. But even advocacy of violation, however reprehensible morally, is not a justification for denying free speech where the advocacy falls short of incitement and there is nothing to indicate that the advocacy would be immediately acted on. The wide difference between advocacy and incitement, between preparation and attempt, between assembling and conspiracy, must be borne in mind. In order to support a finding of clear and present danger it must be shown either that immediate serious violence was to be expected or was advocated, or that the past conduct furnished reason to believe that such advocacy was then contemplated.

Those who won our independence by revolution were not cowards. They did not fear political change. They did not exalt order at the cost of liberty. To courageous, self-reliant men, with confidence in the power of free and fearless reasoning applied through the processes of popular government, no danger flowing from speech can be deemed clear and present, unless the incidence of the evil apprehended is so imminent that it may befall before there is opportunity for full discussion. If there be time to expose through discussion the falsehood and fallacies, to avert the evil by the processes of education, the remedy to be applied is more speech, not enforced silence. Only an emergency can justify repression. Such must be the rule if authority is to be reconciled with freedom. Such, in my opinion, is the command of the Constitution. It is, therefore, always open to Americans to challenge a law abridging free speech and assembly by showing that there was no emergency justifying it.

The Need to Prove Immediate Harm

Moreover, even imminent danger cannot justify resort to prohibition of these functions essential to effective democracy, unless the evil apprehended is relatively serious. Prohibition of free speech and assembly is a measure so stringent that it would be inappropriate as the means for averting a relatively trivial harm to society. A police measure may be unconstitutional merely because the remedy, although effective as means of protection, is unduly harsh or oppressive. Thus, a state might, in the exercise of its police power, make any trespass upon the land of another a crime, regardless of the results or of the intent or purpose of the trespasser. It might, also, punish an attempt, a conspiracy, or an incitement to commit the trespass. But it is hardly conceivable that this court would hold constitutional a statute which punished as a felony the mere voluntary assembly with a society formed to teach that pedestrians had the moral right to cross unenclosed, unposted, waste lands and to advocate their doing so, even if there was imminent danger that advocacy would lead to a trespass. The fact that speech is likely to result in some violence or in destruction of property is not enough to justify its suppression. There must be the probability of serious injury to the state. Among freemen, the deterrents ordinarily to be applied to prevent crime are education and punishment for violations of the law, not abridgment of the rights of free speech and assembly.

CHAPTER 3

The Separation of Church and State

Chapter Preface

The First Amendment begins by stating that "Congress shall make no law respecting an establishment of religion, or prohibiting the free exercise therof." The fact that religion is the first freedom listed indicates its importance to the American people. However, despite its undeniable achievement in creating religious liberty, the precise meaning and implications of this phrase have been the source of considerable controversy.

Most analyses of this part of the Bill of Rights separate its guarantee of religious freedom into two clauses—the establishment clause ("respecting an establishment of religion") and the free exercise clause ("prohibiting the free exercise therof"). Both phrases refer to restrictions on government activity. The establishment clause prohibits government from taking steps to establish an official church or religion. The free exercise clause prohibits government from interfering with the expression of religious beliefs. The implications of these two clauses, and the fact that the rights they protect may sometimes conflict, have been a source of disagreement. Does the establishment clause forbid *any* intermingling of church and state functions, or does it simply forbid the establishment of a national church or the preferential treatment of a particular sect or religion? Do government measures accommodating religious practices violate the establishment clause or fulfill the free exercise clause?

In attempting to ascertain the meaning and implications of the First Amendment, many judges, scholars, and others have looked to an important phrase that does not appear in the Bill of Rights. In an 1802 letter to the Danbury Baptist Association, President Thomas Jefferson stated that the First Amendment had created "a wall of separation between Church & State." What Jefferson meant by that phrase is still debated by historians, but his metaphor is one of several historical pieces of evidence repeatedly cited in the public debate over church-state relations in the United States, as people disagree whether the First Amendment really did create a "wall of separation."

Because the Supreme Court held that the Bill of Rights limited the powers of only the federal government, not the states, it made very few rulings on the religious clauses of the First Amendment from 1789 to 1940. Most freedom of religion issues related to state and local laws. Then in the 1940 case *Cantwell v. Connecticut* the Supreme Court made two significant assertions. One was that the

First Amendment's guarantee of freedom of religion was made applicable to state and local governments by the Fourteenth Amendment's guarantee of due process. In this ruling the Supreme Court followed the precedent set in 1925 in *Gitlow v. New York*. In that case the Court held that the First Amendment's free speech provisions applied to the states. A second significant assertion in *Cantwell v. Connecticut* was that freedom of religion "embraces two concepts—freedom to believe and freedom to act. The first is absolute but, in the nature of things, the second cannot be." In this the Court was affirming a judgment it made in 1879 in *Reynolds v. United States*, when it upheld federal laws against polygamy. Polygamy was then advocated by the Mormon church, but the Court ruled that while government could not prohibit the *belief* in polygamy, it could prohibit its *practice*—a distinction the Supreme Court uses, with some refinements, to this day.

Since 1940 the Supreme Court has made numerous rulings concerning both the establishment and free exercise of religion. Many of these cases involved the proper role of religious belief and practices in the nation's public schools. The controversy many of these rulings created illustrates the continuing national debate over the meaning of religious freedom in America as expressed in the Bill of Rights. Three significant cases and an important historical debate cited in those cases are examined in this chapter.

VIEWPOINT 1

"Should it be thought necessary at present for the Assembly to exert the right of supporting religion in general by an assessment on all the people, we would wish it to be done on the most liberal plan.*"*

A General Religious Tax Can Be Consistent with Religious Freedom

The Presbytery of Hanover

In the years 1784 to 1786, the people of the state of Virginia had a tumultuous and historic debate over the meaning and establishment of religious liberty, a debate that ultimately culminated in the passage of the Statute for Religious Freedom. Although the episode took place before the writing of the U.S. Constitution and the Bill of Rights, many of the protagonists in the Virginia debate also played a major role in the creation of those documents. In the twentieth century the U.S. Supreme Court in several cases looked back to this episode in Virginia's history in an effort to properly interpret the meaning of the religion clause of the First Amendment.

During most of its history, the colony of Virginia viewed the Anglican (later Episcopal) church as its official church. The Anglican church received preferential status in the form of public tax support, land grants, state-compelled church attendance, and state punishment of certain religious offenses, including blasphemy. Most of the church's funds came from a mandatory tax on all Virginians regardless of whether they were church members. Although other sects, including Baptists and Presbyterians, were

From the "Memorial of the Presbytery of Hanover to the Assembly" of Virginia, November 12, 1784.

able to grow and eventually achieve a status of toleration, the Episcopal church remained supreme in the eyes of Virginia's law. This situation continued until the American Revolution. In 1776 Virginia abolished the requirement that nonmembers pay taxes to the Episcopal church; three years later church members were also relieved of compulsory taxation. Virginia's 1776 constitution contained a clause on religious freedom that was partially written by the young legislator James Madison, who would later play an influential role in the creation of the national Bill of Rights:

> Religion . . . can be directed only by reason and conviction, not by force or violence; and therefore, all men are equally entitled to the free exercise of religion according to the dictates of conscience.

Virginia's Episcopal churches suffered in the loss of support during the revolutionary war, and many of Virginia's political leaders worried about a general decline of religion and morality in the new state. In 1784 Patrick Henry, the noted revolutionary orator and political leader, proposed a Bill Establishing a Provision for Teachers of the Christian Religion. Commonly called the General Assessment Bill, it would require a modest annual tax for the support of the Christian religion. Instead of supporting just one established church, however, the bill would allow taxpayers to designate which church would benefit or, alternatively, could designate their tax "for the encouragement of seminaries of learning." Henry and others asserted that such provisions would help support religion but would not violate Virginia's new constitution and its clause on religious liberty.

Of the three main denominations in Virginia at that time, the Episcopalians generally supported the General Assessment, viewing it as a way to at least partially regain some of the support lost during the Revolution. The Baptists, early and consistent advocates of the separation of church and state, firmly opposed the measure. The Presbyterians took a position somewhere in the middle.

The founding of the Hanover Presbytery in 1760 under the leadership of dissenting minister Samuel Davies marked an important development in the struggle of the Presbyterians for religious equality with the established Anglican church. The Hanover Presbytery sent several notable petitions to the Virginia legislature, including one in 1776 advocating reform so that "every religious sect may be protected in the full exercise of their several modes of worship, and exempted from the payment of all taxes for the support of any church whatever." However, when the Presbyterian clergy of the Hanover district met in October 1784, the passage of Henry's General Assessment Bill seemed imminent. Thus, after expressing opposition to the establishment of any official state church, the petition to the legislature cautiously endorsed the idea of a general assessment, providing that it did not interfere with religious practice or assist any particular denomination. The statement was presented to the Virginia legislature on November 12, 1784. Historian H. J. Eckenrode credits John Blair Smith, one of the leaders of the Presbyterian clergy, with writing it.

To the Honourable Speaker and House of Delegates of Virginia:
Gentlemen—The united clergy of the Presbyterian church of Virginia assembled in Presbytery beg leave again to address your honorable house upon a few important subjects in which we find ourselves interested as citizens of this State.

The freedom we possess is so rich a blessing, and the purchase of it has been so high that we would ever wish to cherish a spirit of vigilant attention to it in every circumstance of possible danger. We are anxious to retain a full share of all the privileges which our happy revolution affords, and cannot but feel alarmed at the continued existence of any infringement upon them or even any indirect attempt tending to this. Impressed with this idea as men, whose rights are sacred and dear to them, ought to be, we are obliged to express our sensibility upon the present occasion, and we naturally direct our appeal to you gentlemen as the public guardians of our country's happiness and liberty, who are influenced we hope by that wisdom and justice which your high station requires. Conscious of the rectitude of our intention and the strength of our claim, we wish to speak our sentiments freely upon these occasions, but at the same time with all that respectful regard which becomes us when addressing the representatives of a great and virtuous people. . . . We have understood that a comprehensive incorporating act has been and is at present in aggitation, whereby ministers of the gospel as such, of certain descriptions, shall have legal advantages which are not proposed to be extended to the people at large of any denomination. A proposition has been made by some gentlemen in the house of delegates, we are told, to extend the grace to us amongst others in our professional capacity. If this be so we are bound to acknowledge with gratitude our obligations to such gentlemen for their inclination to favor us with the sanction of public authority in the discharge of our duty. But as the scheme of incorporating clergymen, *independent of the religious communities to which they belong*, is inconsistent with our ideas of propriety, we request the liberty of declining any such solitary honor should it be again proposed. To form clergymen into a distinct order in the community, and especially where it would be possible for them to have the principal direction of a considerable public estate by such incorporation, has a tendency to render them independent, at length, of the churches whose ministers they are; and this has been too often found by experience to produce ignorance, immorality and neglect of the duties of their station.

A Petition for the General Assessment

Among the petitions sent to the Virginia House of Delegates during the General Assessment debate was this one from residents of the Isle of Wight in support of taxes for religion.

A petition of sundry inhabitants of the county of Isle of Wight, whose names are thereunto subscribed, was presented to the House and read; setting forth that they are much concerned to see the countenance of the civil power wholly withdrawn from religion, and the people left without the smallest coercion to contribute to its support; that they consider it as the duty of a wise Legislature to encourage its progress and diffuse its influence; that, being thoroughly convinced that the prosperity and happiness of this country essentially depends on the progress of religion, they beg leave to call the attention of the Legislature to a principle, old as society itself, that whatever is to conduce equally to the advantage of all should be borne equally by all; and praying that an act may pass to compel every one to contribute something, in proportion to his property, to the support of religion.

Besides, if clergymen were to be erected by the State into a distinct political body, detached from the rest of the citizens, with the express design of "enabling them to direct spiritual matters," which we all possess without such formality, it would naturally tend to introduce the antiquated and absurd system in which government is owned in effect to be the fountain head of spiritual influences to the church. It would establish an immediate, a peculiar, and for that very reason, in our opinion, illicit connection between government and such as were thus distinguished. The Legislature in that case would be the head of the religious party, and its dependent members would be entitled to all decent reciprocity to a becoming paternal and fostering care. This we suppose would be given a preference, and creating a distinction between citizens equally good, on account of something entirely foreign from civil merit, which would be a source of endless jealousies, and inadmissible in a Republic of any other well directed government. The principle, too, which this system aims to establish is both false and dangerous to religion, and we take this opportunity to remonstrate and protest against it. . . .

Human Affairs

We conceive that human legislation ought to have human affairs alone for its concern. Legislators in free States possess delegated authority for the good of the community at large in its political and civil capacity.

The existence, preservation and happiness of society should be their only object, and to this their public cares should be confined. Whatever is not materially connected with this lies not within their province as statesmen. The thoughts, the intentions, the faith and the consciences of men, with their modes of worship, lie beyond their reach, and are ever to be referred to a higher and more penetrating tribunal. These internal and spiritual matters cannot be measured by human rule, nor be amenable to human laws. It is the duty of every man for himself to take care of his immortal interests in a future state, where we are to account for our conduct as individuals; and it is by no means the business of the Legislature to attend to this, for *there* governments and states, as collective bodies, shall no more be known.

Religion, therefore, as a spiritual system, and its ministers in a professional capacity, ought not to be under the direction of the State.

Neither is it necessary for their existence that they should be publicly supported by legal provision for the purpose, as tried experience hath often shown; although it is absolutely necessary to the existence and welfare of every political combination of men in society to have the support of religion and its solemn institutions, as it affects the conduct of rational beings more than human laws can possibly do. On this account it is wise policy in legislators to seek its alliance and solicit its aid in a civil view, because of its happy influence upon the morality of its citizens, and its tendency to preserve the veneration of an oath, or an appeal to heaven, which is the cement of the social union. It is upon this principle alone, in our opinion, that a legislative body has right to interfere in religion at all, and of consequence we suppose that this interference ought only to extend to the preserving of the public worship of the Deity, and the supporting of institutions for inculcating the great fundamental principles of all religion, without which society could not easily exist. Should it be thought necessary at present for the Assembly to exert the right of supporting religion in general by an assessment on all the people, we would wish it to be done on the most *liberal plan*. A general assessment of the kind we have heard proposed is an object of such consequence that it excites much anxious speculation amongst your constituents.

We therefore earnestly pray that nothing may be done in the case inconsistent with the proper objects of human legislation, or the Declaration of Rights, as published at the Revolution. We hope that the assessment will not be proposed under the idea of supporting religion as a spiritual system, relating to the care of the soul, and preparing it for its future destiny. We hope that no attempt will be made to point out articles of faith that are not essential to the preservation of society; or to settle modes of worship; or to interfere in the internal government of religious communities; *or to render the ministers of religion independent of the will of the people whom they serve.* We expect from our representatives that careful attention to the political equality of all the citizens which a republic ought ever to cherish, and no scheme of an assessment will be encouraged which will violate the happy privilege we now enjoy of thinking for ourselves in all cases where conscience is concerned.

We request the candid indulgence of the honorable House to the present address, and their most favorable construction of the motives which induce us to obtrude ourselves into public notice. We are urged by a sense of duty. We feel ourselves impressed with the importance of the present crisis. We have expressed ourselves in the plain language of freemen upon the interesting subjects which call for animadversion, and we hope to stand excused with you, gentlemen, for the manner in which it is executed, as well as for the part we take in the public interests of the community. In the present important moment we conceive it criminal to be silent, and have therefore attempted to discharge a duty which we owe our religion as Christians, to ourselves as freemen, and to our posterity, who ought to receive from us a precious birthright of perfect freedom and political equality.

That you may enjoy the direction of heaven in your present deliberations, and possess in a high degree the spirit of your exalted station, is the prayer of your sincere well-wishers,

The Presbytery of Hanover.

VIEWPOINT 2

"The religion, then, of every man must be left to the conviction and conscience of every man."

A General Religious Tax Is Detrimental to Religious Freedom

James Madison (1751-1836)

James Madison, fourth president of the United States, was one of the leading figures in the formation of the U.S. Constitution and the Bill of Rights. In interpreting the Bill of Rights, especially the First Amendment section regarding religion, Supreme Court justices and others have looked back to a document written in 1785 titled *Memorial and Remonstrance Against Religious Assessments*.

The pamphlet, one of Madison's most famous writings on the subject of religious liberty, resulted from a political struggle in 1784-85 over whether to pass a general tax in support of religion, in lieu of maintaining a state-established church. Patrick Henry, Richard Henry Lee, and other prominent Virginia political leaders had sponsored a General Assessment Bill, which declared that "the Christian religion shall in all times coming be deemed and held to be the established religion." To that end they proposed taxes on all Virginians for the support of teachers of the Christian religion. By allowing taxpayers to designate which church the taxes could go to, Henry and others argued, religious liberty would be maintained.

James Madison, then a member of Virginia's General Assembly, opposed official support for religion, Christian or otherwise, as much as he did an official church. In his *Memorial*, he listed fifteen

From James Madison, *Memorial and Remonstrance Against Religious Assessments*, 1785.

reasons for his opposition to the measure. Madison argued that compulsory taxes violated an individual's religious conscience and that entanglement of church and state harmed both institutions. The pamphlet was widely published and distributed.

Madison's efforts, coupled with those of Baptists and other religious dissenters, resulted in the defeat of the General Assessment Bill in 1785. The victory encouraged Madison to bring up for debate a bill on church and state written by Thomas Jefferson in 1779. In 1786 the Virginia Act for Establishing Religious Freedom was passed. It declared:

> No man shall be compelled to frequent or support any religious worship, place or ministry whatsoever, nor shall be enforced, restrained . . . or otherwise suffer on account of his religious opinions or belief; but that all men shall be free to profess, and by argument to maintain, their opinions in matters of religion, and that the same shall in nowise diminish, enlarge, or affect their civil capacities.

We, the subscribers, citizens of the said Commonwealth, having taken into serious consideration a bill printed by order of the last session of General Assembly, entitled "A Bill Establishing a Provision for Teachers of the Christian Religion," and conceiving that the same, if finally armed with the sanctions of a law, will be a dangerous abuse of power, are bound as faithful members of a free state to remonstrate against it, and to declare the reasons by which we are determined. We remonstrate against the said bill:

1. Because we hold it for a fundamental and undeniable truth, "that religion or the duty which we owe to our Creator and the manner of discharging it, can be directed only by reason and conviction, not by force or violence." The religion, then, of every man must be left to the conviction and conscience of every man; and it is the right of every man to exercise it as these may dictate. This right is in its nature an unalienable right. . . . We maintain, therefore, that in matters of religion no man's right is abridged by the institution of civil society, and that religion is wholly exempt from its cognizance. True it is that no other rule exists by which any question which may divide a society can be ultimately determined than the will of the majority; but it is also true that the majority may trespass on the rights of the minority.

2. Because if religion be exempt from the authority of the society at large, still less can it be subject to that of the legislative body. The latter are but the creatures and vicegerents of the former. . . . The preservation of a free government requires not

merely that the metes and bounds which separate each department of power may be invariably maintained, but more especially that neither of them be suffered to overleap the great barrier which defends the rights of the people. The rulers who are guilty of such an encroachment exceed the commission from which they derive their authority, and are tyrants. The people who submit to it are governed by laws made neither by themselves nor by an authority derived from them, and are slaves.

Protecting Our Liberties

3. Because it is proper to take alarm at the first experiment on our liberties. We hold this prudent jealousy to be the first duty of citizens and one of the noblest characteristics of the late Revolution. The freemen of America did not wait till usurped power had strengthened itself by exercise and entangled the question in precedents. They saw all the consequences in the principle, and they avoided the consequences by denying the principle. We revere this lesson too much soon to forget it. Who does not see that the same authority which can establish Christianity, in exclusion of all other religions, may establish with the same ease any particular sect of Christians, in exclusion of all other sects? That the same authority which can force a citizen to contribute threepence only of his property for the support of any one establishment may force him to conform to any other establishment in all cases whatsoever?

4. Because the bill violates that equality which ought to be the basis of every law. . . .

While we assert for ourselves a freedom to embrace, to profess, and to observe the religion which we believe to be of divine origin, we cannot deny an equal freedom to those whose minds have not yet yielded to the evidence which has convinced us. If this freedom be abused, it is an offense against God, not against man: To God, therefore, not to man must an account of it be rendered. . . .

5. Because the bill implies either that the civil magistrate is a competent judge of religious truths, or that he may employ religion as an engine of civil policy. The first is an arrogant pretension falsified by the contradictory opinions of rulers in all ages and throughout the world; the second an unhallowed perversion of the means of salvation.

6. Because the establishment proposed by the bill is not requisite for the support of the Christian religion. To say that it is, is a contradiction to the Christian religion itself; for every page of it disavows a dependence on the powers of this world. It is a contradiction to fact, for it is known that this religion both existed and flourished, not only without the support of human laws but in spite of every opposition from them; and not only during the

period of miraculous aid but long after it had been left to its own evidence and the ordinary care of Providence. Nay, it is a contradiction in terms, for a religion not invented by human policy must have preexisted and been supported before it was established by human policy. It is, moreover, to weaken in those who profess this religion a pious confidence in its innate excellence and the patronage of its Author; and to foster in those who still reject it a suspicion that its friends are too conscious of its fallacies to trust it to its own merits.

The Harms of a General Tax for Religion

The residents of Rockbridge, Virginia, sent a petition to the Virginia House of Delegates on December 1, 1784, opposing a general tax for the support of religion.

We have been . . . informed that it is in contemplation to have a Law passed this Session of Assembly to establish a general Tax for the Support of the Ministers of the Gospel of all Denominations, with this reserve that each Man may say to whom his quota shall be given—This scheme should it take place is the best calculated to destroy Religion that perhaps could be devised and much more dangerous than the establishment of any one Sect for whilst that Sect was corrupted by being independent of the will of the particular Societies or Congregations where they officiated for their Support the rest would remain pure or at least of Good Morals—But by a general tax all will be rendered so independent of the will of the particular Societies for their Support that all will be infected with the Common contagion and we shall be more likely to have the State swarming with Fools, Sots and Gamblers than with a Sober Sensible and Exemplary Clergy—Let the Ministers of the Gospel of all denominations enjoy the Privileges common to every good Citizen protect them in their religious exercises in the Persons Property and Contracts and that we humbly conceive is all they are entitled to and all a Legislature has power to grant. We are extreamly sorry to find our most essential Rights (after all the blood and treasure expended) tottering and uncertain.

---

7. Because experience witnesses that ecclesiastical establishments, instead of maintaining the purity and efficacy of religion, have had a contrary operation. During almost fifteen centuries has the legal establishment of Christianity been on trial. What have been its fruits? More or less in all places, pride and indolence in the clergy; ignorance and servility in the laity; in both, superstition, bigotry, and persecution. Inquire of the teachers of Christianity for the ages in which it appeared in its greatest luster; those of every sect point to the ages prior to its incorporation

with civil policy. Propose a restoration of this primitive state in which its teachers depended on the voluntary rewards of their flocks; many of them predict its downfall. On which side ought their testimony to have greatest weight, when for or when against their interest?

Religion and Government

8. Because the establishment in question is not necessary for the support of civil government. If it be urged as necessary for the support of civil government only as it is a means of supporting religion, and it be not necessary for the latter purpose, it cannot be necessary for the former. If religion be not within the cognizance of civil government, how can its legal establishment be necessary to civil government? What influence in fact have ecclesiastical establishments had on civil society? In some instances they have been seen to erect a spiritual tyranny on the ruins of civil authority; in many instances they have been seen upholding the thrones of political tyranny; in no instance have they been seen the guardians of the liberties of the people. Rulers who wished to subvert the public liberty may have found an established clergy convenient auxiliaries. A just government, instituted to secure and perpetuate it, needs them not. Such a government will be best supported by protecting every citizen in the enjoyment of his religion with the same equal hand which protects his person and his property; by neither invading the equal rights of any sect, nor suffering any sect to invade those of another.

9. Because the proposed establishment is a departure from that generous policy, which, offering an asylum to the persecuted and oppressed of every nation and religion, promised a luster to our country and an accession to the number of its citizens. What a melancholy mark is the bill of sudden degeneracy! Instead of holding forth an asylum to the persecuted, it is itself a signal of persecution. It degrades from the equal rank of citizens all those whose opinions in religion do not bend to those of the legislative authority. Distant as it may be, in its present form, from the Inquisition, it differs from it only in degree. The one is the first step, the other is the last in the career of intolerance. . . .

10. Because it will have a like tendency to banish our citizens. The allurements presented by other situations are every day thinning their number. To superadd a fresh motive to emigration by revoking the liberty which they now enjoy would be the same species of folly which has dishonored and depopulated flourishing kingdoms.

11. Because it will destroy that moderation and harmony which the forbearance of our laws to intermeddle with religion has produced amongst its several sects. Torrents of blood have been

spilled in the Old World [by] vain attempts of the secular arm to extinguish religious discord by proscribing all differences in religious opinion. Time has at length revealed the true remedy. Every relaxation of narrow and rigorous policy, wherever it has been tried, has been found to assuage the disease. The American theater has exhibited proofs that equal and complete liberty, if it does not wholly eradicate it, sufficiently destroys its malignant influence on the health and prosperity of the state. If with the salutary effects of this system under our own eyes we begin to contract the bounds of religious freedom, we know no name that will too severely reproach our folly. At least let warning be taken at the first fruits of the threatened innovation. The very appearance of the bill has transformed "that Christian forbearance, love, and charity," which of late mutually prevailed, into animosities and jealousies, which may not soon be appeased. What mischiefs may not be dreaded should this enemy to the public quiet be armed with the force of a law? . . .

15. Because, finally, "the equal right of every citizen to the free exercise of his religion according to the dictates of conscience" is held by the same tenure with all our other rights. If we recur to its origin, it is equally the gift of nature; if we weigh its importance, it cannot be less dear to us; if we consult the declaration of those rights which pertain to the good people of Virginia as the "basis and foundation of government," it is enumerated with equal solemnity, or rather, studied emphasis. Either then we must say that the will of the legislature is the only measure of their authority; and that in the plenitude of that authority, they may sweep away all our fundamental rights; or that they are bound to leave this particular right untouched and sacred. Either we must say that they may control the freedom of the press, may abolish the trial by jury, may swallow up the executive and judiciary powers of the state, nay, that they may despoil us of our very right of suffrage and erect themselves into an independent and hereditary assembly; or we must say that they have no authority to enact into law the bill under consideration. We, the subscribers, say that the General Assembly of this Commonwealth have no such authority. And . . . that no effort may be omitted on our part against so dangerous an usurpation, we oppose to it this remonstrance; earnestly praying, as we are in duty bound, that the Supreme Lawgiver of the universe, by illuminating those to whom it is addressed, may on the one hand turn their councils from every act which would affront His holy prerogative, or violate the trust committed to them; and on the other, guide them into every measure which may be worthy of His blessing, may redound to their own praise, and establish more firmly the liberties, the prosperity, and the happiness of the Commonwealth.

VIEWPOINT 3

"Conscientious scruples have not, in the course of the long struggle for religious toleration, relieved the individual from obedience to a general law not aimed at the promotion or restriction of religious beliefs."

Mandatory Flag Salutes Are Constitutional

Felix Frankfurter (1882-1965)

One of the earliest Supreme Court cases involving religious freedom was heard in 1940, on the eve of U.S. involvement in World War II. The case involved two children, Lillian and William Gobitis, who were expelled from a Pennsylvania public school after refusing to participate in a mandatory salute of the American flag because of their religious beliefs. Lower federal courts had ruled that the school board rule violated the children's free exercise of religion, citing both the First and Fourteenth amendments. The Fourteenth Amendment to the Constitution adopted in 1868, stipulated that states could not "make or enforce any law which shall abridge the privileges . . . of citizens of the United States, nor shall any State deprive any person of life, liberty, or property, without due process of law." The Supreme Court had in previous cases ruled that the Fourteenth Amendment had made the First Amendment applicable to state and local governments.

The Minersville School District appealed the case to the Supreme

From the majority opinion of the U.S. Supreme Court in *Minersville School District v. Gobitis,* 310 U.S. 586 (1940).

Court. The Court ruled eight to one against the children and in favor of the school board's directive. The majority opinion was written by Justice Felix Frankfurter, who had been appointed to the Supreme Court in 1939. A distinguished Harvard Law School professor, founding member of the American Civil Liberties Union, and close adviser to President Franklin D. Roosevelt, his appointment was hailed by many supporters of civil liberties. However, on the bench he advocated a philosophy of judicial restraint, arguing that the Court should in most cases let stand decisions by the majority of the people, as represented in the state legislatures and other bodies. In his *Minersville* opinion Frankfurter argues that freedom of religion is not an absolute, and that laws which do not directly and purposely restrict or promote religion may be allowed. Frankfurter concludes that the Supreme Court should defer to the judgment of the Minersville School Board and other local authorities in determining whether the goal of upholding national unity by requiring a flag salute overrode civil liberties concerns.

Many sharply criticized the *Minersville* decision. In an unusual development, the Supreme Court essentially reversed its decision three years later in a similar case, with Frankfurter reiterating the views expressed here, but in dissent.

Lillian Gobitis, aged twelve, and her brother William, aged ten, were expelled from the public schools of Minersville, Pennsylvania, for refusing to salute the national flag as part of a daily school exercise. The local Board of Education required both teachers and pupils to participate in this ceremony. The ceremony is a familiar one. The right hand is placed on the breast and the following pledge recited in unison: "I pledge allegiance to my flag, and to the Republic for which it stands; one nation indivisible, with liberty and justice for all." While the words are spoken, teachers and pupils extend their right hands in salute to the flag. The Gobitis family are affiliated with "Jehovah's Witnesses," for whom the Bible as the Word of God is the supreme authority. The children had been brought up conscientiously to believe that such a gesture of respect for the flag was forbidden by command of scripture. . . .

We must decide whether the requirement of participation in such a ceremony, exacted from a child who refuses upon sincere religious grounds, infringes without due process of law the liberty guaranteed by the Fourteenth Amendment.

Centuries of strife over the erection of particular dogmas as exclusive or all-comprehending faiths led to the inclusion of a guar-

The Duty of a Judge

Three years after Supreme Court Justice Felix Frankfurter wrote his Minersville School District v. Gobitis *opinion upholding mandatory flag salute laws, the Supreme Court changed its mind and declared such laws unconstitutional. Writing in dissent, Frankfurter, a Jew, passionately defended his belief that a judge's personal opinions on the wisdom of particular laws should not influence the judgment of whether they violate the Constitution.*

One who belongs to the most vilified and persecuted minority in history is not likely to be insensible to the freedoms guaranteed by our Constitution. Were my purely personal attitude relevant I should wholeheartedly associate myself with the general libertarian views in the Court's opinion, representing as they do the thought and action of a lifetime. But as judges we are neither Jew nor Gentile, neither Catholic nor agnostic. We owe equal attachment to the Constitution and are equally bound by our judicial obligations whether we derive our citizenship from the earliest or the latest immigrants to these shores. As a member of this Court I am not justified in writing my private notions of policy into the Constitution, no matter how deeply I may cherish them or how mischievous I may deem their disregard. The duty of a judge who must decide which of two claims before the Court shall prevail, that of a State to enact and enforce laws within its general competence or that of an individual to refuse obedience because of the demands of his conscience, is not that of the ordinary person. It can never be emphasized too much that one's own opinion about the wisdom or evil of a law should be excluded altogether when one is doing one's duty on the bench. The only opinion of our own even looking in that direction that is material is our opinion whether legislators could in reason have enacted such a law. In the light of all the circumstances, including the history of this question in this Court, it would require more daring than I possess to deny that reasonable legislators could have taken the action which is before us for review. Most unwillingly, therefore, I must differ from my brethren with regard to legislation like this. I cannot bring my mind to believe that the "liberty" secured by the Due Process Clause gives this Court authority to deny to the State of West Virginia the attainment of that which we all recognize as a legitimate legislative end, namely, the promotion of good citizenship, by employment of the means here chosen.

antee for religious freedom in the Bill of Rights. The First Amendment, and the Fourteenth through its absorption of the First, sought to guard against repetition of those bitter religious struggles by prohibiting the establishment of a state religion and by securing to every sect the free exercise of its faith. So pervasive is the acceptance of this precious right that its scope is brought into question, as here, only when the conscience of individuals collides with the felt necessities of society.

Certainly the affirmative pursuit of one's convictions about the ultimate mystery of the universe and man's relation to it is placed beyond the reach of law. Government may not interfere with organized or individual expression of belief or disbelief. Propagation of belief—or even of disbelief in the supernatural—is protected, whether in church or chapel, mosque or synagogue, tabernacle or meetinghouse. Likewise the Constitution assures generous immunity to the individual from imposition of penalties for offending, in the course of his own religious activities, the religious views of others, be they a minority or those who are dominant in government. . . .

In the judicial enforcement of religious freedom, we are concerned with a historic concept. The religious liberty which the Constitution protects has never excluded legislation of general scope not directed against doctrinal loyalties of particular sects. Judicial nullification of legislation cannot be justified by attributing to the framers of the Bill of Rights views for which there is no historic warrant. Conscientious scruples have not, in the course of the long struggle for religious toleration, relieved the individual from obedience to a general law not aimed at the promotion or restriction of religious beliefs. The mere possession of religious convictions which contradict the relevant concerns of a political society does not relieve the citizen from the discharge of political responsibilities. The necessity for this adjustment has again and again been recognized. In a number of situations the exertion of political authority has been sustained, while basic considerations of religious freedom have been left inviolate. In all these cases the general laws in question, upheld in their application to those who refused obedience from religious conviction, were manifestations of specific powers of government deemed by the legislature essential to secure and maintain that orderly, tranquil, and free society without which religious toleration itself is unattainable. . . .

The Need for National Unity

The case before us is not concerned with an exertion of legislative power for the promotion of some specific need or interest of secular society—the protection of the family, the promotion of health, the common defense, the raising of public revenues to defray the cost of government. But all these specific activities of government presuppose the existence of an organized political society. The ultimate foundation of a free society is the binding tie of cohesive sentiment. Such a sentiment is fostered by all those agencies of the mind and spirit which may serve to gather up the traditions of a people, transmit them from generation to generation, and thereby create the continuity of a treasured common life which constitutes a civilization. We live by symbols. The flag is the symbol of our national unity, transcending all internal differences, however large, within the framework of the Constitution. . . .

The wisdom of training children in patriotic impulses by those compulsions which necessarily pervade so much of the educational process is not for our independent judgment. Even were we convinced of the folly of such a measure, such belief would be no proof of its unconstitutionality. For ourselves, we might be tempted to say that the deepest patriotism is best engendered by giving unfettered scope to the most crochety beliefs. Perhaps it is best, even from the standpoint of those interests which ordinances like the one under review seek to promote, to give to the least popular sect leave from conformities like those here in issue. But the court-room is not the arena for debating issues of educational policy. It is not our province to choose among competing considerations in the subtle process of securing effective loyalty to the traditional ideals of democracy, while respecting at the same time individual idiosyncracies among a people so diversified in racial origins and religious allegiances. So to hold would in effect make us the school board for the country. That authority has not been given to this Court, nor should we assume it.

"The action of the local authorities in compelling the flag salute . . . invades the sphere of intellect and spirit which it is the purpose of the First Amendment . . . to reserve from all official control."

Mandatory Flag Salutes Violate the First Amendment

Robert H. Jackson (1892-1954)

One of the more dramatic instances of the Supreme Court changing its course occurred in 1943, when the Court overruled a decision made three years earlier. In the 1940 case *Minersville School District v. Gobitis* the Supreme Court had upheld a school practice mandating the salute of the American flag, with the penalty of expulsion for noncompliance. Seventeen states had passed such laws, aimed primarily at Jehovah's Witnesses who believe that saluting the flag violates the biblical rule against worshipping false idols. In the months following the *Minersville* decision, mobs attacked the dwellings and churches of Jehovah's Witnesses. Hundreds of Jehovah's Witnesses children were expelled from the schools after being taunted and abused as traitors. Among the expelled children were those of Walter Barnette in West Virginia. In addition to expelling the seven children, local authorities had prosecuted the parents for causing delinquency and had threatened to send the children to reformatories.

From the majority opinion of the U.S. Supreme Court in *West Virginia State Board of Education v. Barnette*, 319 U.S. 624 (1943).

The Barnettes appealed to the Supreme Court, which had undergone its own changes. Two new justices had been appointed, Robert H. Jackson and Wiley Rutledge. Harlan F. Stone, the lone dissenter in *Minersville*, was now chief justice. And in a highly unusual move, three justices, Hugo Black, William O. Douglas, and Frank Murphy wrote in an opinion in an unrelated matter that *Minersville* was "wrongly decided." This combination of events resulted in a dramatic reversal as the Supreme Court voted six to three to overturn the West Virginia law.

Jackson wrote the majority opinion. A holder of several federal posts under President Franklin D. Roosevelt, including attorney general, Jackson was appointed associate justice by Roosevelt in 1941 and served until his death in 1954. In overturning the West Virginia law, Jackson argued that the compulsory flag salute violated the children's First and Fourteenth Amendment rights of freedom of speech and conscience, which he reasoned included a right to remain silent. He criticized the previous *Gobitis* decision on several grounds, arguing that the Supreme Court does have the prerogative to overturn oppressive and unconstitutional legislation, and that the creation of national unity should not include compulsory acts. In a frequently quoted passage, Jackson writes, "If there is any fixed star in our constitutional constellation, it is that no official, high or petty, can prescribe what shall be orthodox in politics, nationalism, religion, or other matters of opinion."

The Board of Education on January 9, 1942, adopted a resolution containing recitals taken largely from the Court's *Gobitis* opinion and ordering that the salute to the flag become "a regular part of the program of activities in the public schools," that all teachers and pupils "shall be required to participate in the salute honoring the Nation represented by the Flag; provided, however, that refusal to salute the Flag be regarded as an Act of insubordination, and shall be dealt with accordingly."...

Appellees, citizens of the United States and of West Virginia, brought suit in the United States District Court for themselves and others similarly situated asking its injunction to restrain enforcement of these laws and regulations against Jehovah's Witnesses. The Witnesses are an unincorporated body teaching that the obligation imposed by law of God is superior to that of laws enacted by temporal government. Their religious beliefs include a literal version of Exodus, Chapter 20, verses 4 and 5, which says: "Thou shalt not make unto thee any graven image, or any likeness of anything that is in heaven above, or that is in the earth beneath, or that is in the water under the earth; thou shalt not bow down thyself to them, nor serve them." They consider that the flag is an "image" within this command. For this reason they refuse to salute it.

Children of this faith have been expelled from school and are threatened with exclusion for no other cause. Officials threaten to send them to reformatories maintained for criminally inclined juveniles. Parents of such children have been prosecuted and are threatened with prosecutions for causing delinquency. . . .

This case calls upon us to reconsider a precedent decision, as the Court throughout its history often has been required to do. Before turning to the *Gobitis Case*, however, it is desirable to notice certain characteristics by which this controversy is distinguished.

The freedom asserted by these appellees does not bring them into collision with rights asserted by any other individuals. It is such conflicts which most frequently require intervention of the State to determine where the rights of one end and those of another begin. But the refusal of these persons to participate in the ceremony does not interfere with or deny rights of others to do so. Nor is there any question in this case that their behavior is peaceable and orderly. The sole conflict is between authority and rights of the individual. The State asserts power to condition access to public education on making a prescribed sign and profession and at the same time to coerce attendance by punishing both parent and child. The latter stand on a right of self-determination in matters that touch individual opinion and personal attitude. . . .

A Form of Speech

There is no doubt that, in connection with the pledges, the flag salute is a form of utterance. Symbolism is a primitive but effective way of communicating ideas. The use of an emblem or flag to symbolize some system, idea, institution, or personality, is a short cut from mind to mind. Causes and nations, political parties, lodges, and ecclesiastical groups seek to knit the loyalty of their followings to a flag or banner, a color or design. . . .

Over a decade ago Chief Justice Hughes led this Court in holding that the display of a red flag as a symbol of opposition by peaceful and legal means to organized government was protected by the free speech guaranties of the Constitution. *Stromberg* v. *California*, 283 US 359. Here it is the State that employs a flag as a symbol of adherence to government as presently organized. It requires the individual to communicate by word and sign his acceptance of the political ideas it thus bespeaks. Objection to this form of communication when coerced is an old one, well known to the framers of the Bill of Rights.

It is also to be noted that the compulsory flag salute and pledge requires affirmation of a belief and an attitude of mind. It is not clear whether the regulation contemplates that pupils forego any contrary convictions of their own and become unwilling converts to the prescribed ceremony or whether it will be acceptable if they simulate assent by words without belief and by a gesture barren of meaning. It is now a commonplace that censorship or suppression of expression of opinion is tolerated by our Constitution only when the expression presents a clear and present danger of action of a kind the State is empowered to prevent and punish. It would seem that involuntary affirmation could be commanded only on even more immediate and urgent grounds than silence. But here the power of compulsion is invoked without any allegation that remaining passive during a flag salute ritual creates a clear and present danger that would justify an effort even to muffle expression. To sustain the compulsory flag salute we are required to say that a Bill of Rights which guards the individual's right to speak his own mind, left it open to public authorities to compel him to utter what is not in his mind.

Whether the First Amendment to the Constitution will permit officials to order observance of ritual of this nature does not depend upon whether as a voluntary exercise we would think it to be good, bad or merely innocuous. . . .

Nor does the issue as we see it turn on one's possession of particular religious views or the sincerity with which they are held. While religion supplies appellees' motive for enduring the discomforts of making the issue in this case, many citizens who do not share these religious views hold such a compulsory rite to infringe constitutional liberty of the individual. It is not necessary to inquire whether nonconformist beliefs will exempt from the duty to salute unless we first find power to make the salute a legal duty.

Reexamining the *Gobitis* Decision

The *Gobitis* decision, however, *assumed*, as did the argument in that case and in this, that power exists in the State to impose the flag salute discipline upon school children in general. The Court only examined and rejected a claim based on religious beliefs of immunity from an unquestioned general rule. The question which underlies the flag salute controversy is whether such a ceremony so touching matters of opinion and political attitude may be imposed upon the individual by official authority under powers committed to any political organization under our Constitution. We examine rather than assume existence of this power and, against this broader definition of issues in this case, reexamine specific grounds assigned for the *Gobitis* decision. . . .

It was . . . considered in the *Gobitis Case* that functions of educational officers in states, counties and school districts were such that to interfere with their authority "would in effect make us the school board for the country."

The Fourteenth Amendment, as now applied to the States, protects the citizen against the State itself and all of its creatures—Boards of Education not excepted. These have, of course, important, delicate, and highly discretionary functions, but none that they may not perform within the limits of the Bill of Rights. That they are educating the young for citizenship is reason for scrupulous protection of constitutional freedoms of the individual, if we are not to strangle the free mind at its source and teach youth to discount important principles of our government as mere platitudes.

Mandatory flag salutes were common in American public schools in the 1940s before they were ruled unconstitutional.

Such Boards are numerous and their territorial jurisdiction often small. But small and local authority may feel less sense of responsibility to the Constitution, and agencies of publicity may be less vigilant in calling it to account. The action of Congress in making flag observance voluntary and respecting the conscience of the objector in a matter so vital as raising the Army contrasts sharply with these local regulations in matters relatively trivial to the welfare of the nation. There are village tyrants as well as village Hampdens, but none who acts under color of law is beyond reach of the Constitution.

The *Gobitis* opinion reasoned that this is a field "where courts possess no marked and certainly no controlling competence," that it is committed to the legislatures as well as the courts to guard cherished liberties and that it is constitutionally appropriate to "fight out the wise use of legislative authority in the forum of public opinion and before legislative assemblies rather than to transfer such a contest to the judicial arena," since all the "effective means of inducing political changes are left free."

The very purpose of a Bill of Rights was to withdraw certain subjects from the vicissitudes of political controversy, to place them beyond the reach of majorities and officials and to establish them as legal principles to be applied by the courts. One's right to life, liberty, and property, to free speech, a free press, freedom of worship and assembly, and other fundamental rights may not be submitted to vote; they depend on the outcome of no elections. . . .

National Unity

Lastly, and this is the very heart of the *Gobitis* opinion, it reasons that "national unity is the basis of national security," that the authorities have "the right to select appropriate means for its attainment," and hence reaches the conclusion that such compulsory measures toward "national unity" are constitutional. Upon the verity of this assumption depends our answer in this case.

National unity as an end which officials may foster by persuasion and example is not in question. The problem is whether under our Constitution compulsion as here employed is a permissible means for its achievement.

Struggles to coerce uniformity of sentiment in support of some end thought essential to their time and country have been waged by many good as well as by evil men. Nationalism is a relatively recent phenomenon but at other times and places the ends have been racial or territorial security, support of a dynasty or regime, and particular plans for saving souls. As first and moderate methods to attain unity have failed, those bent on its accomplishment must resort to an ever increasing severity. As governmental pressure toward unity becomes greater, so strife becomes more bitter as to whose unity it shall be. Probably no deeper division of our people could proceed from any provocation than from finding it necessary to choose what doctrine and whose program public educational officials shall compel youth to unite in embracing. Ultimate futility of such attempts to compel coherence is the lesson of every such effort from the Roman drive to stamp out Christianity as a disturber of its pagan unity, the Inquisition, as a means to religious and dynastic unity, the Siberian exiles as a means to Russian unity, down to the fast failing efforts of our present totalitarian enemies. Those who begin coercive elimination of dissent soon find themselves exterminating dissenters. Compulsory unification of opinion achieves only the unanimity of the graveyard.

It seems trite but necessary to say that the First Amendment to our Constitution was designed to avoid these ends by avoiding these beginnings. There is no mysticism in the American concept of the State or of the nature or origin of its authority. We set up government by consent of the governed, and the Bill of Rights denies those in power any legal opportunity to coerce that consent. Authority here is to be controlled by public opinion, not public opinion by authority.

The case is made difficult not because the principles of its decision are obscure but because the flag involved is our own. Nevertheless, we apply the limitations of the Constitution with no fear that freedom to be intellectually and spiritually diverse or even contrary will disintegrate the social organization. To believe that patriotism will not flourish if patriotic ceremonies are voluntary and spontaneous instead of a compulsory routine is to make an unflattering estimate of the appeal of our institutions to free minds. We can have intellectual individualism and the rich cultural diversities that we owe to exceptional minds only at the price of occasional eccentricity and abnormal attitudes. When they are so harmless to others or to the State as those we deal with here, the price is not too great. But freedom to differ is not limited to things that do not matter much. That would be a mere shadow of freedom. The test of its substance is the right to differ as to things that touch the heart of the existing order.

If there is any fixed star in our constitutional constellation, it is that no official, high or petty, can prescribe what shall be orthodox in politics, nationalism, religion, or other matters of opinion or force citizens to confess by word or act their faith therein. If there are any circumstances which permit an exception, they do not now occur to us.

We think the action of the local authorities in compelling the flag salute and pledge transcends constitutional limitations on their power and invades the sphere of intellect and spirit which it is the purpose of the First Amendment to our Constitution to reserve from all official control.

VIEWPOINT 5

"The First Amendment has erected a wall between church and state. That wall must be kept high and impregnable."

The First Amendment Clearly Separates Church and State

Hugo Black (1886-1971)

The Supreme Court did not extensively interpret the meaning of the First Amendment prohibition of laws "respecting an establishment of religion" until 1947. The case of *Everson v. Board of Education* involved a New Jersey program that provided bus transportation to all students regardless of whether they attended a public or religious private school. The Supreme Court held that because of the Fourteenth Amendment, the Bill of Rights prohibition on religious establishment applied to state and local as well as federal laws. They then examined just what was meant by the clause in the First Amendment prohibiting the "establishment of religion."

The majority opinion was written by Hugo Black, associate justice from 1937 to 1971. Black, a former Alabama senator and judge, is considered by many historians to be one of the most influential justices of the Supreme Court's history. He gained a reputation as a strong defender of the Bill of Rights and an advocate

From the majority opinion of the U.S. Supreme Court in *Everson v. Board of Education of Ewing Township*, 330 U.S. 1 (1947).

of overturning both state and federal government laws when, in his view, they violated the first ten amendments.

In the *Everson* opinion excerpted here, Justice Black looks back on history to try to ascertain the views of the writers of the Constitution. Among the historical evidence he considers are the views of Thomas Jefferson and James Madison and their struggle against religious taxes in Virginia. Black concludes that the historical evidence indicates that the First Amendment erected "a wall of separation between church and state" (the phrase originated in an 1811 letter by Jefferson). It is a wall, he said, that prohibits both federal and state governments from passing laws "which aid one religion, aid all religions, or prefer one religion over another."

Black's judgment was met with criticism by some historians and other scholars, who maintained that the founding fathers intended to forbid the federal government from establishing a church, not to completely sever the public and religious spheres. However, Black's interpretation was shared by other members of the Supreme Court (including the dissenters, who differed mainly on the application for this particular case), and his interpretation was the basis for many future Supreme Court rulings overturning laws as violations of the First Amendment.

The New Jersey statute is challenged as a "law respecting the establishment of religion." The First Amendment, as made applicable to the states by the Fourteenth, . . . commands that a state "shall make no law respecting an establishment of religion, or prohibiting the free exercise thereof." . . . These words of the First Amendment reflected in the minds of early Americans a vivid mental picture of conditions and practices which they fervently wished to stamp out in order to preserve liberty for themselves and for their posterity. Doubtless their goal has not been entirely reached; but so far has the Nation moved toward it that the expression, "law respecting the establishment of religion," probably does not so vividly remind present-day Americans of the evils, fears, and political problems that caused that expression to be written into our Bill of Rights. Whether this New Jersey law is one respecting an "establishment of religion" requires an understanding of the meaning of that language, particularly with respect to the imposition of taxes. Once again, therefore, it is not inappropriate briefly to review the background and environment of the period in which that constitutional language was fashioned and adopted.

Hugo Black, associate justice of the Supreme Court from 1937 to 1971, played a key role in the interpretation of the religious guarantees of the First Amendment.

A large proportion of the early settlers of this country came here from Europe to escape the bondage of laws which compelled them to support and attend government favored churches. The centuries immediately before and contemporaneous with the colonization of America had been filled with turmoil, civil strife, and persecutions, generated in large part by established sects determined to maintain their absolute political and religious supremacy. With the power of government supporting them, at various times and places, Catholics had persecuted Protestants, Protestants had persecuted Catholics, Protestant sects had persecuted other Protestant sects, Catholics of one shade of belief had persecuted Catholics of another shade of belief, and all of these had from time to time persecuted Jews. In efforts to force loyalty to whatever religious group happened to be on top and in league with the government of a particular time and place, men and women had been fined, cast in jail, cruelly tortured, and killed. Among the offenses for which these punishments had been inflicted were such things as speaking disrespectfully of the views of ministers of government-established churches, non-attendance at those churches, expressions of non-belief in their doctrine, and failure to pay taxes and tithes to support them.

These practices of the old world were transplanted to and began to thrive in the soil of the new America. The very charters granted by the English Crown to the individuals and companies designated to make the laws which would control the destinies of the colonials authorized these individuals and companies to erect religious establishments which all, whether believers or nonbelievers, would be required to support and attend. An exercise of this authority was accompanied by a repetition of many of the old-world practices and persecutions. Catholics found themselves hounded and proscribed because of their faith; Quakers who followed their conscience went to jail; Baptists were peculiarly obnoxious to certain dominant Protestant sects; men and women of varied faiths who happened to be in a minority in a particular locality were persecuted because they steadfastly persisted in worshipping God only as their own consciences dictated. And all of these dissenters were compelled to pay tithes and taxes to support government-sponsored churches whose ministers preached inflammatory sermons designed to strengthen and consolidate the established faith by generating a burning hatred against dissenters.

These practices became so commonplace as to shock the freedom-loving colonials into a feeling of abhorrence. The imposition of taxes to pay ministers' salaries and to build and maintain churches and church property aroused their indignation. It was these feelings which found expression in the First Amendment. No one locality and no one group throughout the Colonies can rightly be given entire credit for having aroused the sentiment that culminated in adoption of the Bill of Rights' provisions embracing religious liberty. But Virginia, where the established church had achieved a dominant influence in political affairs and where many excesses attracted wide public attention, provided a great stimulus and able leadership for the movement. The people there, as elsewhere, reached the conviction that individual religious liberty could be achieved best under a government which was stripped of all power to tax, to support, or otherwise to assist any or all religions, or to interfere with the beliefs of any religious individual or group.

Debate in Virginia

The movement toward this end reached its dramatic climax in Virginia in 1785-86 when the Virginia legislative body was about to renew Virginia's tax levy for the support of the established church. Thomas Jefferson and James Madison led the fight against this tax. Madison wrote his great Memorial and Remonstrance against the law. In it, he eloquently argued that a true religion did not need the support of law; that no person, either believer or nonbeliever, should be taxed to support a religious institution of any kind; that the best interest of a society required that the minds of men always be wholly free; and that cruel persecutions were the inevitable result of government-established religions. Madison's Remonstrance received strong support throughout Virginia, and the Assembly postponed consideration of the proposed tax measure until its next session. When the proposal came up for consideration at that session, it not only died in committee, but the Assembly enacted the famous "Virginia Bill for Religious Liberty" originally written by Thomas Jefferson. The preamble to that Bill stated among other things that

> Almighty God hath created the mind free; that all attempts to influence it by temporal punishments or burthens, or by civil incapacitations, tend only to beget habits of hypocrisy and meanness, and are a departure from the plan of the Holy author of our religion, who being Lord both of body and mind, yet chose not to propagate it by coercions on either . . .; that to compel a man to furnish contributions of money for the propagation of opinions which he disbelieves, is sinful and tyrannical; that even the forcing him to support this or that teacher of his own religious persuasion, is depriving him of the comfortable liberty of giving his contributions to the particular pastor, whose morals he would make his pattern. . . .

And the statute itself enacted

> That no man shall be compelled to frequent or support any religious worship, place, or ministry whatsoever, nor shall be enforced, restrained, molested or burthened in his body or goods, nor shall otherwise suffer on account of his religious opinions or belief. . . .

This Court has previously recognized that the provisions of the First Amendment, in the drafting and adoption of which Madison and Jefferson played such leading roles, had the same objective and were intended to provide the same protection against governmental intrusion on religious liberty as the Virginia statute. . . . Prior to the adoption of the Fourteenth Amendment, the First Amendment did not apply as a restraint against the states. Most of them did soon provide similar constitutional protections for religious liberty. But some states persisted for about half a century in imposing restraints upon the free exercise of religion and in discriminating against particular religious group[s]. In recent years, so far as the provision against the establishment of a religion is concerned, the question has most frequently arisen in connection with proposed state aid to church schools and efforts to carry on religious teachings in the public schools in accordance with the tenets of a particular sect. Some churches have either sought or accepted state financial support for their schools. Here again the efforts to obtain state aid or acceptance of it have not been limited to any one particular faith. The state courts, in the main, have remained faithful to the language of their own constitutional provisions designed to protect religious freedom and to separate religions and governments. Their decisions, however, show the difficulty in drawing the line between tax legislation which provides funds for the welfare of the general public and that which is designed to support institutions which teach religion.

A Wall of Separation

In a letter to the Danbury Baptist Association on January 1, 1802, President Thomas Jefferson expressed his views that the First Amendment had created "a wall of separation" between church and state. The letter has been cited in a number of Supreme Court opinions.

Believing with you that religion is a matter which lies solely between Man & his God, that he owes account to none other for his faith or his worship, that the legitimate powers of government reach actions only, & not opinions. I contemplate with sovereign reverence that act of the whole American people which declared that *their* legislature should "make no law regarding an establishment of religion, or prohibiting the free exercise thereof," thus building a wall of separation between Church & State. Adhering to this expression of the supreme will of the nation in behalf of the rights of conscience, I shall see with sincere satisfaction the progress of those sentiments which tend to restore to men all his natural rights, convinced he has no natural right in opposition to his social duties.

The meaning and scope of the First Amendment, preventing establishment of religion or prohibiting the free exercise thereof, in the light of its history and the evils it was designed forever to suppress, have been several times elaborated by the decisions of this Court prior to the application of the First Amendment to the states by the Fourteenth. The broad meaning given the Amendment by these earlier cases has been accepted by this Court in its decisions concerning an individual's religious freedom rendered since the Fourteenth Amendment was interpreted to make the prohibitions of the First applicable to state action abridging religious freedom. There is every reason to give the same application and broad interpretation to the "establishment of religion" clause. . . .

Establishing a Religion

The "establishment of religion" clause of the First Amendment means at least this: Neither a state nor the Federal Government can set up a church. Neither can pass laws which aid one religion, aid all religions, or prefer one religion over another. Neither can force nor influence a person to go to or to remain away from church against his will or force him to profess a belief or disbelief in any religion. No person can be punished for entertaining or professing religious beliefs or disbeliefs, for church attendance or non-attendance. No tax in any amount, large or small, can be levied to support any religious activities or institutions, whatever they may be called, or whatever form they may adopt to teach or practice religion. Neither a state nor the Federal Government can, openly or secretly, participate in the affairs of any religious organizations or groups and vice versa. In the words of Jefferson, the clause against establishment of religion by law was intended to erect "a wall of separation between Church and State.". . .

We must consider the New Jersey statute in accordance with the foregoing limitations imposed by the First Amendment. But we must not strike that state statute down if it is within the State's constitutional power even though it approaches the verge of that power. . . . New Jersey cannot consistently with the "establishment of religion" clause of the First Amendment contribute tax-raised funds to the support of an institution which teaches the tenets and faith of any church. On the other hand, other language of the amendment commands that New Jersey cannot hamper its citizens in the free exercise of their own religion. Consequently, it cannot exclude individual Catholics, Lutherans, Mohammedans, Baptists, Jews, Methodists, Non-believers, Presbyterians, or the members of any other faith, *because of their faith, or lack of it*, from receiving the benefits of public welfare legislation. While we do not mean to intimate that a state could not provide transportation only to children attending public schools, we must be careful, in protecting the citizens of New Jersey against state-established churches, to be sure that we do not inadvertently prohibit New Jersey from extending its general state law benefits to all its citizens without regard to their religious belief.

The New Jersey Program

Measured by these standards, we cannot say that the First Amendment prohibits New Jersey from spending tax-raised funds to pay the bus fares of parochial school pupils as a part of a general program under which it pays the fares of pupils attending public and other schools. . . .

The State contributes no money to the [parochial] schools. It does not support them. Its legislation, as applied, does no more than provide a general program to help parents get their children, regardless of their religion, safely and expeditiously to and from accredited schools.

The First Amendment has erected a wall between church and state. That wall must be kept high and impregnable. We could not approve the slightest breach. New Jersey has not breached it here.

VIEWPOINT 6

"It would be an utter distortion of American history and law to make . . . the exclusion of cooperation between religion and government implied in the term 'separation of Church and State.'"

The First Amendment Does Not Absolutely Separate Church and State

American Roman Catholic Bishops

Since 1947 there has been much historical and public policy debate over the clause in the First Amendment stating that "Congress shall make no laws respecting an establishment of religion or forbidding the free exercise thereof." Did the nation's founders intend to keep government completely neutral in religious matters? Or did they simply wish to prevent the establishment of an official church, or the favoring of one particular religious sect over another? A case for the latter view is presented here by American bishops of the Roman Catholic church in a public statement released in November 1948.

The bishops were reacting to two cases, *Everson v. Board of Education* and *McCollum v. Board of Education*. In the first case, the Supreme Court upheld a New Jersey law that provided state aid for transporting students who attended Catholic schools. In the second case the Court ruled that programs giving release time for public school students to attend religious classes violated the First Amendment's prohibition against "the establishment of religion." In both cases, the Supreme Court stated that the First Amendment had created a wall of separation between church and state that, in the words of Justice Hugo Black in the *Everson* case, "must be kept high and impregnable."

The Catholic bishops in their statement question the reasoning of Justice Black. They assert that government involvement and assistance of religious institutions and practices has a long history in the United States. They argue that Thomas Jefferson, James Madison, and other founders did not intend for a "wall of separation" between church and state in the way the Supreme Court has defined it, and they conclude that attempts to separate government and religion are examples of "secularism" which threaten to weaken religion in the United States.

Human life centers in God. The failure to center life in God is secularism—which is the most deadly menace to our Christian and American way of living. We shall not successfully combat this evil merely by defining and condemning it. Constructive effort is called for to counteract this corrosive influence in every phase of life where individual attitudes are a determining factor—in the home, in the school, at work, and in civil polity. For as man is, so ultimately are all the institutions of human society. . . .

Religion and Citizenship

The inroads of secularism in civil life are a challenge to the Christian citizen—and indeed to every citizen with definite religious convictions. The essential connection between religion and good citizenship is deep in our American tradition. Those who took the lead in establishing our independence and framing our Constitution were firm and explicit in the conviction that religion and morality are the strong supports of national well-being, that national morality cannot prevail in the absence of religious principle, and that impartial encouragement of religious influence on its citizens is a proper and practical function of good government.

This American tradition clearly envisioned the school as the meeting place of these helpful interacting influences. The third article of the Northwest Ordinance passed by Congress in 1787, reenacted in 1790, and included in the Constitutions of many states, enjoins: "Religion, morality and knowledge being necessary to good citizenship and the happiness of mankind, schools and the means of education shall forever be encouraged." This is our authentic American tradition on the philosophy of education for citizenship.

In the field of law, our history reveals the same fundamental connection between religion and citizenship. It is through law that government exercises control over its citizens for the common good and establishes a balance between their rights and duties. The American concept of government and law started with the recognition that man's inalienable rights—which it is the function of government to protect—derive from God, his Creator. It thus bases human law, which deals with man's rights and their correlative duties in society, on foundations that are definitely religious, on principles that emerge from the definite view of man as a creature of God.

This view of man anchors human law to the natural law, which is the moral law of God made clear to us through the judgments of human reason and the dictates of conscience. The natural law, as an outstanding modern legal commentator has written, "is binding over all the globe, in all countries and at all times; no human laws are of any validity if contrary to this." Thus human law is essentially an ordinance of reason, not merely a dictate of will on the part of the state. In our authentic American tradition, this is the accepted philosophy of law.

Secularism Corrodes Tradition

On this basically religious tradition concerning the preparation of the citizen through education and the direction of the citizen through law, secularism has in the past century exercised a corrosive influence. It has banned religion from tax-supported education and is now bent on destroying all cooperation between government and organized religion in the training of our future citizens. It has undermined the religious foundations of law in the minds of many men in the legal profession and has predisposed them to accept the legalistic tyranny of the omnipotent State. It has cleverly exploited, to the detriment of religion and good citizenship, the delicate problem of cooperation between Church and State in a country of divided religious allegiance. That concrete problem, delicate as it is, can, without sacrifice of principle, be solved in a practical way when goodwill and a spirit of fairness prevail.

Authoritative Catholic teaching on the relations between Church and State, as set forth in papal encyclicals and in the treatises of recognized writers on ecclesiastical law, not only states clearly what these relations should normally be under ideal conditions, but also indicates to what extent the Catholic Church can adapt herself to the particular conditions that may obtain in different countries. Examining, in the full perspective of that teaching, the position which those who founded our nation and framed its basic law took on the problem of Church-State relations in our own country, we find that the First Amendment to our Constitution solved that problem in a way that was typically American in its practical recognition of existing conditions and its evident desire to be fair to all citizens of whatever religious faith.

To one who knows something of history and law, the meaning of the First Amendment is clear enough from its own words: "Congress shall make no laws respecting an establishment of religion or forbidding the free exercise thereof." The meaning is even clearer in the records of the Congress that enacted it. Then, and throughout English and colonial history, an "establishment of religion" meant the setting up by law of an official Church which would receive from the government favors not equally accorded to others in the cooperation between government and religion—which was simply taken for granted in our country at that time and has, in many ways, continued to this day.

Christian Religion and the Constitution

Thomas Cooley was a nineteenth-century judge, legal author, and public official. His influential study The General Principles of Constitutional Law in the United States of America *was published in 1898.*

It was never intended by the Constitution that the government should be prohibited from recognizing religion, or that religious worship should never be provided for in cases where a proper recognition of Divine Providence in the working of government might seem to require it, and where it might be done without drawing any invidious distinctions between different religious beliefs, organizations, or sects. The Christian religion was always recognized in the administration of the common law; and so far as that law continues to be the law of the land, the fundamental principles of that religion must continue to be recognized in the same cases and to the same extent as formerly.

Under the First Amendment, the federal government could not extend this type of preferential treatment to one religion as against another, nor could it compel or forbid any state to do so. If this practical policy be described by the loose metaphor "a wall of separation between Church and State," that term must be understood in a definite and typically American sense. It would be an utter distortion of American history and law to make that practical policy involve the indifference to religion and the exclusion of cooperation between religion and government implied in the term "separation of Church and State" as it has become the shibboleth of doctrinaire secularism.

Within the past two years secularism has scored unprecedented victories in its opposition to governmental encouragement of religious and moral training, even where no preferential treatment of one religion over another is involved. In two recent cases, the Supreme Court of the United States has adopted an entirely novel and ominously extensive interpretation of the "establishment of religion" clause of the First Amendment.

This interpretation would bar any cooperation between government and organized religion which would aid religion, even where no discrimination between religious bodies is in question. This reading of the First Amendment, as a group of non-Catholic religious leaders recently noted, will endanger "forms of cooperation between Church and State which have been taken for granted by the American people," and "greatly accelerate the trend toward the secularization of our culture."

Reluctant as we are to criticize our supreme judicial tribunal, we cannot but observe that when the members of that tribunal write long and varying opinions in handing down a decision, they must expect that intelligent citizens of a democracy will study and appraise these opinions. The "Journal of the American Bar Association," in a critical analysis of one of the cases in question, pertinently remarks: "The traditionally religious sanctions of our law, life and government are challenged by a judicial propensity which deserves the careful thought and study of lawyers and people."

Lawyers trained in the American tradition of law will be amazed to find that in the McCollum case the majority opinions pay scant attention to logic, history or accepted norms of legal interpretation. Logic would demand that what is less clear be defined by what is more clear. In the present instance we find just the reverse. The carefully chiselled phrases of the First Amendment are defined by the misleading metaphor, "the wall of separation between Church and State."

This metaphor of Jefferson specifies nothing except that there shall be no "established Church," no State religion. All the rest of its content depends on the letter of the law that sets it up, and can in the concrete imply anything, from the impartial cooperation between government and free religious bodies (as in Holland and traditionally in our own country) all the way down to bitter persecution of religion (as in France at the turn of the century). As was pointedly remarked in a dissenting opinion: "A rule of law cannot be drawn from a metaphor."

A glance at the history of Jefferson's own life and work would have served as a warning against the broad and devastating application of his "wall of separation" metaphor that we find in this case. The expression first appears in a letter written by Jefferson in 1802 and, significantly enough, in a context that makes it refer to the "free exercise of religion" clause rather than to the "establishment of religion" clause of the First Amendment.

Twenty years later, Jefferson clearly showed in action that his concept of "separation of Church and State" was far different from the concept of those who now appeal to his metaphor as a norm of interpretation. As the rector of the State University of Virginia, Jefferson proposed a system of cooperation between the various religious groups and the university which goes far beyond anything under consideration in the case at hand. And Mr. Madison, who had proposed the First Amendment and who led in carrying it through to enactment by Congress was one of the Visitors of the University of Virginia who approved Jefferson's plan.

Even one who is not a lawyer would expect to find in the opinion of the court some discussion of what was in the mind of the members of Congress when they framed and adopted the First Amendment. For it would seem that the intent of the legislator should be of capital importance in interpreting any law when a doubt is raised as to the objective meaning of the words in which it is framed.

In regard to the "establishment of religion" clause, there is no doubt of the intent of the legislator. It is clear in the record of the Congress that framed it and of the state legislatures that ratified it. To them it meant no official Church for the country as a whole, no preferment of one religion over another by the federal government—and at the same time, no interference by the federal government in the Church-State relations of the individual states. . . .

Reaffirmation of Tradition Asked

We, therefore, hope and pray that the novel interpretation of the First Amendment recently adopted by the Supreme Court will in due process be revised. To that end we shall peacefully, patiently and perseveringly work.

We feel with deep conviction that for the sake of both good citizenship and religion there should be a reaffirmation of our original American tradition of free cooperation between government and religious bodies—cooperation involving no special privilege to any group and no restriction on the religious liberty of any citizen. We solemnly disclaim any intent or desire to alter this prudent and fair American policy of government in dealing with the delicate problems that have their source in the divided religious allegiance of our citizens.

*"The constitutional prohibition
against . . . establishment of religion must at least
mean that in this country it is no part of the
business of government to compose official prayers
for . . . people to recite."*

School Prayers Violate
the First Amendment

Hugo Black (1886-1971)

One of the most controversial decisions of the Supreme Court concerning church and state occurred in 1962, when in *Engel v. Vitale* the Court declared unconstitutional state-sponsored prayers in public schools. The decision, in which the Court further developed and applied the reasoning from the 1947 case *Everson v. Board of Education*, inspires controversy to this day.

The prayer in question was composed by the New York State Board of Regents, and read "Almighty God, we acknowledge our dependence upon Thee, and we beg Thy blessings upon us, our parents, our teachers, and our country." The State Board recommended daily recital of this prayer on a voluntary basis. One school district went a step further and began to require every class to recite the prayer at the beginning of each day, permitting children to remain silent or to be excused from the classroom if they did not wish to participate. In 1959 parents of ten children in

From the majority opinion of the U.S. Supreme Court in *Engel v. Vitale*, 370 U.S. 421 (1962).

the district sought legal action to discontinue the prayer, arguing that it violated Bill of Rights provisions calling for separation of church and state. The lower state courts and the New York Court of Appeals held that the prayer was constitutional as long as students had the right not to participate. The case was heard before the Supreme Court in 1962. On June 25, 1962, the Court struck down the "Regents' Prayer" as unconstitutional.

The majority opinion was written by Hugo Black, an associate justice from 1937 to 1971. Black had written the 1947 *Everson* opinion, and in that and other writings had been a consistent advocate of the strict separation of church and state. As in the *Everson* opinion, Black used U.S. colonial history and the writings of James Madison and Thomas Jefferson to support his conclusions. Black agreed with the plaintiffs that the prayer amounted to an establishment of religion, which is prohibited by the Bill of Rights. He concluded by stating that the ruling should not be seen as being hostile toward religion, but that religion is better served by government noninterference.

The respondent Board of Education of Union Free School District No. 9, New Hyde Park, New York, acting in its official capacity under state law, directed the School District's principal to cause the following prayer to be said aloud by each class in the presence of a teacher at the beginning of each school day:

> Almighty God, we acknowledge our dependence upon Thee, and we beg Thy blessings upon us, our parents, our teachers and our country.

This daily procedure was adopted on the recommendation of the State Board of Regents, a governmental agency created by the State Constitution to which the New York Legislature has granted broad supervisory, executive, and legislative powers over the State's public school system. These state officials composed the prayer which they recommended and published as a part of their "Statement on Moral and Spiritual Training in the Schools," saying: "We believe that this Statement will be subscribed to by all men and women of good will, and we call upon all of them to aid in giving life to our program."

Shortly after the practice of reciting the Regents' prayer was adopted by the School District, the parents of ten pupils brought this action in a New York State Court insisting that use of this official prayer in the public schools was contrary to the beliefs, religions, or religious practices of both themselves and their children.

Among other things, these parents challenged the constitutionality of both the state law authorizing the School District to direct the use of prayer in public schools and the School District's regulation ordering the recitation of this particular prayer on the ground that these actions of official governmental agencies violate that part of the First Amendment of the Federal Constitution which commands that "Congress shall make no law respecting an establishment of religion"—a command which was "made applicable to the State of New York by the Fourteenth Amendment of the said Constitution." The New York Court of Appeals, over the dissents of Judges Dye and Fuld, sustained an order of the lower state courts which had upheld the power of New York to use the Regents' prayer as a part of the daily procedures of its public schools so long as the schools did not compel any pupil to join in the prayer over his or his parents' objection. We granted certiorari to review this important decision involving rights protected by the First and Fourteenth Amendments.

A Position of Neutrality

Associate Justice William O. Douglas wrote a concurring opinion in Engel v. Vitale, *in which he stated that government must remain strictly neutral in religious matters.*

The First Amendment leaves the Government in a position not of hostility to religion but of neutrality. The philosophy is that the atheist or agnostic—the nonbeliever—is entitled to go his own way. The philosophy is that if the government interferes in matters spiritual, it will be a divisive force. The First Amendment teaches that a government neutral in the field of religion better serves all religious interests.

We think that by using its public school system to encourage recitation of the Regents' prayer, the State of New York has adopted a practice wholly inconsistent with the Establishment Clause. There can, of course, be no doubt that New York's program of daily classroom invocation of God's blessings as prescribed in the Regents' prayer is a religious activity. It is a solemn avowal of divine faith and supplication for the blessings of the Almighty. . . .

The petitioners contend among other things that the state laws requiring or permitting use of the Regents' prayer must be struck down as a violation of the Establishment Clause because that prayer was composed by governmental officials as a part of a governmental program to further religious beliefs. For this reason, petitioners argue, the State's use of the Regents' prayer in its public school system breaches the constitutional wall of separation between Church and State. We agree with that contention since we think that the constitutional prohibition against laws respecting an establishment of religion must at least mean that in this country it is no part of the business of government to compose official prayers for any group of the American people to recite as a part of a religious program carried on by government.

A Matter of History

It is a matter of history that this very practice of establishing governmentally composed prayers for religious services was one of the reasons which caused many of our early colonists to leave England and seek religious freedom in America. . . .

It is an unfortunate fact of history that when some of the very groups which had most strenuously opposed the established Church of England found themselves sufficiently in control of colonial governments in this country to write their own prayers into law, they passed laws making their own religion the official religion of their respective colonies. Indeed, as late as the time of the Revolutionary War, there were established churches in at least eight of the thirteen former colonies and established religions in at least four of the other five. But the successful Revolution against English political domination was shortly followed by intense opposition to the practice of establishing religion by law. This opposition crystallized rapidly into an effective political force in Virginia where the minority religious groups such as Presbyterians, Lutherans, Quakers and Baptists had gained such strength that the adherents to the established Episcopal Church were actually a minority themselves. In 1785-1786, those opposed to the established Church, led by James Madison and Thomas Jefferson, who, though themselves not members of any of these dissenting religious groups, opposed all religious establishments by law on grounds of principle, obtained the enactment of the famous "Virginia Bill for Religious Liberty" by which all religious groups were placed on an equal footing so far as the State was concerned. Similar though less far-reaching legislation was being considered and passed in other States.

By the time of the adoption of the Constitution, our history shows that there was a widespread awareness among many Americans of the dangers of a union of Church and State. These people knew, some of them from bitter personal experience, that one of the greatest dangers to the freedom of the individual to worship in his own way lay in the Government's placing its official stamp of approval upon one particular kind of prayer or one particular form of religious services. They knew the anguish, hardship and bitter strife that could come when zealous religious groups struggled with one another to obtain the Government's stamp of approval from each King, Queen, or Protector that came to temporary power. The Constitution was intended to avert a part of this danger by leaving the government of this country in the hands of the people rather than in the hands of any monarch. But this safeguard was not enough. Our Founders were no more willing to let the content of their prayers and their privilege of praying whenever they pleased be influenced by the ballot box than they were to let these vital matters of personal conscience depend upon the succession of monarchs. The First Amendment was added to the Constitution to stand as a guarantee that neither the power nor the prestige of the Federal Government would be used to control, support or influence the kinds of prayer the American people can say—that the people's religions must not be subjected to the pressures of government for change each time a new political administration is elected to office. Under that Amendment's prohibition against governmental establishment of religion, as reinforced by the provisions of the Fourteenth Amendment, government in this country, be it state or federal, is without power to prescribe by law any particular form of prayer which is to be used as an official prayer in carrying on any program of governmentally sponsored religious activity.

The New York Program

There can be no doubt that New York's state prayer program officially establishes the religious beliefs embodied in the Regents' prayer. The respondents' argument to the contrary, which is largely based upon the contention that the Regents' prayer is "non-denominational" and the fact that the program, as modified and approved by state courts, does not require all pupils to recite the prayer but permits those who wish to do so to remain silent or be excused from the room, ignores the essential nature of the program's constitutional defects. Neither the fact that the prayer may be denominationally neutral, nor the fact that its observance on the part of the students is voluntary can serve to free it from the limitations of the Establishment Clause, as it might from the Free Exercise Clause, of the First Amendment, both of which are operative against the States by virtue of the Fourteenth Amendment. Although these two clauses may in certain instances overlap, they forbid two quite different kinds of governmental encroachment upon religious freedom. The Establishment Clause, unlike the Free Exercise Clause, does not depend upon any showing of direct governmental compulsion and is violated by the enactment of laws which establish an official religion whether those laws operate directly to coerce nonobserving individuals or not. This is not to say, of course, that laws officially prescribing a particular form of religious worship do not involve coercion of such

The Place of Religion

The Supreme Court reaffirmed its Engel v. Vitale *ruling one year later, when in* Abington School District v. Schempp *it forbade states from passing laws requiring teachers to read Bible passages in class. The opinion was written by Associate Justice Tom C. Clark.*

The place of religion in our society is an exalted one, achieved through a long tradition of reliance on the home, the church and the inviolable citadel of the individual heart and mind. We have come to recognize through bitter experience that it is not within the power of government to invade that citadel, whether its purpose or effect be to aid or oppose, to advance or retard. In the relationship between man and religion, the State is firmly committed to a position of neutrality. Though the application of that rule requires interpretation of a delicate sort, the rule itself is clearly and concisely stated in the words of the First Amendment.

individuals. When the power, prestige and financial support of government is placed behind a particular religious belief, the indirect coercive pressure upon religious minorities to conform to the prevailing officially approved religion is plain. But the purposes underlying the Establishment Clause go much further than that. Its first and most immediate purpose rested on the belief that a union of government and religion tends to destroy government and to degrade religion. The history of governmentally established religion, both in England and in this country, showed that whenever government had allied itself with one particular form of religion, the inevitable result had been that it had incurred the hatred, disrespect and even contempt of those who held contrary beliefs. That same history showed that many people had lost their respect for any religion that had relied upon the support of government to spread its faith. The Establishment Clause thus stands as an expression of principle on the part of the Founders of our Constitution that religion is too personal, too sacred, too holy, to permit its "unhallowed perversion" by a civil magistrate. Another purpose of the Establishment Clause rested upon an awareness of the historical fact that governmentally established religions and religious persecutions go hand in hand. The Founders knew that only a few years after the Book of Common Prayer became the only accepted form of religious services in the established Church of England, an Act of Uniformity was passed to compel all Englishmen to attend those services and to make it a criminal offense to conduct or attend religious gatherings of any other kind—a law which was consistently flouted by dissenting religious groups in England and which contributed to widespread persecutions of people like John Bunyan who persisted in holding "unlawful [religious] meetings . . . to the great disturbance and distraction of the good subjects of this kingdom. . . ." And they knew that similar persecutions had received the sanction of law in several of the colonies in this country soon after the establishment of official religions in those colonies. It was in large part to get completely away from this sort of systematic religious persecution that the Founders brought into being our Nation, our Constitution, and our Bill of Rights with its prohibition against any governmental establishment of religion. The New York laws officially prescribing the Regents' prayer are inconsistent with both the purposes of the Establishment Clause and with the Establishment Clause itself.

Constitution Not Hostile to Religion

It has been argued that to apply the Constitution in such a way as to prohibit state laws respecting an establishment of religious services in public schools is to indicate a hostility toward religion or toward prayer. Nothing, of course, could be more wrong. The history of man is inseparable from the history of religion. And perhaps it is not too much to say that since the beginning of that history many people have devoutly believed that "More things are wrought by prayer than this world dreams of." It was doubtless largely due to men who believed this that there grew up a sentiment that caused men to leave the cross-currents of officially established state religions and religious persecution in Europe and come to this country filled with the hope that they could find a place in which they could pray when they pleased to the God of their faith in the language they chose. And there were men of this same faith in the power of prayer who led the fight for adoption of our Constitution and also for our Bill of Rights with the very guarantees of religious freedom that forbid the sort of governmental activity which New York has attempted here. These men knew that the First Amendment, which tried to put an end to governmental control of religion and of prayer, was not written to destroy either. They knew rather that it was written to quiet well-justified fears which nearly all of them felt arising out of an awareness that governments of the past had shackled men's tongues to make them speak only the religious thoughts that government wanted them to speak and to pray only to the God that government wanted them to pray to. It is neither sacrilegious nor antireligious to say that each separate government in this country should stay out of the business of writing or sanctioning official prayers and leave that purely religious function to the people themselves and to those the people chose to look to for religious guidance.

VIEWPOINT 8

"It should be difficult for any American to find much, if anything, to quarrel with in that brief school prayer."

School Prayers Do Not Violate the First Amendment

Strom Thurmond (1902-)

In 1962 the Supreme Court ruled in *Engel v. Vitale* that a short "nondenominational" prayer recited by students at public schools in New York was unconstitutional because it violated the First Amendment's prohibition against laws "respecting an establishment of religion." The decision was met with protest and controversy. Republican congressman Frank J. Becker of New York stated that it was "the most tragic decision in the history of the United States." Becker led the first of several efforts to amend the Constitution to allow school prayer.

The following viewpoint is taken from a speech before the U.S. Senate by Strom Thurmond three days after the Supreme Court decision was handed down. It is in many respects typical of the outcry caused by the controversial decision. Thurmond argues that the Supreme Court decision is in error and that Hugo Black has misread American history and its religious heritage. He asserts that the First Amendment was meant to prevent the national government from establishing a particular church or denomination as an official church, not to create a total separation of church

From Strom Thurmond's speech before the U.S. Senate, June 28, 1962.

and state. He concludes by stating that the decision threatened America's future by disregarding religion. Thurmond has been a South Carolina senator since 1954. He first gained national attention in 1948 when he ran for president as a member of the States' Rights party, a group of conservative Democrats who objected to the Democratic party's civil rights platform.

The Supreme Court of the United States has overstepped its bounds in loose and distorted interpretations of the United States Constitution on many occasions, particularly in recent years. No Court decision, however, has shocked the conscience of the American people as has the ruling in the now famous school prayer decision of Engel against Vitale, on June 25, 1962. The Court ruled in this case that a simple, nondenominational prayer as devised by the New York State Board of Regents for schoolchildren without compulsion is offensive to the Constitution. The prayer reads as follows:

> Almighty God, we acknowledge our dependence upon Thee, and we beg Thy blessings upon us, our parents, our teachers, and our country.

The constitutional provision which this simple prayer purportedly violates is a portion of the first amendment, which reads as follows:

> Congress shall make no law respecting an establishment of religion, or prohibiting the free exercise thereof.

It should be difficult for any American to find much, if anything, to quarrel with in that brief school prayer which merely acknowledges the existence of a Supreme Being recognizing in a small way our national religious heritage and traditions. The constitutional provision appears to carry little or no ambiguity as to its meaning, particularly if one studies the contemporaneous events leading up to its adoption as a part of the Constitution. It is clear that the framers of this provision were concerned about the establishment of a national religion which would suppress all other religions. They were, as Dr. Billy Graham has so ably pointed out, concerned with maintaining freedom of religion not freedom from religion. In fact, the late Justice Joseph Story informs us in his famous "Commentaries on the Constitution" that "an attempt to level all religion and to make it a matter of state policy to hold all in utter indifference, would have created universal disapprobation, if not universal indignation." An other expert on constitutional law, Mr. [Thomas] Cooley, made the point in his important work, "Principles of Constitutional Law," that "it was never intended by the Constitution that the Government should be prohibited from recognizing religion, where it might be done without drawing any invidious distinctions between different religious beliefs, organizations, or sects."

A Simple Prayer

What the Court found to be invidious or dangerous in this case was the New York Board's attempt to establish a religion with this simple, nondenominational prayer. The *Wall Street Journal* has stated in an editorial comment of June 27 that "this attitude bespeaks considerable confusion and no abundance of common-sense." It is indeed the height of legal absurdity and distortion to state or even imply that the State of New York was attempting to establish a State religion by use of this noncompulsory, 22-word prayer which was carefully worded to avoid making any "invidious distinctions" so as to give preference to one religion over another.

Besides, the constitutional provision contains a prohibition not against the States, but against the Congress establishing a religion or interfering with the free exercise of religion. Justice Story also made a strong point when he stated in his "Commentaries" that "the whole power over the subject of religion is left exclusively to the State governments, to be acted upon according to their own sense of justice and the State constitution; and the Catholic and the Protestant, the Calvinist and the Arminian, the Jew and the Infidel, may sit down at the common table of the national councils without any inquisition into their faith or mode of worship."

The Supreme Court, however, has attempted to tie the 14th amendment into the 1st amendment in another loose interpretation of the Constitution, and this combination of the "no establishment" clause with the "equal protection and immunities" clause has been used to rule out the action of the New York State Board of Regents in authorizing this school prayer.

Americans all across this great land of ours are concerned about this decision because it reflects a pattern of national actions designed, as Dr. Billy Graham warned in the February 17, 1962, issue of the *Saturday Evening Post*, "to take the traditional concept of God out of our national life." This is the disturbing fact about this lamentable decision. It signals the come-on of more antireligion decisions to follow in the wake of the precedent set in this judicial amendment to the Constitution. If this decision stands, then any action in public schools or in our national life carrying the "taint" of religion or acknowledgment of a Supreme Being can be swept away. . . .

The American people are proud of our national heritage and

traditions, especially our spiritual ties to a Supreme Being. The history of America has been marked by religious features from the very beginning, just as the map of America is marked with names of religious origin and meaning. The first discoverers and settlers of the Americas came with the Bible and the cross. From each country of the old world with each expedition or attempted colony went missionaries, ministers, priests, for the conversion of the . . . Indians and to provide the ministrations of religion for the colonists.

Many of the colonists came to the New World to escape religious persecution and to worship in freedom. They determined to establish a new world whose government would be based on religious foundations but which would retain for each individual the right to worship in freedom and determine his own destiny.

Voluntary Prayer Does Not Establish Religion

The only dissenting Supreme Court justice in the case Engel v. Vitale *was Potter Stewart, who was an associate justice from 1958 to 1981. He asserted that the school prayer in question posed no First Amendment conflicts because it was both voluntary and nondenominational.*

With all due respect, I think the Court has misapplied a great constitutional principle. I cannot see how an "official religion" is established by letting those who want to say a prayer say it. On the contrary, I think that to deny the wish of these school children to join in reciting this prayer is to deny them the opportunity of sharing in the spiritual heritage of the Nation.

Charters, compacts, constitutions—all the different kinds of formal paper establishing the individual Colonies and States are marked by a highly religious seriousness of tone. It is usual for them to open with an appeal to God, coupled with a declaration of moral and religious purpose, and to close with some phrase petitioning for God's blessing, or submitting to His will. Typical is the Mayflower Compact, which set up a form of democratic government that was to be a model to the many American governments which followed. In the Mayflower Compact, the Pilgrims declared that they had established that government in the presence of God, and in service to God and the Christian faith.

This compact was signed in the year of our Lord 1620. A century and a half later, the same religious basis for political action was invoked in the Declaration of Independence. The rights for which the colonists contended, and upon which they based all their claims to individual freedom and national independence, were the "unalienable rights" with which all men "are endowed by their Creator." They appealed for justice on the basis of the "Laws of Nature and of Nature's God," and their final pledge of loyalty and constancy among themselves was made "with a firm reliance on the protection of divine providence." The Declaration of Independence is basic to our independent, national existence, and its philosophy permeates our political thinking to this day. . . .

After proclaiming our independence in the Declaration of Independence and winning it in the American Revolution, our forefathers sought to secure our independence and newly won liberties for all our people for generations to come. When they met in Philadelphia in 1787 at the Constitutional Convention, the Founding Fathers determined to establish a government which would be separate from any religious faith and one which would place a premium on individual liberty, individual initiative, and individual responsibility. In making certain that church and state would not be mixed, they did not rule God out of our national life as the Supreme Court is attempting to do today. Indeed, they based their ideals as a nation on those given us by Christ. . . .

We are all very familiar with the blessings that have been showered on the American people as a result of the actions—which I believe to have been divinely inspired—at that great convention in 1787. Since that time America has grown and prospered, and our liberties—though constricted of late by the rapid and vast growth of the Central Government—have made us the envy of the world.

Down through the years since the founding of our great Republic, each president has asked the protection and help of God in taking his oath of office, as have Members of the Congress and most other National, State, and local officeholders. In the dissenting opinion in Engel against Vitale, Justice Potter Stewart has pointed out that even in the Supreme Court there has been a traditional recognition of God—the wisdom of which is specifically questioned by Justice William Douglas—by the crier of the Court, in opening each session with the petition: "God save the United States and this Honorable Court.". . .

Religious Traditions

These words, these actions, and these traditions are only a few of many examples of our national acknowledgment of a Supreme Being, to whom we look individually and collectively for divine guidance and inspiration. The Congress has itself approved actions which have put our Nation on the side of God, in accordance with President Lincoln's admonition that we insure not only that God is on our side, but, more importantly, that we are on God's side. Some of these actions have been passed in very recent years while our religious traditions have been taking a vicious beating in the courts of our land in other twisted and distorted interpretations of the first amendment to the Constitution. . . .

Just as the Congress has provided itself with chaplains, so has the Congress provided our armed services with chaplains to give our service men and women moral and spiritual guidance and training. In fact, each year we appropriate funds to pay the salaries and allowances of these armed services chaplains and also to maintain the chapels in which they minister.

By and large, these actions of the Congress which have acknowledged and emphasized and reinforced our religious heritage have not fallen under the hammer of any assault from minorities within our Government. However, in 1928, the Supreme Court considered and rejected a challenge of congressional appropriations to pay the salaries of the chaplains of the Congress, the Army, and the Navy.

The road between the decisions in the chaplains' case, as stated in Elliott against White, in 1928, and in the school prayer case, as stated in Engel against Vitale of June 25, 1962, is pockmarked with holes of irrational and unrealistic mental gymnastics which have so undermined and weakened the constitutional concept of federalism and States rights as to set the stage for the prohibition of State action permitting a simple, non-compulsory, interdenominational prayer in a public school.

The irrational—and, I think, irreverent—decision in Engel against Vitale comes at a time when the world is locked in a cold war struggle between the forces of freedom which look to a Supreme Being for divine guidance and supplication and the forces of tyranny which are presided over by an ideology which does not recognize true freedom or any god except man himself and the worship of materialism. In this time of the most critical period in our national life, we need to increase rather than decrease individual and national attention to spiritual and moral values which undergird our Nation in this struggle, which is essentially a fight between those who do and do not believe in a Supreme Being. Every time we turn our young people—or any of our people for that matter—away from God, we turn them down the road toward the enemy camp of reliance on man and devotion to materialism. . . .

In closing, I commend Justice Stewart for taking a stand—albeit a lonesome stand on the Court—in favor of fostering and promoting our religious heritage and traditions rather than joining in the action which attempts to interpret God out of our national life. In the end his dissent will prevail, not only because his position is supported by the overwhelming majority of the American people, who still hold the reins of Government, but because it is right.

CHAPTER 4

National Security

Chapter Preface

The question of how to balance the civil liberties enshrined in the Bill of Rights with national security concerns has been a perennial one in American politics. The issue becomes especially acute at times of national crisis. This chapter looks at how American leaders reconciled the sometimes opposing claims of freedom and security at three different junctures: the Civil War, World War II, and the beginning of the cold war.

Abraham Lincoln faced the secession of eleven southern states. In his determined efforts to win the Civil War and preserve the Union, the "Constitution was put into a deep freeze," in the words of historian Michael Linfield. Military authorities imposed press censorship by seizing and shutting down newspapers that criticized the war or Lincoln's policies and by arresting or banishing the newspaper editors. Telegraph lines were placed under military control. Tens of thousands of citizens were arrested for resisting the draft or criticizing the war. They were detained by military authorities acting with little regard for constitutional protections. The Supreme Court tried to limit Lincoln's actions in several cases, but its pronouncements were essentially ignored until the war was over.

In the next eighty years the influence of the Bill of Rights grew considerably, both in the reach of Supreme Court decisions and in the public consciousness. Ironically, it was laws passed during World War I to stifle dissent that helped bring this development about. The Court upheld these laws and generally ruled that in times of war and national crisis the rules regarding free speech change. Still, the series of Supreme Court decisions of that period laid the groundwork for ultimately increasing the Court's role in defining and protecting freedom of speech. The first decades of the twentieth century also witnessed the founding of several organizations, such as the American Civil Liberties Union (ACLU) and the American Bar Association's Committee on the Bill of Rights, that gave the Bill of Rights greater public and legal respectability. In 1941 the Bill of Rights had its 150th anniversary. It was celebrated with unprecedented attention by the American public.

However, the United States was soon to face two major crises that, like the Civil War, threatened to imperil its existence—World War II against the fascist powers Germany and Japan and the subsequent cold war against the communist Soviet Union. In both cases disputes arose over whether steps taken to protect national security violated the Bill of Rights, even as the ten amendments were being celebrated as a benchmark of American freedom.

Zechariah Chafee, a noted civil liberties scholar, wrote in 1941 that the United States should not repeat the repressive measures taken in the Civil War and World War I:

> Let us not in our anxiety to protect ourselves from foreign tyrants imitate some of their worse acts, and sacrifice in the process of national defense the very liberties which we are defending.

Most historians would agree with criminal justice professor Samuel Walker when he wrote that Chafee's warnings were generally heeded, with one glaring exception:

> The fate of civil liberties during World War II dramatized how much the country had changed since the first Great War [World War I]. . . . With one notable exception . . . there was remarkably little suppression of civil liberties. . . .
>
> The great exception to this generally favorable picture, of course, was the evacuation and internment of Japanese-Americans. About 120,000 people . . . lost their liberty and millions of dollars in property. Even more appalling was the limited opposition to the government's action. . . .
>
> The treatment of Japanese-Americans was a sobering reminder of the fragility of civil liberties. Despite the recent progress, the episode illustrated the extent to which the government, the Supreme Court, and most of the public could countenance a gross violation of civil rights.

With the exception of the Japanese-American internment, the United States had largely passed the test suggested by Chafee in not sacrificing civil liberties for the sake of national security. However, the United States was soon to be faced with a new threat and a new test—the rise of the Soviet Union and the cold war. During the late forties and early fifties, a series of events caused Americans to become more fearful for national security. Some of the events and threats were external: the Soviet development of the atomic bomb in 1949, the Chinese communist revolution that same year, and the attack on South Korea by North Korea in 1950. Some of the events were internal: the 1953 conviction and execution of Julius and Ethel Rosenberg for passing atomic secrets to the Soviet Union and the controversial debate over whether Alger Hiss, a high-ranking U.S. State Department official, was a communist spy. These events contributed to an atmosphere of fear of communism as both a foreign enemy and an internal subversive threat to America. Federal government, local government, and private groups all embarked on anticommunist crusades that destroyed many people's careers and reputations and that trampled the Bill of Rights. Many people agreed with Attorney General (later Supreme Court Justice) Tom C. Clark, when he warned in a speech on Bill of Rights Day, December 15, 1947, that Americans must be wary of "those who cloak themselves under the Bill of Rights and who would undermine our form of government."

Does the First Amendment extend free speech protection to those advocating communism and its call for a violent overthrow of government? Should people who are being investigated by Congress and who refuse to answer questions, citing the Fifth Amendment as prohibition against self-incrimination, be judged guilty? Should organizations deemed potentially harmful to national security have the right to keep their membership and other information secret? These are but a few of the questions concerning the Bill of Rights and national security that the United States has wrestled with at different times in its history, questions that still reverberate today.

VIEWPOINT 1

"The Constitution is not in its application in all respects the same in cases of rebellion or invasion involving the public safety, as it is in times of . . . peace."

War Justifies the Restriction of Civil Liberties

Abraham Lincoln (1809-1865)

The question of how and whether to maintain civil liberties while conducting a war confronted leaders on both sides of the American Civil War (1861-1865). Abraham Lincoln, the sixteenth president of the United States, and Jefferson Davis, the first and only president of the Confederacy, took contrasting approaches. Davis maintained civil liberties for most Southerners except slaves. Abraham Lincoln, however, arrested and detained thousands of suspected Confederate sympathizers, suppressing their constitutional rights, including *habeas corpus*, a constitutional provision forbidding unlawful detention, and the procedural rights guaranteed in the fifth through eighth amendments of the Bill of Rights.

In 1863 a group of Democrats from Albany, New York, wrote to Lincoln, offering general support of the war but decrying the civil liberties violations. High among their concerns was the fate of

From Abraham Lincoln's letter to Erastus Corning and others, dated June 12, 1863.

Clement L. Vallandigham, a Democratic congressman who had actively opposed conscription and denounced Lincoln and other Union leaders. Lincoln had Vallandigham arrested for treasonable utterances. He was subsequently convicted and ultimately banished to the Confederacy.

Lincoln replied to the Albany Democrats in a June 12, 1863, letter, excerpted in the following viewpoint, in which he made one of his most developed arguments defending his war policies. He argues that the "inherent power" of the executive justifies using whatever measures are necessary to protect national security at a time of crisis. He also asserts that his actions would do no permanent harm to the liberties protected under the Constitution and the Bill of Rights.

Gentlemen:

Your letter of May 19, inclosing the resolutions of a public meeting held at Albany, New York, on the 16th of the same month, was received several days ago. . . .

Critical Resolutions

The resolutions promise to support me in every constitutional and lawful measure to suppress the rebellion; and I have not knowingly employed, nor shall knowingly employ, any other. But the meeting, by their resolutions, assert and argue that certain military arrests and proceedings following them, for which I am ultimately responsible are unconstitutional. I think they are not. The resolutions quote from the Constitution the definition of treason, and also the limiting safeguards and guarantees therein provided for the citizen on trials for treason, and on his being held to answer for capital or otherwise infamous crimes, and in criminal prosecutions his right to a speedy and public trial by an impartial jury. They proceed to resolve "that these safeguards of the rights of the citizen against the pretensions of arbitrary power were intended more especially for his protection in times of civil commotion." And, apparently to demonstrate the proposition, the resolutions proceed: "They were secured substantially to the English people after years of protracted civil war, and were adopted into our Constitution at the close of the revolution." Would not the demonstration have been better if it could have been truly said that these safeguards had been adopted and applied during the civil wars and during our revolution, instead of after the one and at the close of the other? I, too, am devotedly for them after civil war and before civil war, and at all times, "except when, in cases of rebellion or invasion, the public safety may require" their suspension. . . . But these provisions of the Constitution have no application to the case we have in hand, because the arrests complained of were not made for treason—that is, not for the treason defined in the Constitution, and upon the conviction of which the punishment is death— nor yet were they made to hold persons to answer for any capital or otherwise infamous crimes; nor were the proceedings following, in any constitutional or legal sense, "criminal prosecutions." The arrests were made on totally different grounds, and the proceedings following accorded with the grounds of the arrests. . . . [The rebel] sympathizers pervaded all departments of the government and nearly all communities of the people. From this material, under cover of "liberty of speech," "liberty of the press," and *"habeas corpus,"* they hoped to keep on foot amongst us a most efficient corps of spies, informers, suppliers and aiders and abettors of their cause in a thousand ways. They knew that in times such as they were inaugurating, by the Constitution itself the *"habeas corpus"* might be suspended; but they also knew they had friends who would make a question as to who was to suspend it; meanwhile their spies and others might remain at large to help on their cause. Or if, as has happened, the Executive should suspend the writ without ruinous waste of time, instances of arresting innocent persons might occur, as are always likely to occur in such cases; and then a clamor could be raised in regard to this. . . . Yet . . . I was slow to adopt the strong measures which [are] . . . indispensable to the public safety. Nothing is better known to history than that courts of justice are utterly incompetent to such cases. Civil courts are organized chiefly for trials of individuals, or, at most, a few individuals acting in concert—and this in quiet times, and on charges of crimes well defined in the law. Even in times of peace bands of horse-thieves and robbers frequently grow too numerous and powerful for the ordinary courts of justice. But what comparison, in numbers, have such bands ever borne to the insurgent sympathizers even in many of the loyal States? Again, a jury too frequently has at least one member more ready to hang the panel than to hang the traitor. And yet again, he who dissuades one man from volunteering, or induces one soldier to desert, weakens the Union cause as much as he who kills a Union soldier in battle. Yet this dissuasion or inducement may be so conducted as to be no defined crime of which any civil court would take cognizance.

Rebellion

Ours is a case of rebellion. . . . [The Suspension Clause] plainly attests the understanding of those who made the Constitution that ordinary courts of justice are inadequate to "cases of rebellion"—attests their purpose that, in such cases, men may be held in custody whom the courts, acting on ordinary rules, would discharge. *Habeas corpus* does not discharge men who are proved to be guilty of defined crime; and its suspension is allowed by the Constitution on purpose that men may be arrested and held who cannot be proved to be guilty of defined crime, "when, in cases of rebellion or invasion, the public safety may require it."

Abraham Lincoln, president of the United States from 1861 to 1865, faced criticism for his suspension of certain civil liberties while prosecuting the Civil War.

This is precisely our present case—a case of rebellion wherein the public safety does require the suspension. . . . Arrests in cases of rebellion do not proceed altogether upon the same basis. In the latter case arrests are made not so much for what has been done, as for what probably would be done. The latter is more for the preventive and less for the vindictive than the former. In such cases the purposes of men are much more easily understood than in cases of ordinary crime. The man who stands by and says nothing when the peril of his government is discussed, cannot be misunderstood. If not hindered, he is sure to help the enemy; much more if he talks ambiguously—talks for his country with "buts," and "ifs" and "ands." [Several Confederate leaders] were all within the power of the government since the rebellion began, and were nearly as well known to be traitors then as now. Unquestionably if we had seized and held them, the insurgent cause would be much weaker. But no one of them had then committed any crime defined in the law. Every one of them, if arrested, would have been discharged on *habeas corpus* were the writ allowed to operate. In view of these and similar cases, I think the time not unlikely to come when I shall be blamed for having made too few arrests rather than too many.

By the third resolution the meeting indicate their opinion that military arrests may be constitutional in localities where rebellion actually exists, but that such arrests are unconstitutional in localities where rebellion or insurrection does not actually exist. They insist that such arrests shall not be made "outside of the lines of necessary military occupation and the scenes of insurrection." Inasmuch, however, as the Constitution itself makes no such distinction, I am unable to believe that there is any such constitutional distinction. I concede that the class of arrests complained of can be constitutional only when, in cases of rebellion or invasion, the public safety may require them; and I insist that in such cases they are constitutional wherever the public safety does require them, as well in places to which they may prevent the rebellion extending, as in those where it may be already prevailing; as well where they may restrain mischievous interference with the raising and supplying of armies to suppress the rebellion, as where the rebellion may actually be; as well where they may restrain the enticing men out of the army, as where they would prevent mutiny in the army; equally constitutional at all places where they will conduce to the public safety, as against the dangers of rebellion or invasion.

Clement L. Vallandigham

Take the particular case mentioned by the meeting. It is asserted in substance, that Mr. Vallandigham was, by a military commander, seized and tried "for no other reason than words addressed to a public meeting in criticism of the course of the administration, and in condemnation of the military orders of the general." Now, if there be no mistake about this, if this assertion is the truth and the whole truth, if there was no other reason for the arrest, then I concede that the arrest was wrong. But the arrest, as I understand, was made for a very different reason. Mr. Vallandigham avows his hostility to the war on the part of the Union; and his arrest was made because he was laboring, with some effect, to prevent the raising of troops, to encourage desertions from the army, and to leave the rebellion without an adequate military force to suppress it. He was not arrested because he was damaging the political prospects of the administration or the personal interests of the commanding general but because he was damaging the army, upon the existence and vigor of which the life of the nation depends. He was warring upon the military, and this gave the military constitutional jurisdiction to lay hands upon him. . . . Long experience has shown that armies cannot be maintained unless desertion shall be punished by the severe penalty of death. . . . Must I shoot a simple-minded soldier boy who deserts, while I must not touch a hair of a wily agitator who induces him to desert? This is none the less injurious when effected by getting a father, or brother, or friend into a public meeting, and there working upon his feelings till he is persuaded to write the soldier boy that he is fighting in a bad cause, for a wicked administration of a contemptible government, too weak to arrest and punish him if he shall desert. I think that, in such a case, to silence the agitator and save the boy is not only constitutional, but withal a great mercy.

If I be wrong . . . my error lies in believing . . . that the Constitution is not in its application in all respects the same in cases of rebellion or invasion involving the public safety, as it is in times of profound peace and public security. The Constitution itself makes the distinction, and I can no more be persuaded that the government can constitutionally take no strong measures in times of rebellion, because it can be shown that the same could not be lawfully taken in time of peace, than I can be persuaded that a particular drug is not good medicine for a sick man because it can be shown to not be good food for a well one. Nor am I able to appreciate the danger apprehended by the meeting, that the American people will by means of military arrests during the rebellion lose the right of public discussion, the liberty of speech and the press, the law of evidence, trial by jury, and *habeas corpus* throughout the indefinite peaceful future which I trust lies before them, any more than I am able to believe that a man could contract so strong an appetite for emetics during temporary illness as to persist in feeding upon them during the remainder of his healthful life. . . .

I am specifically called on to discharge Mr. Vallandigham. . . . In response to such appeal I have to say . . . it will afford me great pleasure to discharge him so soon as I can by any means believe the public safety will not suffer by it.

VIEWPOINT 2

"The Constitution of the United States is a law for rulers and people, equally in war and in peace, and covers with the shield of its protection all classes of men, at all times, and under all circumstances."

War Does Not Always Justify the Restriction of Civil Liberties

David Davis (1815-1886)

Over the course of the Civil War, President Abraham Lincoln suspended many of the provisions of the Bill of Rights and the Constitution by authorizing the military arrest and detainment without trial of thousands of suspected Confederate sympathizers. One such person was Lambdin P. Milligan, an Indiana civilian who was arrested in his home in October 1864 and charged with conspiring to aid rebel forces in Indiana, Kentucky, and Illinois. He was tried by a military commission without any of the procedural protections found in the Constitution and the Bill of Rights, and he was sentenced to be hanged. Milligan appealed to the federal courts in Indiana, stating that his trial and sentence by the military authorities deprived him of his rights guaranteed by the Bill of Rights.

His case eventually reached the Supreme Court, which issued its ruling in 1866, one year after the Civil War's end and Abra-

From the majority opinion of the U.S. Supreme Court in *Ex Parte Milligan*, 71 U.S. (4 Wall.) 2 (1866).

ham Lincoln's assassination. The Supreme Court unanimously held that Milligan's rights were violated and that the president had no authority to set up such military courts, except in the active theater of war when the regular courts were not functioning. (A minority of justices held that in such situations only Congress, not the president, had such authority.) The landmark decision created important judicial protections against military and executive invasion of individual rights. The opinion was written by David Davis, a former close friend of Lincoln and associate justice of the Supreme Court from 1862 to 1877.

The importance of the main question presented by this record cannot be overstated, for it involves the very framework of the government and the fundamental principles of American liberty.

During the late wicked Rebellion, the temper of the times did not allow that calmness in deliberation and discussion so necessary to a correct conclusion of a purely judicial question. Then, considerations of safety were mingled with the exercise of power, and feelings and interests prevailed which are happily terminated. Now that the public safety is assured, this question, as well as all others, can be discussed and decided without passion or the admixture of any element not required to form a legal judgment. We approach the investigation of this case fully sensible of the magnitude of the inquiry and the necessity of full and cautious deliberation. . . .

The controlling question in the case is this: Upon the facts stated in Milligan's petition, and the exhibits filed, had the Military Commission mentioned in it jurisdiction, legally, to try and sentence him? Milligan, not a resident of one of the rebellious states, or a prisoner of war, but a citizen of Indiana for twenty years past, and never in the military or naval service, is, while at his home, arrested by the military power of the United States, imprisoned and, on certain criminal charges preferred against him, tried, convicted, and sentenced to be hanged by a military commission, organized under the direction of the military commander of the military district of Indiana. Had this tribunal the legal power and authority to try and punish this man?

A Fundamental Question

No graver question was ever considered by this court, nor one which more nearly concerns the rights of the whole people; for it is the birthright of every American citizen when charged with crime, to be tried and punished according to law. The power of punishment is alone through the means which the laws have provided for that purpose, and if they are ineffectual, there is an immunity from punishment, no matter how great an offender the individual may be, or how much his crimes may have shocked the sense of justice of the country, or endangered its safety. By the protection of the law human rights are secured; withdraw that protection, and they are at the mercy of wicked rulers, or the clamor of an excited people. If there was law to justify this military trial, it is not our province to interfere; if there was not, it is our duty to declare the nullity of the whole proceedings. The decision of this question does not depend on argument or judicial precedents, numerous and highly illustrative as they are. These precedents inform us of the extent of the struggle to preserve liberty and to relieve those in civil life from military trials. The founders of our government were familiar with the history of that struggle; and secured in a written Constitution every right which the people had wrested from power during a contest of ages. By that Constitution and the laws authorized by it, this question must be determined. The provisions of that instrument on the administration of criminal justice are too plain and direct to leave room for misconstruction or doubt of their true meaning. Those applicable to this case are found in that clause of the original Constitution which says "that the trial of all crimes, except in case of impeachment, shall be by jury;" and in the fourth, fifth, and sixth articles of the amendments. . . .

Time has proven the discernment of our ancestors; for even these provisions, expressed in such plain English words, that it would seem the ingenuity of man could not evade them, are now, after the lapse of more than seventy years, sought to be avoided. Those great and good men foresaw that troublous times would arise, when rulers and people would become restive under restraint, and seek by sharp and decisive measures to accomplish ends deemed just and proper, and that the principles of constitutional liberty would be in peril, unless established by irrepealable law. The history of the world had taught them that what was done in the past might be attempted in the future. The Constitution of the United States is a law for rulers and people, equally in war and in peace, and covers with the shield of its protection all classes of men, at all times, and under all circumstances. No doctrine involving more pernicious consequences, was ever invented by the wit of man than that any of its provisions can be suspended during any of the great exigencies of government. Such a doctrine leads directly to anarchy or despotism, but the theory of necessity on which it is based is false; for the government, within the Constitution, has all the powers granted to it which are necessary to preserve its existence, as has been happily proved by the result of the great effort to throw off its just authority.

Have any of the rights guaranteed by the Constitution been violated in the case of Milligan? and if so, what are they?

Every trial involves the exercise of judicial power; and from what source did the Military Commission that tried him derive their authority? Certainly no part of the judicial power of the country was conferred on them; because the Constitution expressly vests it "in one Supreme Court and such inferior courts as the Congress may from time to time ordain and establish," and it is not pretended that the commission was a court ordained and established by Congress. They cannot justify on the mandate of the President; because he is controlled by law, and has his appropriate sphere of duty, which is to execute, not to make, the laws; and there is "no unwritten criminal code to which resort can be had as a source of jurisdiction."

But it is said that the jurisdiction is complete under the "laws and usages of war."

It can serve no useful purpose to inquire what those laws and usages are, whence they originated, where found, and on whom they operate; they can never be applied to citizens in states which have upheld the authority of the government, and where the courts are open and their process unobstructed. This court has judicial knowledge that in Indiana the Federal authority was always unopposed, and its courts always open to hear criminal accusations and redress grievances; and no usage of war could sanction a military trial there for any offense whatever of a citizen in civil life, in nowise connected with the military service. Congress could grant no such power; and to the honor of our national legislature be it said, it had never been provoked by the state of the country even to attempt its exercise. One of the plainest constitutional provisions was, therefore, infringed when Milligan was tried by a court not ordained and established by Congress, and not composed of judges appointed during good behavior. . . .

Trial by Jury

Another guarantee of freedom was broken when Milligan was denied a trial by jury. The great minds of the country have differed on the correct interpretation to be given to various provisions of the Federal Constitution; and judicial decision has been often invoked to settle their true meaning; but until recently no one ever doubted that the right of trial by jury was fortified in the organic law against the power of attack. It is now assailed; but if ideas can be expressed in words, and language has any meaning, this right—one of the most valuable in a free country—is preserved to every one accused of a crime who is not attached to the Army, or Navy, or Militia in actual service. The sixth amendment affirms that "in all criminal prosecutions the accused shall enjoy the right to a speedy and public trial by an impartial jury," language broad enough to embrace all persons and cases; but the fifth, recognizing the necessity of an indictment, or presentment, before any one can be held to answer for high crimes, "except cases arising in the land or naval forces, or in the militia, when in actual service, in time of war or public danger"; and the framers of the Constitution, doubtless, meant to limit the right to trial by jury, in the Sixth Amendment, to those persons who were subject to indictment or presentment in the Fifth. . . .

It is claimed that martial law covers with its broad mantle the proceedings of this Military Commission. The proposition is this: That in a time of war the commander of an armed force (if in his opinion the exigencies of the country demand it, and of which he is to judge) has the power, within the lines of his military district, to suspend all civil rights and their remedies, and subject citizens as well as soldiers to the rule of his will; and in the exercise of his lawful authority cannot be restrained, except by his superior officer or the President of the United States.

If this position is sound to the extent claimed, then when war exists, foreign or domestic, and the country is subdivided into military departments for mere convenience, the commander of one of them can, if he chooses, within the limits, on the plea of necessity, with the approval of the Executive, substitute military force for and [to] the exclusion of the laws, and punish all persons, as he thinks right and proper, without fixed or certain rules.

The statement of this proposition shows its importance; for, if true, republican government is a failure, and there is an end of liberty regulated by law. Martial law, established on such a basis, destroys every guarantee of the Constitution, and effectually renders the "military independent of and superior to the civil power"—the attempt to do which by the King of Great Britain was deemed by our fathers such an offense, that they assigned it to the world as one of the causes which impelled them to declare their independence. Civil liberty and this kind of martial law cannot endure together; the antagonism is irreconcilable and, in the conflict, one or the other must perish.

This nation, as experience has proved, cannot always remain at peace, and has no right to expect that it will always have wise and humane rulers, sincerely attached to the principles of the Constitution. Wicked men, ambitious of power, with hatred of liberty and contempt of law, may fill the place once occupied by Washington and Lincoln; and if this right is conceded, and the calamities of war again befall us, the dangers to human liberty are frightful to contemplate. If our fathers had failed to provide for just such a contingency, they would have been false to the trust reposed in them. They knew—the history of the world told them—the nation they were founding, be its existence short or long, would be involved in war; how often or how long continued, human foresight could not tell; and that unlimited power, wherever lodged at such a time, was especially hazardous to freemen. For this, and other equally weighty reasons, they secured the inheritance they had fought to maintain, by incorporating in a written Constitution the safeguards which time had proved were essential to its preservation. Not one of these safeguards can the President or Congress or the Judiciary disturb, except the one concerning the writ of habeas corpus.

Habeas Corpus

It is essential to the safety of every government that, in a great crisis, like the one we have just passed through, there should be a power somewhere of suspending the writ of habeas corpus. In every war, there are men of previously good character, wicked enough to counsel their fellow citizens to resist the measures deemed necessary by a good government to sustain its just authority and overthrow its enemies; and their influence may lead to dangerous combinations. In the emergency of the times, an immediate public investigation according to law may not be possible; and yet, the peril to the country may be too imminent to suffer such persons to go at large. Unquestionably, there is then an exigency which demands that the government, if it should see fit, in the exercise of a proper discretion, to make arrests, should not be required to produce the person arrested in answer to a writ of habeas corpus. The Constitution goes no further. It does not say after a writ of habeas corpus is denied a citizen, that he shall be tried otherwise than by the course of common law. If it had intended this result, it was easy by the use of direct words to have accomplished it. The illustrious men who framed that instrument were guarding the foundations of civil liberty against the abuses of unlimited power; they were full of wisdom, and the lessons of history informed them that a trial by an established court, assisted by an impartial jury, was the only sure way of protecting the citizen against oppression and wrong. Knowing this, they limited the suspension to one great right, and left the rest to remain forever inviolable. But, it is insisted that the safety of the country in time of war demands that this broad claim for martial law shall be sustained. If this were true, it could be well said that a country, preserved at the sacrifice of all the cardinal principles of liberty, is not worth the cost of preservation. Happily, it is not so.

VIEWPOINT 3

"When under conditions of modern warfare our shores are threatened by hostile forces, the power to protect must be commensurate with the threatened danger."

Interning Japanese-Americans During World War II Was Justified

Hugo Black (1886-1971)

Following the Japanese attack on Pearl Harbor, Hawaii, the United States declared war on Japan on December 8, 1941. At the time, approximately 110,000 Japanese-Americans, two-thirds of whom were American citizens, resided on the West Coast of the United States. They quickly became objects of fear and suspicion. Officials and citizens worried that they would sabotage America's military effort and assist a possible Japanese invasion. In 1942, under authority of an executive order by President Franklin D. Roosevelt, the U.S. military declared the entire West Coast a vital military area and forcibly evacuated from their homes all Japanese-Americans residing there. They detained these people in barbed wire-enclosed "relocation centers" constructed in California, Montana, and other states, holding them for the duration of the war.

From the majority opinion of the U.S. Supreme Court in *Korematsu v. United States*, 319 U.S. 624 (1944).

The relocation program received several legal challenges during World War II that reached the Supreme Court. One such case involved Fred Korematsu, a shipyard worker who challenged the order to leave his home in San Leandro, California. The Supreme Court, in a six to three vote, ruled against him in 1944. Writing for the majority was Hugo Black, an associate justice from 1937 to 1971 and remembered today as a staunch defender of the Bill of Rights. Citing a previous case, *Hirabayashi v. United States*, in which the Supreme Court upheld a curfew regulation on Japanese-Americans as a necessary war measure, Black defends the evacuation program of the U.S. government. While declaring that the civil rights restrictions on the basis of race were "immediately suspect," he ultimately upholds the military evacuation measures as justifiable because of national security concerns.

The petitioner, an American citizen of Japanese descent, was convicted in a federal district court for remaining in San Leandro, California, a "Military Area," contrary to Civilian Exclusion Order No. 34 of the Commanding General of the Western Command, U.S. Army, which directed that after May 9, 1942, all persons of Japanese ancestry should be excluded from that area. No question was raised as to petitioner's loyalty to the United States. The Circuit Court of Appeals affirmed, and the importance of the constitutional question involved caused us to grant certiorari.

It should be noted, to begin with, that all legal restrictions which curtail the civil rights of a single racial group are immediately suspect. That is not to say that all such restrictions are unconstitutional. It is to say that courts must subject them to the most rigid scrutiny. Pressing public necessity may sometimes justify the existence of such restrictions; racial antagonism never can. . . .

War Powers

The 1942 Act was attacked in the *Hirabayashi* case as an unconstitutional delegation of power; it was contended that the curfew order and other orders on which it rested were beyond the war powers of the Congress, the military authorities and of the President, as Commander in Chief of the Army; and finally that to apply the curfew order against none but citizens of Japanese ancestry amounted to a constitutionally prohibited discrimination solely on account of race. To these questions, we gave the serious consideration which their importance justified. We upheld the curfew order as an exercise of the power of the government to take steps necessary to prevent espionage and sabotage in an area threatened by Japanese attack.

The people pictured here were among the 110,000 Japanese-Americans who were forcibly evacuated from their homes during World War II. In 1988 Congress granted $20,000 restitution payments for each of the 60,000 survivors.

In the light of the principles we announced in the *Hirabayashi* case, we are unable to conclude that it was beyond the war power of Congress and the Executive to exclude those of Japanese ancestry from the West Coast war area at the time they did. True, exclusion from the area in which one's home is located is a far greater deprivation than constant confinement to the home from 8 p.m. to 6 a.m. Nothing short of apprehension by the proper military authorities of the gravest imminent danger to the public safety can constitutionally justify either. But exclusion from a threatened area, no less than curfew, has a definite and close relationship to the prevention of espionage and sabotage. The military authorities, charged with the primary responsibility of defending our shores, concluded that curfew provided inadequate protection and ordered exclusion. They did so, as pointed out in our *Hirabayashi* opinion, in accordance with Congressional authority to the military to say who should, and who should not, remain in the threatened areas.

In this case the petitioner challenges the assumptions upon which we rested our conclusions in the *Hirabayashi* case. He also urges that by May 1942, when Order No. 34 was promulgated, all danger of Japanese invasion of the West Coast had disappeared. After careful consideration of these contentions we are compelled to reject them.

Here, as in the *Hirabayashi* case, *supra*, p. 99, ". . . we cannot reject as unfounded the judgment of the military authorities and of Congress that there were disloyal members of that population, whose number and strength could not be precisely and quickly ascertained. We cannot say that the war-making branches of the Government did not have ground for believing that in a critical hour such persons could not readily be isolated and separately dealt with, and constituted a menace to the national defense and safety, which demanded that prompt and adequate measures be taken to guard against it."

Like curfew, exclusion of those of Japanese origin was deemed necessary because of the presence of an unascertained number of disloyal members of the group, most of whom we have no doubt were loyal to this country. It was because we could not reject the finding of the military authorities that it was impossible to bring about an immediate segregation of the disloyal from the loyal that we sustained the validity of the curfew order as applying to the whole group. In the instant case, temporary exclusion of the entire group was rested by the military on the same ground. The judgment that exclusion of the whole group was for the same reason a military imperative answers the contention that the exclusion was in the nature of group punishment based on antagonism to those of Japanese origin. That there were members of the group who retained loyalties to Japan has been confirmed by investigations made subsequent to the exclusion. Approximately five thousand American citizens of Japanese ancestry refused to swear unqualified allegiance to the United States and to renounce allegiance to the Japanese Emperor, and several thousand evacuees requested repatriation to Japan.

The Burdens of Citizenship

We uphold the exclusion order as of the time it was made and when the petitioner violated it. . . . In doing so, we are not unmindful of the hardships imposed by it upon a large group of American citizens. . . . But hardships are part of war and war is an aggregation of hardships. All citizens alike, both in and out of uniform, feel the impact of war in greater or lesser measure. Citizenship has its responsibilities as well as its privileges, and in time of war the burden is always heavier. Compulsory exclusion of large groups of citizens from their homes, except under circumstances of direst emergency and peril, is inconsistent with our basic governmental institutions. But when under conditions of modern warfare our shores are threatened by hostile forces, the power to protect must be commensurate with the threatened danger. . . .

It is said that we are dealing here with the case of imprisonment of a citizen in a concentration camp solely because of his ancestry, without evidence or inquiry concerning his loyalty and good disposition towards the United States. Our task would be simple, our duty clear, were this a case involving the imprisonment of a loyal citizen in a concentration camp because of racial prejudice. Regardless of the true nature of the assembly and relocation centers—and we deem it unjustifiable to call them concentration camps with all the ugly connotations that term implies—we are dealing specifically with nothing but an exclusion order. To cast this case into outlines of racial prejudice, without reference to the real military dangers which were presented, merely confuses the issue. Korematsu was not excluded from the Military Area because of hostility to him or his race. He *was* excluded because we are at war with the Japanese Empire, because the properly constituted military authorities feared an invasion of our West Coast and felt constrained to take proper security measures, because they decided that the military urgency of the situation demanded that all citizens of Japanese ancestry be segregated from the West Coast temporarily, and finally, because Congress, reposing its confidence in this time of war in our military leaders—as inevitably it must—determined that they should have the power to do just this. There was evidence of disloyalty on the part of some, the military authorities considered that the need for action was great, and time was short. We cannot—by availing ourselves of the calm perspective of hindsight—now say that at that time these actions were unjustified.

VIEWPOINT 4

"This racial restriction . . . is one of the most sweeping and complete deprivations of constitutional rights in the history of this nation in the absence of martial law."

Interning Japanese-Americans During World War II Was Not Justified

Frank Murphy (1890-1949)

During World War II the United States forcibly moved thousands of Japanese-Americans from their homes on the West Coast and forced them to live in barbed wire-enclosed detention centers. The evacuations provoked sharp debate as to whether such curtailment of civil liberties was justified in the case of war. The debate continued well after the war, and in 1988 Congress enacted legislation awarding restitution payments to surviving internees.

The following viewpoint is taken from a dissenting opinion on the 1944 Supreme Court case *Korematsu v. United States*, in which shipyard worker Fred Korematsu challenged his evacuation from his California home. The majority of the Supreme Court voted to uphold the evacuation proceedings. One of the dissenters was Frank Murphy, an associate justice of the Supreme Court from

From Frank Murphy's dissenting opinion in the U.S. Supreme Court decision in *Korematsu v. United States*, 319 U.S. 624 (1944).

1940 to 1949. As a Michigan governor, a U.S. attorney general who established the first civil liberties unit in the Justice Department, and a Supreme Court justice, Murphy gained a reputation as a strong advocate and defender of civil liberties. In his minority opinion, excerpted here, Murphy attacks the wartime evacuation and internment of Japanese-Americans as racist and as a serious and unjustifiable abridgement of liberties guaranteed in the Bill of Rights.

This exclusion of "all persons of Japanese ancestry, both alien and non-alien," from the Pacific Coast area on a plea of military necessity in the absence of martial law ought not to be approved. Such exclusion goes over "the very brink of constitutional power" and falls into the ugly abyss of racism.

In dealing with matters relating to the prosecution and progress of a war, we must accord great respect and consideration to the judgments of the military authorities who are on the scene and who have full knowledge of the military facts. The scope of their discretion must, as a matter of necessity and common sense, be wide. And their judgments ought not to be overruled lightly by those whose training and duties ill-quip them to deal intelligently with matters so vital to the physical security of the nation.

At the same time, however, it is essential that there be definite limits to military discretion, especially where martial law has not been declared. . . .

Violating Constitutional Rights

The judicial test of whether the Government, on a plea of military necessity, can validly deprive an individual of any of his constitutional rights is whether the deprivation is reasonably related to a public danger that is so "immediate, imminent, and impending" as not to admit of delay and not to permit the intervention of ordinary constitutional processes to alleviate the danger. . . . Civilian Exclusion Order No. 34, banishing from a prescribed area of the Pacific Coast "all persons of Japanese ancestry, both alien and non-alien," clearly does not meet that test. Being an obvious racial discrimination, the order deprives all those within its scope of the equal protection of the laws as guaranteed by the Fifth Amendment. It further deprives these individuals of their constitutional rights to live and work where they will, to establish a home where they choose and to move about freely. In excommunicating them without benefit of hearings, this order also deprives them of all their constitutional rights to procedural due process. Yet no reasonable relation to an "immediate, imminent, and impending" public danger is evident to support this racial restriction which is one of the most sweeping and complete deprivations of constitutional rights in the history of this nation in the absence of martial law.

It must be conceded that the military and naval situation in the spring of 1942 was such as to generate a very real fear of invasion of the Pacific Coast, accompanied by fears of sabotage and espionage in that area. The military command was therefore justified in adopting all reasonable means necessary to combat these dangers. In adjudging the military action taken in light of the then apparent dangers, we must not erect too high or too meticulous standards; it is necessary only that the action have some reasonable relation to the removal of the dangers of invasion, sabotage and espionage. But the exclusion, either temporarily or permanently, of all persons with Japanese blood in their veins has no such reasonable relation. And that relation is lacking because the exclusion order necessarily must rely for its reasonableness upon the assumption that *all* persons of Japanese ancestry may have a dangerous tendency to commit sabotage and espionage and to aid our Japanese enemy in other ways. It is difficult to believe that reason, logic or experience could be marshalled in support of such an assumption.

That this forced exclusion was the result in good measure of this erroneous assumption of racial guilt rather than bona fide military necessity is evidenced by the Commanding General's Final Report on the evacuation from the Pacific Coast area. In it he refers to all individuals of Japanese descent as "subversive," as belonging to "an enemy race" whose "racial strains are undiluted," and as constituting "over 112,000 potential enemies . . . at large today" along the Pacific Coast. In support of this blanket condemnation of all persons of Japanese descent, however, no reliable evidence is cited to show that such individuals were generally disloyal, or had generally so conducted themselves in this area as to constitute a special menace to defense installations or war industries, or had otherwise by their behavior furnished reasonable ground for their exclusion as a group.

Racial Prejudice

Justification for the exclusion is sought, instead, mainly upon questionable racial and sociological grounds not ordinarily within the realm of expert military judgment, supplemented by certain semi-military conclusions drawn from an unwarranted use of circumstantial evidence. Individuals of Japanese ancestry are condemned because they are said to be "a large, unassimilated, tightly knit racial group, bound to an enemy nation by strong ties of race, culture, custom and religion." They are claimed to be given to "emperor worshipping ceremonies" and to "dual citizenship." Japanese language schools and allegedly pro-Japanese organizations are cited as evidence of possible group disloyalty, together with facts as to certain persons being educated and residing at length in Japan. It is intimated that many of these individuals deliberately resided "adjacent to strategic points," thus enabling them "to carry into execution a tremendous program of sabotage on a mass scale should any considerable number of them have been inclined to do so." . . . Finally, it is intimated, though not directly charged or proved, that persons of Japanese ancestry were responsible for three minor isolated shellings and bombings of the Pacific Coast area, as well as for unidentified radio transmissions and night signalling.

The main reasons relied upon by those responsible for the forced evacuation, therefore, do not prove a reasonable relation between the group characteristics of Japanese Americans and the dangers of invasion, sabotage and espionage. The reasons appear, instead, to be largely an accumulation of much of the misinformation, half-truths and insinuations that for years have been directed against Japanese Americans by people with racial and economic prejudices—the same people who have been among the foremost advocates of the evacuation. A military judgment based upon such racial and sociological considerations is not entitled to the great weight ordinarily given the judgments based upon strictly military considerations. Especially is this so when every charge relative to race, religion, culture, geographical location, and legal and economic status has been substantially discredited by independent studies made by experts in these matters. . . .

No adequate reason is given for the failure to treat these Japanese Americans on an individual basis by holding investigations and hearings to separate the loyal from the disloyal, as was done in the case of persons of German and Italian ancestry. . . . It is asserted merely that the loyalties of this group "were unknown and time was of the essence." Yet nearly four months elapsed after Pearl Harbor before the first exclusion order was issued; nearly eight months went by until the last order was issued; and the last of these "subversive" persons was not actually removed until almost eleven months had elapsed. Leisure and deliberation seem to have been more of the essence than speed. And the fact that conditions were not such as to warrant a declaration of martial law adds strength to the belief that the factors of time and military necessity were not as urgent as they have been represented to be.

Moreover, there was no adequate proof that the Federal Bureau of Investigation and the military and naval intelligence services did not have the espionage and sabotage situation well in hand during this long period. Nor is there any denial of the fact that not one person of Japanese ancestry was accused or convicted of espionage or sabotage after Pearl Harbor while they were still free, a fact which is some evidence of the loyalty of the vast majority of these individuals and of the effectiveness of the established methods of combatting these evils. It seems incredible that under these circumstances it would have been impossible to hold loyalty hearings for the mere 112,000 persons involved—or at least for the 70,000 American citizens—especially when a large part of this number represented children and elderly men and women. . . .

All Americans Have Equal Constitutional Rights

I dissent, therefore, from this legalization of racism. Racial discrimination in any form and in any degree has no justifiable part whatever in our democratic way of life. It is unattractive in any setting but it is utterly revolting among a free people who have embraced the principles set forth in the Constitution of the United States. All residents of this nation are kin in some way by blood or culture to a foreign land. Yet they are primarily and necessarily a part of the new and distinct civilization of the United States. They must accordingly be treated at all times as the heirs of the American experiment and as entitled to all the rights and freedoms guaranteed by the Constitution.

VIEWPOINT 5

"Overthrow of the Government by force and violence is certainly a substantial enough interest for the Government to limit speech."

Advocacy of Communism Is Not Protected by the Bill of Rights

Fred M. Vinson (1890-1953)

In 1940 Congress passed the Smith Act, the first peacetime sedition act since the 1798 Sedition Act. The law, modeled after New York's 1902 Criminal Anarchy Act, prohibited speech or publication that advocated overthrowing the government "by force and violence." In 1948 the federal government prosecuted Eugene Dennis and ten other leaders of the American Communist Party for violating the Smith Act in their advocacy of and writings on the Communist revolution. They appealed to the Supreme Court, arguing that the Smith Act was unconstitutional and that their convictions had violated freedoms granted under the Bill of Rights.

The following is taken from the majority opinion, written by Fred M. Vinson, chief justice of the Supreme Court from 1946 to 1953. Vinson asserts the constitutionality of the Smith Act. In doing so, he examines previous court cases, especially those dealing

From the majority opinion of the U.S. Supreme Court in *Dennis v. United States*, 341 U.S. 494 (1951).

with the "clear and present danger" test in determining whether speech should be protected. Among the cases Vinson cites are *Schenck v. United States* and *Gitlow v. New York*, in which the Supreme Court ruled that free speech could be restricted if it posed a "clear and present danger" to the public. Vinson broadened and reinterpreted the clear and present danger test to mean that Congress could determine that some ideas, such as advocacy of Communism, are so inherently dangerous that prohibiting their expression is justified.

The indictment charged the petitioners with wilfully and knowingly conspiring (1) to organize as the Communist Party of the United States of America a society, group and assembly of persons who teach and advocate the overthrow and destruction of the Government of the United States by force and violence, and (2) knowingly and wilfully to advocate and teach the duty and necessity of overthrowing and destroying the Government of the United States by force and violence. The indictment further alleged that § 2 of the Smith Act proscribes these acts and that any conspiracy to take such action is a violation of § 3 of the Act.

The trial of the case extended over nine months, six of which were devoted to the taking of evidence, resulting in a record of 16,000 pages. Our limited grant of the writ of certiorari has removed from our consideration any question as to the sufficiency of the evidence to support the jury's determination that petitioners are guilty of the offense charged. Whether on this record petitioners did in fact advocate the overthrow of the Government by force and violence is not before us, and we must base any discussion of this point upon the conclusions stated in the opinion of the Court of Appeals, which treated the issue in great detail. That court held that the record in this case amply supports the necessary finding of the jury that petitioners, the leaders of the Communist Party in this country, were unwilling to work within our framework of democracy, but intended to initiate a violent revolution whenever the propitious occasion appeared. . . .

Protecting the Government

The obvious purpose of the statute is to protect existing Government, not from change by peaceable, lawful and constitutional means, but from change by violence, revolution and terrorism. That it is within the *power* of the Congress to protect the Government of the United States from armed rebellion is a proposition which requires little discussion. Whatever theoretical merit there may be to the argument that there is a "right" to rebellion against dictatorial governments is without force where the existing structure of the government provides for peaceful and orderly change. We reject any principle of governmental helplessness in the face of preparation for revolution, which principle, carried to its logical conclusion, must lead to anarchy. No one could conceive that it is not within the power of Congress to prohibit acts intended to overthrow the Government by force and violence. The question with which we are concerned here is not whether Congress has such *power*, but whether the *means* which it has employed conflict with the First and Fifth Amendments to the Constitution.

Communism Poses a Clear and Present Danger

Sidney Hook, a professor of philosophy at New York University for many years, was a former Marxist who became active in anti-Communist causes. In a 1954 book, Heresy, Yes—Conspiracy, No, *he defended the Supreme Court decision in* Dennis v. United States.

All of the opinions in the Smith Act (*Dennis* case), except for the dissents of Justices Black and Douglas, recognize that the phrase "clear and present danger" is no shibboleth, and that in every case its intelligent use requires an analysis of the particular situation. Some consistency there must be, however, if these words are not to become entirely arbitrary. What seems extremely puzzling to me is how anyone can approve of the determination that a clear and present danger existed in the *Schenck* case—when Justice Holmes first formulated his principle—and contest the finding that a clear and present danger exists in the case of *Dennis, et al.,* who are an integral part of a highly organized international conspiracy. . . .

It seems to me that sufficient evidence was introduced, or could easily have been introduced, to convince any but Communists, their sympathizers, and doctrinaire pacifists who believe Stalin has a loving heart, that the international Communist movement, of which these defendants were trusted members, constitutes a clear and present threat to the preservation of free American institutions and our national independence.

One of the bases for the contention that the means which Congress has employed are invalid takes the form of an attack on the face of the statute on the grounds that by its terms it prohibits academic discussion of the merits of Marxism-Leninism, that it stifles ideas and is contrary to all concepts of a free speech and a free press. Although we do not agree that the language itself has that significance, we must bear in mind that it is the duty of the federal courts to interpret federal legislation in a manner not inconsistent with the demands of the Constitution. *American Communications Assn.* v. *Douds*, 339 U.S. 382, 407 (1950). . . .

The very language of the Smith Act negates the interpretation which petitioners would have us impose on that Act. It is directed at advocacy, not discussion. Thus, the trial judge properly charged the jury that they could not convict if they found that petitioners did "no more than pursue peaceful studies and discussions or teaching and advocacy in the realm of ideas." He further charged that it was not unlawful "to conduct in an American college or university a course explaining the philosophical theories set forth in the books which have been placed in evidence." Such a charge is in strict accord with the statutory language, and illustrates the meaning to be placed on those words. Congress did not intend to eradicate the free discussion of political theories, to destroy the traditional rights of Americans to discuss and evaluate ideas without fear of governmental sanction. Rather Congress was concerned with the very kind of activity in which the evidence showed these petitioners engaged.

But although the statute is not directed at the hypothetical cases which petitioners have conjured, its application in this case has resulted in convictions for the teaching and advocacy of the overthrow of the Government by force and violence, which, even though coupled with the intent to accomplish that overthrow, contains an element of speech. For this reason, we must pay special heed to the demands of the First Amendment marking out the boundaries of speech.

Examining Previous Cases

We pointed out in *Douds, supra,* that the basis of the First Amendment is the hypothesis that speech can rebut speech, propaganda will answer propaganda, free debate of ideas will result in the wisest governmental policies. It is for this reason that this Court has recognized the inherent value of free discourse. An analysis of the leading cases in this Court which have involved direct limitations on speech, however, will demonstrate that both the majority of the Court and the dissenters in particular cases have recognized that this is not an unlimited, unqualified right, but that the societal value of speech must, on occasion, be subordinated to other values and considerations.

No important case involving free speech was decided by this Court prior to *Schenck* v. *United States*, 249 U.S. 47 (1919). . . . That case involved a conviction under the Criminal Espionage Act, 40 Stat. 217. The question the Court faced was whether the evidence was sufficient to sustain the conviction. Writing for a unanimous Court Justice Holmes stated that the "question in every case is whether the words used are used in such circumstances and are of such a nature as to create a clear and present danger that they will bring about the substantive evils that Congress has a right to prevent."....

The next important case before the Court in which free speech was the crux of the conflict was *Gitlow* v. *New York*, 268 U.S. 652 (1925). There New York had made it a crime to advocate "the necessity or propriety of overthrowing . . . organized government by force. . . ." The evidence of violation of the statute was that the defendant had published a Manifesto attacking the Government and capitalism. The convictions were sustained, Justices Holmes and Brandeis dissenting. The majority refused to apply the "clear and present danger" test to the specific utterance. Its reasoning was as follows: The "clear and present danger" test was applied to the utterance itself in *Schenck* because the question was merely one of sufficiency of evidence under an admittedly constitutional statute. *Gitlow*, however, presented a different question. There a legislature had found that a certain kind of speech was, itself, harmful and unlawful. The constitutionality of such a state statute had to be adjudged by this Court just as it determined the constitutionality of any state statute, namely, whether the statute was "reasonable." Since it was entirely reasonable for a state to attempt to protect itself from violent overthrow, the statute was perforce reasonable. The only question remaining in the case became whether there was evidence to support the conviction, a question which gave the majority no difficulty. Justices Holmes and Brandeis refused to accept this approach, but insisted that wherever speech was the evidence of the violation, it was necessary to show that the speech created the "clear and present danger" of the substantive evil which the legislature had the right to prevent. Justices Holmes and Brandeis, then, made no distinction between a federal statute which made certain acts unlawful, the evidence to support the conviction being speech, and a statute which made speech itself the crime. This approach was emphasized in *Whitney* v. *California*, 274 U.S. 357 (1927), where the Court was confronted with a conviction under the California Criminal Syndicalist statute. The Court sustained the conviction, Justices Brandeis and Holmes concurring in the result. In their concurrence they repeated that even though the legislature had designated certain speech as criminal, this could not prevent the defendant from showing that there was no danger that the substantive evil would be brought about.

Although no case subsequent to *Whitney* and *Gitlow* has expressly overruled the majority opinions in those cases, there is little doubt that subsequent opinions have inclined toward the Holmes-Brandeis rationale. And in *American Communications Assn.* v. *Douds, supra*, we . . . suggested that the Holmes-Brandeis philosophy insisted that where there was a direct restriction upon speech, a "clear and present danger" that the substantive evil would be caused was necessary before the statute in question could be constitutionally applied. . . . But we further suggested that neither Justice Holmes nor Justice Brandeis ever envisioned that a shorthand phrase should be crystallized into a rigid rule to be applied inflexibly without regard to the circumstances of each case. Speech is not an absolute, above and beyond control by the legislature when its judgment, subject to review here, is that certain kinds of speech are so undesirable as to warrant criminal sanction. Nothing is more certain in modern society than the principle that there are no absolutes, that a name, a phrase, a standard has meaning only when associated with the considerations which gave birth to the nomenclature. . . . To those who would paralyze our Government in the face of impending threat by encasing it in a semantic straitjacket we must reply that all concepts are relative.

A Clear and Present Danger

In this case we are squarely presented with the application of the "clear and present danger" test, and must decide what that phrase imports. We first note that many of the cases in which this Court has reversed convictions by use of this or similar tests have been based on the fact that the interest which the State was attempting to protect was itself too insubstantial to warrant restriction of speech. . . . Overthrow of the Government by force and violence is certainly a substantial enough interest for the Government to limit speech. Indeed, this is the ultimate value of any society, for if a society cannot protect its very structure from armed internal attack, it must follow that no subordinate value can be protected. If, then, this interest may be protected, the literal problem which is presented is what has been meant by the use of the phrase "clear and present danger" of the utterances bringing about the evil within the power of Congress to punish.

Obviously, the words cannot mean that before the Government may act, it must wait until the *putsch* is about to be executed, the plans have been laid and the signal is awaited. If Government is aware that a group aiming at its overthrow is attempting to indoctrinate its members and to commit them to a course whereby they will strike when the leaders feel the circumstances permit, action by the Government is required. The argument that there is no need for Government to concern itself, for Government is strong, it possesses ample powers to put down a rebellion, it may defeat the revolution with ease needs no answer. For that is not the question. Certainly an attempt to overthrow the Government by force, even though doomed from the outset because of inadequate numbers or power of the revolutionists, is a sufficient evil for Congress to prevent. The damage which such attempts create both physically and politically to a nation makes it impossible to measure the validity in terms of the probability of success, or the immediacy of a successful attempt. In the instant case the trial judge charged the jury that they could not convict unless they found that petitioners intended to overthrow the Government "as speedily as circumstances would permit." This does not mean, and could not properly mean, that they would not strike until there was certainty of success. What was meant was that the revolutionists would strike when they thought the time was ripe. We must therefore reject the contention that success or probability of success is the criterion.

The Smith Act

Title I of the Alien Registration Act of 1940 was named the Smith Act after Virginia congressman Howard W. Smith. It proscribed certain speech, publishing, and organizing activities.

It shall be unlawful for any person—
(1) to knowingly or willfully advocate, abet, advise, or teach the duty, necessity, desirability, or propriety of overthrowing or destroying any government in the United States by force or violence, or by the assassination of any officer of any such government;
(2) with the intent to cause the overthrow or destruction of any government in the United States, to print, publish, edit, issue, circulate, sell, distribute, or publicly display any written or printed matter advocating, advising, or teaching the duty, necessity, desirability, or propriety of overthrowing or destroying any government in the United States by force or violence;
(3) to organize or help to organize any society, group, or assembly of persons who teach, advocate, or encourage the overthrow or destruction of any government in the United States by force or violence; or to be or become a member of, or affiliate with, any such society, group, or assembly of persons, knowing the purposes thereof.

The situation with which Justices Holmes and Brandeis were concerned in *Gitlow* was a comparatively isolated event, bearing little relation in their minds to any substantial threat to the safety of the community. . . . They were not confronted with any situation comparable to the instant one—the development of an apparatus signed and dedicated to the overthrow of the Government, in the context of world crisis after crisis.

Chief Judge Learned Hand, writing for the majority below, interpreted the phrase as follows: "In each case [courts] must ask whether the gravity of the 'evil,' discounted by its improbability, justifies such invasion of free speech as is necessary to avoid the danger.". . . We adopt this statement of the rule. As articulated by Chief Judge Hand, it is as succinct and inclusive as any other we might devise at this time. It takes into consideration those factors which we deem relevant, and relates their significances. More we cannot expect from words.

Likewise, we are in accord with the court below, which affirmed the trial court's finding that the requisite danger existed. The mere fact that from the period 1945 to 1948 petitioners' activities did not result in an attempt to overthrow the Government by force and violence is of course no answer to the fact that there was a group that was ready to make the attempt. The formation by petitioners of such a highly organized conspiracy, with rigidly disciplined members subject to call when the leaders, these petitioners, felt that the time had come for action, coupled with the inflammable nature of world conditions, similar uprisings in other countries, and the touch-and-go nature of our relations with countries with whom petitioners were in the very least ideologically attuned, convince us that their convictions were justified on this score. And this analysis disposes of the contention that a conspiracy to advocate, as distinguished from the advocacy itself, cannot be constitutionally restrained, because it comprises only the preparation. It is the existence of the conspiracy which creates the danger. . . . If the ingredients of the reaction are present, we cannot bind the Government to wait until the catalyst is added. . . .

The Question of Vagueness

There remains to be discussed the question of vagueness whether the statute as we have interpreted it is too vague, not sufficiently advising those who would speak of the limitations upon their activity. It is urged that such vagueness contravenes the First and Fifth Amendments. . . .

We hold that sections 2(a) (1), (2) (a) (3) and 3 of the Smith act, do not inherently, or as construed or applied in the instant case, violate the First Amendment and other provisions of the Bill of Rights, or the First and Fifth Amendments because of indefiniteness. Petitioners intended to overthrow the Government of the United States as speedily as the circumstances would permit. Their conspiracy to organize the Communist Party and to teach and advocate the overthrow of the Government of the United States by force and violence created a "clear and present danger" of an attempt to overthrow the Government by force and violence. They were properly and constitutionally convicted for violation of the Smith Act.

VIEWPOINT 6

"The First Amendment['s] . . . philosophy is that violence is rarely, if ever, stopped by denying civil liberties to those advocating . . . force."

Advocacy of Communism Should Be Protected by the Bill of Rights

William O. Douglas (1898-1980)

William O. Douglas was appointed associate justice of the Supreme Court by Franklin D. Roosevelt in 1939. He served until 1975, longer than any previous associate justice, and he was noted for his strong advocacy of civil liberties.

One of his most important dissenting opinions comes from the 1951 case *Dennis v. United States*, in which national officials of the American Communist Party were convicted under the 1940 Smith Act of conspiring to advocate the forcible overthrow of the U.S. government. The majority of the Court ruled that the probable danger of Communist conspiracy justified the restrictions on speech. In his dissenting opinion Douglas disagreed with such a view, arguing that the Smith Act violated the First Amendment.

From William O. Douglas's dissenting opinion in the U.S. Supreme Court decision in *Dennis v. United States*, 341 U.S. 494 (1951).

If this were a case where those who claimed protection under the First Amendment were teaching the techniques of sabotage, the assassination of the President, the filching of documents from public files, the planting of bombs, the art of street warfare, and the like, I would have no doubts. The freedom to speak is not absolute; the teaching of methods of terror and other seditious conduct should be beyond the pale along with obscenity and immorality. This case was argued as if those were the facts. The argument imported much seditious conduct into the record. That is easy and it has popular appeal, for the activities of Communists in plotting and scheming against the free world are common knowledge. But the fact is that no such evidence was introduced at the trial. There is a statute which makes a seditious conspiracy unlawful. Petitioners, however, were not charged with a "conspiracy to overthrow" the Government. They were charged with a conspiracy to form a party and groups and assemblies of people who teach and advocate the overthrow of our Government by force or violence and with a conspiracy to advocate and teach its overthrow by force and violence. It may well be that indoctrination in the techniques of terror to destroy the Government would be indictable under either statute. But the teaching which is condemned here is of a different character.

So far as the present record is concerned, what petitioners did was to organize people to teach and themselves teach the Marxist-Leninist doctrine contained chiefly in four books: Stalin, *Foundations of Leninism* (1924); Marx and Engels, *Manifesto of the Communist Party* (1848); Lenin, *The State and Revolution* (1917); *History of the Communist Party of the Soviet Union* (B.) (1939).

Those books are to Soviet Communism what *Mein Kampf* was to Nazism. If they are understood, the ugliness of Communism is revealed, its deceit and cunning are exposed, the nature of its activities becomes apparent, and the chances of its success less likely. That is not, of course, the reason why petitioners chose these books for their classrooms. They are fervent Communists to whom these volumes are gospel. They preached the creed with the hope that some day it would be acted upon.

Thought Crimes

The opinion of the Court does not outlaw these texts nor condemn them to the fire, as the Communists do literature offensive to their creed. But if the books themselves are not outlawed, if they can lawfully remain on library shelves, by what reasoning does their use in a classroom become a crime? It would not be a crime under the Act to introduce these books to a class, though that would be teaching what the creed of violent overthrow of the Government is. The Act, as construed, requires the element of intent—that those who teach the creed believe in it. The crime then depends not on what is taught but on who the teacher is. That is to make freedom of speech turn not on *what is said*, but on the *intent* with which it is said. Once we start down that road we enter territory dangerous to the liberties of every citizen.

There was a time in England when the concept of constructive treason flourished. Men were punished not for raising a hand against the king but for thinking murderous thoughts about him. The Framers of the Constitution were alive to that abuse and took steps to see that the practice would not flourish here. Treason was defined to require overt acts—the evolution of a plot against the country into an actual project. The present case is not one of treason. But the analogy is close when the illegality is made to turn on intent, not on the nature of the act. We then start probing men's minds for motive and purpose; they become entangled in the law not for what they did but *for what they thought*; they get convicted not for what they said but for the purpose with which they said it.

Intent, of course, often makes the difference in the law. An act otherwise excusable or carrying minor penalties may grow to an abhorrent thing if the evil intent is present. We deal here, however, not with ordinary acts but with speech, to which the Constitution has given a special sanction.

The Exalted Position of Free Speech

Free speech has occupied an exalted position because of the high service it has given our society. Its protection is essential to the very existence of a democracy. The airing of ideas releases pressures which otherwise might become destructive. When ideas compete in the market for acceptance, full and free discussion exposes the false and they gain few adherents. Full and free discussion even of ideas we hate encourages the testing of our own prejudices and preconceptions. Full and free discussion keeps a society from becoming stagnant and unprepared for the stresses and strains that work to tear all civilizations apart.

Full and free discussion has indeed been the first article of our faith. We have founded our political system on it. It has been the safeguard of every religious, political, philosophical, economic, and racial group amongst us. We have counted on it to keep us from embracing what is cheap and false; we have trusted the common sense of our people to choose the doctrine true to our genius and to reject the rest. This has been the one single outstanding tenet that has made our institutions the symbol of freedom and equality. We have deemed it more costly to liberty to suppress a despised minority than to let them vent their spleen. We have above all else feared the political censor. We have wanted a land where our people can be exposed to all the diverse creeds and cultures of the world.

Watering Down the First Amendment

Hugo Black was the only Supreme Court justice besides William O. Douglas to dissent in the case Dennis v. United States. *He wrote that the majority opinion weakened the freedoms guaranteed under the First Amendment.*

So long as this Court exercises the power of judicial review of legislation, I cannot agree that the First Amendment permits us to sustain laws suppressing freedom of speech and press on the basis of Congress' or our own notions of mere "reasonableness." Such a doctrine waters down the First Amendment so that it amounts to little more than an admonition to Congress. The Amendment as so construed is not likely to protect any but those "safe" or orthodox views which rarely need its protection. . . .

Public opinion being what it now is, few will protest the conviction of these Communist petitioners. There is hope, however, that in calmer times, when present pressures, passions, and fears subside, this or some later Court will restore the First Amendment liberties to the high preferred place where they belong in a free society.

There comes a time when even speech loses its constitutional immunity. Speech innocuous one year may at another time fan such destructive flames that it must be halted in the interests of the safety of the Republic. That is the meaning of the clear and present danger test. When conditions are so critical that there will be no time to avoid the evil that the speech threatens, it is time to call a halt. Otherwise, free speech which is the strength of the Nation will be the cause of its destruction.

Yet free speech is the rule, not the exception. The restraint to be constitutional must be based on more than fear, on more than passionate opposition against the speech, on more than a revolted dislike for its contents. There must be some immediate injury to society that is likely if speech is allowed. The classic statement of these conditions was made by Mr. Justice Brandeis in his concurring opinion in *Whitney v. California*, 274 U.S. 357,

Fear of serious injury cannot alone justify suppression of free speech and assembly. Men feared witches and burnt women. It is the function of speech to free men from the bondage of irrational fears. To justify suppression of free speech there must be reasonable ground to fear that serious evil will result if free speech is practiced. There must be reasonable ground to believe that the danger apprehended is imminent. There must be reasonable ground to believe that the evil to be prevented is a serious one. . . .

If there be time to expose through discussion the falsehood and fallacies, to avert the evil by the processes of education, the remedy to be applied is more speech, not enforced silence. (Italics added.)

This record contains no evidence whatsoever showing that the acts charged, *viz.*, the teaching of the Soviet theory of revolution with the hope that it will be realized, have created any clear and present danger to the Nation. . . .

The nature of Communism as a force on the world scene would, of course, be relevant to the issue of clear and present danger of petitioners' advocacy within the United States. But the primary consideration is the strength and tactical position of petitioners and their converts in this country. On that there is no evidence in the record. If we are to take judicial notice of the threat of Communists within the nation, it should not be difficult to conclude that *as a political party* they are of little consequence. Communists in this country have never made a respectable or serious showing in any election. I would doubt that there is a village, let alone a city or county or state, which the Communists could carry. Communism in the world scene is no bogeyman; but Communism as a political faction or party in this country plainly is. Communism has been so thoroughly exposed in this country that it has been crippled as a political force. Free speech has destroyed it as an effective political party. It is inconceivable that those who went up and down this country preaching the doctrine of revolution which petitioners espouse would have any success. In days of trouble and confusion, when bread lines were long, when the unemployed walked the streets, when people were starving, the advocates of a short-cut by revolution might have a chance to gain adherents. But today there are no such conditions. The country is not in despair; the people know Soviet Communism; the doctrine of Soviet revolution is exposed in all of its ugliness and the American people want none of it.

How it can be said that there is a clear and present danger that this advocacy will succeed is, therefore, a mystery. Some nations less resilient than the United States, where illiteracy is high and where democratic traditions are only budding, might have to take drastic steps and jail these men for merely speaking their creed. But in America they are miserable merchants of unwanted ideas; their wares remain unsold. The fact that their ideas are abhorrent does not make them powerful.

The political impotence of the Communists in this country does not, of course, dispose of the problem. Their numbers; their positions in industry and government; the extent to which they have in fact infiltrated the police, the armed services, transportation, stevedoring, power plants, munitions works, and other critical places—these facts all bear on the likelihood that their advocacy of the Soviet theory of revolution will endanger the Republic. But the record is silent on these facts. If we are to proceed on the basis of judicial notice, it is impossible for me to say that the Communists in this country are so potent or so strategically deployed that they must be suppressed for their speech. I could not so hold unless I were willing to conclude that the activities in recent years of committees of Congress, of the Attorney General, of labor unions, of state legislatures, and of Loyalty Boards were so futile as to leave the country on the edge of grave peril. To believe that petitioners and their following are placed in such critical positions as to endanger the Nation is to believe the incredible. It is

Only Action, Not Speech, Can Be Punished

The 1957 Supreme Court case Yates v. U.S. *partially reversed its* Dennis v. U.S. *decision and significantly weakened the scope of the Smith Act. Justice John F. Harlan, writing for the majority, stated that a criminal prosecution for advocacy had to be for some future action, as opposed to a general belief that future action was desirable.*

Petitioners contend that the instructions to the jury were fatally defective in that the trial court refused to charge that, in order to convict, the jury must find that the advocacy which the defendants conspired to promote was of a kind calculated to "incite" persons to action for the forcible overthrow of the Government. It is argued that advocacy of forcible overthrow as mere *abstract doctrine* is within the free speech protection of the First Amendment; that the Smith Act, consistently with that constitutional provision, must be taken as proscribing only the sort of advocacy which incites to illegal *action*; and that the trial court's charge, by permitting conviction for mere advocacy, unrelated to its tendency to produce forcible action, resulted in an unconstitutional application of the Smith Act. The Government, which at the trial also requested the court to charge in terms of "incitement," now takes the position, however, that the true constitutional dividing line is not between inciting and abstract advocacy of forcible overthrow, but rather between advocacy as such, irrespective of its inciting qualities, and the mere discussion or exposition of violent overthrow as an abstract theory. . . .

We are thus faced with the question whether the Smith Act prohibits advocacy and teaching of forcible overthrow as an abstract principle, divorced from any effort to instigate action to that end, so long as such advocacy or teaching is engaged in with evil intent. We hold that it does not.

safe to say that the followers of the creed of Soviet Communism are known to the F.B.I.; that in case of war with Russia they will be picked up overnight as were all prospective saboteurs at the commencement of World War II; that the invisible army of petitioners is the best known, the most beset, and the least thriving of any fifth column in history. Only those held by fear and panic could think otherwise.

This is my view if we are to act on the basis of judicial notice. But the mere statement of the opposing views indicates how important it is that we know the facts before we act. Neither prejudice nor hate nor senseless fear should be the basis of this solemn act. Free speech—the glory of our system of government—should not be sacrificed on anything less than plain and objective proof of danger that the evil advocated is imminent. On this record no one can say that petitioners and their converts are in such a strategic position as to have even the slightest chance of achieving their aims.

The First Amendment provides that "Congress shall make no law . . . abridging the freedom of speech." The Constitution provides no exception. This does not mean, however, that the Nation need hold its hand until it is in such weakened condition that there is no time to protect itself from incitement to revolution. Seditious conduct can always be punished. But the command of the First Amendment is so clear that we should not allow Congress to call a halt to free speech except in the extreme case of peril from the speech itself. The First Amendment makes confidence in the common sense of our people and in their maturity of judgment the great postulate of our democracy. Its philosophy is that violence is rarely, if ever, stopped by denying civil liberties to those advocating resort to force. The First Amendment reflects the philosophy of Jefferson "that it is time enough for the rightful purposes of civil government, for its officers to interfere when principles break out into overt acts against peace and good order." The political censor has no place in our public debates. Unless and until extreme and necessitous circumstances are shown, our aim should be to keep speech unfettered and to allow the processes of law to be invoked only when the provocateurs among us move from speech to action.

Andrei Vishinsky wrote in 1938 in The Law of the Soviet State, "In our state, naturally, there is and can be no place for freedom of speech, press, and so on for the foes of socialism."

Our concern should be that we accept no such standard for the United States. Our faith should be that our people will never give support to these advocates of revolution, so long as we remain loyal to the purposes for which our nation was founded.

CHAPTER 5

The Warren Court and the Due Process Revolution

Chapter Preface

The four words "due process of law" form a phrase that has a paradoxically simple yet difficult to define meaning: the government must be fair in its actions. The clause is one of the key phrases of the Bill of Rights. It appears twice in the Constitution: in the Fifth Amendment of the Bill of Rights, and in the Fourteenth Amendment, which was adopted in 1868 and which in the twentieth century led to a revolution in how the Bill of Rights was applied to state governments. To understand the importance of this phrase, it is necessary to look at American constitutional history.

At the time the Bill of Rights was adopted in 1791, it was expected to apply only to the new national government. James Madison had included in the amendments he introduced in Congress in 1789 a provision forbidding state governments from violating "the rights of conscience, or the freedom of the press, or the right to trial by jury in criminal cases"—a proposal he once wrote was "the most valuable amendment in the whole list." The Senate, for reasons unknown today because debate was not recorded, dropped the measure.

In several Supreme Court cases prior to the Civil War, people tried to cite the Bill of Rights in cases involving state governments, but to no avail. In *Barron v. Baltimore* the Supreme Court under Chief Justice John Marshall dismissed a case in which a person sued the city of Baltimore for damaged property under the Fifth Amendment's prohibition against the government taking private property "without just compensation." Marshall stated that the Bill of Rights contained "no expression indicating an intention to apply them to the State governments. This court cannot so apply them." In an 1845 case in which a Roman Catholic priest argued that his religious liberties were being violated by a New Orleans yellow fever ordinance limiting funerals to one designated chapel, the Supreme Court again dismissed the case, arguing that questions on local laws are "left to State constitutions."

This limited role of the Bill of Rights was, as was so much else of America's government and society, greatly altered by the Civil War. The Thirteenth, Fourteenth, and Fifteenth Amendments, also known as the Civil War Amendments, significantly altered America's Constitution. Of these the Fourteenth Amendment, which aimed at protecting the civil rights of the former slaves who were freed under the Thirteenth Amendment, had the greatest effect. Its first section reads:

All persons born or naturalized in the United States and subject to the jurisdiction thereof, are citizens of the United States and of the state wherein they reside. No state shall make or enforce any law which shall abridge the privileges or immunities of citizens of the United States; nor shall any state deprive any person of life, liberty, or property, without due process of law; nor deny to any person within its jurisdiction the equal protection of the laws.

It fell to the Supreme Court to interpret what these new restrictions on *state* governments meant. Did they refer to the restrictions on government activity listed in the Bill of Rights?

Some people believed that the clause in the Fourteenth Amendment stating that no state law can "abridge the privileges or immunities of citizens of the United States" made the Bill of Rights applicable to the states. However, in the *Slaughterhouse* cases (1873), the Supreme Court refused to concur with that interpretation. The five-justice majority based their refusal on the belief that such an interpretation would "change the whole theory of state and federal governments" and would make the Court "a perpetual censor upon all legislation of the states." In subsequent cases, the Court refused to change its interpretation. People seeking to change state laws or cases which they believed were unfair began to argue on the basis of the Due Process Clause ("nor shall any state deprive any person of life, liberty, or property, without due process of law") instead.

However, beginning with the 1884 *Hurtado* case, the Supreme Court's reading of the Due Process Clause was just as narrow as its *Slaughterhouse* reading of the Privileges and Immunities Clause. The Court again refused to use the Fourteenth Amendment to nationalize the Bill of Rights. For the next few decades the most successful litigants under the Fourteenth Amendment were business corporations arguing that their rights under "due process" were violated by minimum wage and other economic legislation.

Finally, in the 1897 case of *Chicago, Burlington & Quincy Railroad Company v. Chicago*, the Court departed from its previous stance and decided that the Due Process Clause required states, when they took property for public use, to compensate the owners, just as the Fifth Amendment required the federal government to do. For the first time, a right embodied in the Bill of Rights had been applied to the states via the Due Process Clause of the Fourteenth Amendment.

Thus began a long, slow process of what became known as the "selective incorporation" of the Bill of Rights within the Due Process Clause of the Fourteenth Amendment. Constitution scholar Linda R. Monk writes in *The Bill of Rights: A User's Guide:*

The Supreme Court applied the Bill of Rights to the states in a piecemeal fashion, rather than all at once. The Court determined whether a right was important enough to be included in "due process of law." If so, that right was applied to the states. In *Palko* v. *Connecticut* (1937), Justice Benjamin Cardozo set forth the test for whether a right should be incorporated. Only those rights that were "fundamental" and essential to "a scheme of ordered liberty" would be incorporated.

The peak of "selective incorporation" occurred in the 1960s, when Chief Justice Earl Warren issued numerous rulings incorporating key provisions in the Bill of Rights. The greatest effect was on the criminal justice system, since most of the Bill of Rights after the First Amendment deals with criminal justice procedural matters. This effect was not without controversy, both within legal journals debating the meaning of the Fourteenth Amendment and the proper role of judges, and in public arenas where many accused the Supreme Court of unfairly helping criminals. The viewpoints in this chapter examine a small sampling of the many issues surrounding "due process of law."

VIEWPOINT 1

"In the sense of the Constitution, 'due process of law' was not meant or intended to include . . . the institution and procedure of a grand jury in any case."

Due Process Does Not Necessarily Include All Bill of Rights Provisions

Stanley Matthews (1824-1889)

In 1868 the Fourteenth Amendment to the Constitution was ratified. Unlike the Bill of Rights, it was directed at the state governments, and read in part:

> No State shall . . . deprive any person of life, liberty, or property, without due process of law.

The U.S. Supreme Court was soon faced with the question of what constituted "due process of law." Did the Fourteenth Amendment mean that state governments were subject to the same Bill of Rights restrictions that had previously applied only to the federal government? The Supreme Court's answer to this question has changed over time.

One of the first significant cases dealing with the Fourteenth Amendment and the Bill of Rights was decided in 1884. Joseph

From the majority opinion of the U.S. Supreme Court in *Hurtado v. California*, 110 U.S. 516 (1884).

Hurtado had been convicted of murder by the state of California and sentenced to be hanged. He claimed that he was denied due process because his criminal proceedings under California law did not include an indictment from a grand jury. The Fifth Amendment of the Bill of Rights states in part:

> No person shall be held to answer for a capital, or otherwise infamous crime, unless on presentment or indictment of a grand jury.

The Fifth Amendment goes on to include almost identical language to the Fourteenth: "nor shall [the accused] be deprived of life, liberty, or property, without due process of law."

Hurtado claimed that California was bound by due process of law to use a grand jury. The Supreme Court, however, rejected that argument. In his majority opinion excerpted here, Justice Stanley Matthews argues that if the specific guarantees of the Bill of Rights were meant to be considered part of "due process," they would have been explicitly included in the Fourteenth Amendment. Because the Fourteenth Amendment does not include any provisions about grand juries, grand juries are not included in the meaning of "due process of law." Matthews concludes that Hurtado's rights were not violated and that the Fourteenth Amendment's guarantee of "due process" does not necessarily mean that Bill of Rights restrictions now apply to the states.

Matthews, a former abolitionist, state attorney general for Ohio, and U.S. senator, served as an associate justice of the Supreme Court from 1881 until his death in 1889.

The proposition of law we are asked to affirm is, that an indictment or presentment by a grand jury, as known to the common law of England, is essential to that "due process of law," when applied to prosecutions for felonies, which is secured and guaranteed by this provision of the Constitution of the United States, and which accordingly it is forbidden to the States respectively to dispense with in the administration of criminal law.

The question . . . involves a consideration of what additional restrictions upon the legislative policy of the States have been imposed by the 14th Amendment to the Constitution. . . .

The Constitution of the United States was ordained, it is true, by descendants of Englishmen, who inherited the traditions of English law and history; but it was made for an undefined and expanding future, and for a people gathered and to be gathered from many Nations and of many tongues. And while we take just pride in the principles and institutions of the common law, we are not to forget that in lands where other systems of jurisprudence prevail, the ideas and processes of civil justice are also not unknown. . . .

We are to construe this phrase in the 14th Amendment by the *usus loquendi* [usage in speaking] of the Constitution itself. The same words are contained in the 5th Amendment. That article makes specific and express provision for perpetuating the institution of the grand jury, so far as relates to prosecutions, for the more aggravated crimes under the laws of the United States. It declares that "No person shall be held to answer for a capital or otherwise infamous crime, unless on a presentment or indictment of a grand jury, except in cases arising in the land or naval forces, or in the militia when in actual service in time of war or public danger; nor shall any person be subject for the same offense to be twice put in jeopardy of life or limb; nor shall he be compelled in any criminal case to be a witness against himself." It then immediately adds: "nor be deprived of life, liberty or property, without due process of law." According to a recognized canon of interpretation, especially applicable to formal and solemn instruments of constitutional law, we are forbidden to assume, without clear reason to the contrary, that any part of this most important Amendment is superfluous. The natural and obvious inference is, that in the sense of the Constitution, "due process of law" was not meant or intended to include, *ex vi termini* [by the force or meaning of the term], the institution and procedure of a grand jury in any case. The conclusion is equally irresistible, that when the same phrase was employed in the 14th Amendment to restrain the action of the States, it was used in the same sense and with no greater extent; and that if in the adoption of that Amendment it had been part of its purpose to perpetuate the institution of the grand jury in all the States, it would have embodied, as did the 5th Amendment, express declarations to that effect. Due process of law in the latter refers to that law of the land, which derives its authority from the legislative powers conferred upon Congress by the Constitution of the United States, exercised within the limits therein prescribed, and interpreted according to the principles of the common law. In the 14th Amendment, by parity of reason, it refers to that law of the land in each State, which derives its authority from the inherent and reserved powers of the State, exerted within the limits of those fundamental principles of liberty and justice which lie at the base of all our civil and political institutions, and the greatest security for which resides in the right of the people to make their own laws, and alter them at their pleasure. "The 14th Amendment," as was said by Mr. Justice Joseph Bradley in Mo. v. Lewis [1880], "does not profess to secure to all persons in the United States the benefit of the same laws and the same remedies. Great diversities in these respects may exist in two States separated only by an imaginary line. On one side of this line there may be a right of trial by jury, and on the other side no such right. Each State prescribes its own modes of judicial proceeding."

But it is not to be supposed that these legislative powers are absolute and despotic, and that the Amendment prescribing due process of law is too vague and indefinite to operate as a practical restraint. It is not every Act, legislative in form, that is law. Law is something more than mere will exerted as an act of power. . . . Arbitrary power, enforcing its edicts to the injury of the persons and property of its subjects, is not law, whether manifested as the decree of a personal monarch or of an impersonal multitude. And the limitations imposed by our constitutional law upon the action of the governments, both state and national, are essential to the preservation of public and private rights, notwithstanding the representative character of our political institutions. . . .

It follows that any legal proceeding enforced by public authority, whether sanctioned by age and custom, or newly devised in the discretion of the legislative power, in furtherance of the general public good, which regards and preserves these principles of liberty and justice, must be held to be due process of law.

VIEWPOINT 2

"'Due process of law,' within the meaning of the national Constitution, does not import one thing with reference to . . . the States, and another with reference to . . . the general government."

Due Process Should Incorporate All Bill of Rights Provisions

John Marshall Harlan (1833-1911)

John Marshall Harlan served as an associate justice on the Supreme Court from 1877 to 1911. He is best remembered for his dissenting opinions, many of which have had greater influence on subsequent generations than on his own. For instance, he cast the only dissenting vote in *Plessy v. Ferguson*, the 1896 case that defended racial segregation laws on the "separate but equal" doctrine. Harlan's dissenting views were eventually vindicated by the 1954 case *Brown v. Board of Education*.

Another important case in which Harlan was the sole dissenter was the 1884 case *Hurtado v. California*. The question to be decided was whether the procedural guarantees of the Bill of Rights (including the right to a grand jury indictment for capital offenses) was now binding to the state governments because of the Fourteenth Amendment of the Constitution and its call for "due process of law." Harlan, the sole dissenting justice in the case, asserts

From John Marshall Harlan's dissenting opinion in the U.S. Supreme Court decision in *Hurtado v. California*, 110 U.S. 516 (1884).

in his minority opinion that the guarantees of criminal procedure in the Bill of Rights are fundamental to "due process of law" and thus should apply to states as well as to the federal government. Harlan criticizes the reasoning of the majority, arguing that it could be used to exempt states from other Bill of Rights protections (a prediction which proved correct). Joel M. Gora wrote of the implications of *Hurtado* in his 1977 book *Due Process of Law*:

> The lines of judicial battle were thus clearly drawn. On one side was the view of the *Hurtado* majority that the due process guarantee in the Fourteenth Amendment was to be interpreted flexibly, with English traditions serving only as a guide, and with the specific guarantees of the original Bill of Rights not automatically embodied as part of the due process clause. On the other side was Justice Harlan's view that those specific guarantees were central to the meaning of "due process of law," that they limited the states no less than the federal government, and that the preservation of liberty was better assured by adherence to those specifics than by a flexible judicial interpretation.

The plaintiff in error, Joseph Hurtado, now under sentence of death pronounced in one of the courts of California, brings this writ of error upon the ground that the proceedings against him are in violation of the Constitution of the United States. The Crime charged, and of which he was found guilty, is murder. The prosecution against him is not based upon any presentment or indictment of a grand jury, but upon an information filed by the district attorney of the county in which the crime was alleged to have been committed. His contention is that an information for a capital offence is forbidden by that clause of the Fourteenth Amendment of the Constitution of the United States which declares that no State shall "deprive any person of life, liberty, or property without due process of law." As I cannot agree that the State may, consistently with due process of law, require a person to answer for a capital offence, except upon the presentment or indictment of a grand jury, and as human life is involved in the judgment rendered here, I do not feel at liberty to withhold a statement of the reasons for my dissent from the opinion of the court. . . .

"Due process of law," within the meaning of the national Constitution, does not import one thing with reference to the powers of the States, and another with reference to the powers of the general government. If particular proceedings conducted under the authority of the general government, and involving life, are prohibited, because not constituting that due process of law required by the Fifth Amendment of the Constitution of the United States, similar proceedings, conducted under the authority of a State, must be deemed illegal as not being due process of law within the meaning of the Fourteenth Amendment. . . .

According to the settled usages and modes of proceeding existing under the common and statute law of England at the settlement of this country, information in capital cases was not consistent with the "law of the land," or with "due process of law." Such was the understanding of the patriotic men who established free institutions upon this continent. Almost the identical words of Magna Charta were incorporated into most of the State Constitutions before the adoption of our national Constitution. When they

---

The Fourteenth Amendment and the Bill of Rights

John Marshall Harlan's opinion in Hurtado *that the Fourteenth Amendment applied the Bill of Rights to the states was repeated sixty-three years later by Justice Hugo Black.*

My study of the historical events that culminated in the Fourteenth Amendment . . . persuades me that one of the chief objects that the provisions of the amendment's first section . . . were intended to accomplish was to make the Bill of Rights applicable to the states. With full knowledge of the import of the *Barron* decision, the framers and backers of the Fourteenth Amendment proclaimed its purpose to be to overturn the constitutional rule that case had announced. . . .

I cannot consider the Bill of Rights to be an outworn eighteenth-century "straight jacket.". . . Its provisions may be thought outdated abstractions by some. And it is true that they were designed to meet ancient evils. But they are the same kind of human evils that have emerged from century to century wherever excessive power is sought by the few at the expense of the many. In my judgment the people of no nation can lose their liberty so long as a Bill of Rights like ours survives. . . . I fear to see the consequences of the Court's practice of substituting its own concepts of decency and fundamental justice for the language of the Bill of Rights as its point of departure in interpreting and enforcing that Bill of Rights. If the choice must be between the selective process of the *Palko* decision applying some of the Bill of Rights to the states, or . . . applying none of them, I would choose the *Palko* selective process. But rather than accept either of these choices, I would follow what I believe was the original purpose of the Fourteenth Amendment—to extend to all the people of the nation the complete protection of the Bill of Rights. To hold that this Court can determine what, if any, provisions of the Bill of Rights will be enforced, and if so to what degree, is to frustrate the great design of a written Constitution.

declared, in substance, that no person should be deprived of life, liberty, or property, except by the judgment of his peers or the law of the land, they intended to assert his right to the same guaranties that were given in the mother country by the great charter and the laws passed in furtherance of its fundamental principles.

My brethren concede that there are principles of liberty and justice, lying at the foundation of our civil and political institutions, which no State can violate consistently with that due process of law required by the Fourteenth Amendment in proceedings involving life, liberty, or property. Some of these principles are enumerated in the opinion of the court. But, for reasons which do not impress my mind as satisfactory, they exclude from that enumeration the exemption from prosecution, by information, for a public offence involving life. By what authority is that exclusion made? Is it justified by the settled usages and modes of procedure existing under the common and statute law of England at the emigration of our ancestors, or at the foundation of our government? Does not the fact that the people of the original States required an amendment of the national Constitution, securing exemption from prosecution, for a capital offence, except upon the indictment or presentment of a grand jury, prove that, in their judgment, such an exemption was essential to protection against accusation and unfounded prosecution, and, therefore, was a fundamental principle in liberty and justice? . . .

The Intent of the Framers

But it is said that the framers of the Constitution did not suppose that due process of law necessarily required for a capital offence the institution and procedure of a grand jury, else they would not in the same amendment prohibiting the deprivation of life, liberty, or property, without due process of law, have made specific and express provision for a grand jury where the crime is capital or otherwise infamous; therefore, it is argued, the requirement by the Fourteenth Amendment of due process of law in all proceedings involving life, liberty, and property, without specific reference to grand juries in any case whatever, was not intended as a restriction upon the power which it is claimed the States previously had, so far as the express restrictions of the national Constitution are concerned, to dispense altogether with grand juries.

This line of argument, it seems to me, would lead to results which are inconsistent with the vital principles of republican government. If the presence in the Fifth Amendment of a specific provision for grand juries in capital cases, alongside the provision for due process of law in proceedings involving life, liberty, or property, is held to prove that "due process of law" did not, in the judgment of the framers of the Constitution, necessarily require a grand jury in capital cases, inexorable logic would require it to be, likewise, held that the right not to be put twice in jeopardy of life and limb for the same offence, nor compelled in a criminal case to testify against one's self—rights and immunities also specifically recognized in the Fifth Amendment—were not protected by that due process of law required by the settled usages and proceedings existing under the common and statute law of England at the settlement of this country. More than that, other amendments of the Constitution proposed at the same time, expressly recognize the right of persons to just compensation for private property taken for public use; their right, when accused of crime, to be informed of the nature and cause of the accusation against them, and to a speedy and public trial, by an impartial jury of the State and district wherein the crime was committed; to be confronted by the witnesses against them; and to have compulsory process for obtaining witnesses in their favor. Will it be claimed that these rights were not secured by the "law of the land" or by "due process of law," as declared and established at the foundation of our government? Are they to be excluded from the enumeration of the fundamental principles of liberty and justice, and, therefore, not embraced by "due process of law?"...

It seems to be that too much stress is put upon the fact that the framers of the Constitution made express provision for the security of those rights which at common law were protected by the requirement of due process of law, and, in addition, declared, generally, that no person shall "be deprived of life, liberty or property without due process of law." The rights, for the security of which these express provisions were made, were of a character so essential to the safety of the people that it was deemed wise to avoid the possibility that Congress, in regulating the processes of law, would impair or destroy them. Hence, their specific enumeration in the earlier amendments of the Constitution, in connection with the general requirement of due process of law, the latter itself being broad enough to cover every right of life, liberty or property secured by the settled usages and modes of proceeding existing under the common and statute law of England at the time our government was founded. . . .

Fundamental Principles of Liberty

The court, in this case, while conceding that the requirement of due process of law protects the fundamental principles of liberty and justice, adjudges, in effect, that an immunity or right, recognized at the common law to be essential to personal security, jealously guarded by our national Constitution against violation by any tribunal or body exercising authority under the general government, and expressly or impliedly recognized, *when the Four-*

teenth Amendment was adopted, in the Bill of Rights or Constitution of every State in the Union, is, yet, not a fundamental principle in governments established, as those of the States of the Union are, to secure to the citizen liberty and justice, and, therefore, is not involved in that due process of law required in proceedings conducted under the sanction of a State. My sense of duty constrains me to dissent from this interpretation of the supreme law of the land.

Viewpoint 3

"The due process clause of the Fourteenth Amendment does not incorporate, as such, the specific guarantees found in the Sixth Amendment."

Due Process Does Not Include the Right to a Lawyer at Public Expense

Owen J. Roberts (1875-1955)

> The Sixth Amendment to the Constitution reads in part:
>
> > In all criminal prosecutions the accused shall enjoy the right . . . to have the assistance of counsel in his defense.

In interpreting and applying this clause, the Supreme Court has grappled with two central questions. One is whether this provision requires the court to provide a lawyer at public expense if the person cannot afford one. Until 1938 this was held to be true only of capital cases. Then in *Johnson v. Herbst*, a 1938 case involving a federal counterfeiting prosecution, the Supreme Court ruled that "the Sixth Amendment withholds from federal courts, in all criminal cases, the power and authority to deprive an accused of his life or liberty unless he has or waives the assistance of counsel."

The second major question facing the Supreme Court was whether such a rule applies also to state courts, where the vast majority of criminal cases are heard. The answer to this question depends on the Court's interpretation of the Fourteenth Amendment—an interpretation that has evolved over the years.

From the majority opinion of the U.S. Supreme Court in *Betts v. Brady*, 316 U.S. 455 (1942).

At first, the Supreme Court, in cases such as *Hurtado v. California* and others, formed a narrow interpretation of the Fourteenth Amendment, asserting that its due process clause did not necessarily mean the Bill of Rights now applied to the states. It was not until 1925 in the case *Gitlow v. New York* that the Court decided that parts of the Bill of Rights (in this case, freedom of speech and the press as mentioned in the First Amendment) applied to state governments.

The Supreme Court first examined the Sixth Amendment's right to counsel provision with regard to state courts in the 1932 case *Powell v. Alabama*, also known as the Scottsboro case. The Supreme Court overturned the convictions of eight black youths for the alleged rape of two white women on the grounds that the defendants had received inadequate counsel at their trial. Historian David J. Bodenhamer writes in *Crucible of Liberty:*

> The U.S. Supreme Court ruled, 7-2, that the right to counsel was part of the due process clause of the Fourteenth Amendment and thus binding on the states. But this right was only similar to, not identical with, the same right guaranteed by the Sixth Amendment. . . . Five years later, in *Palko v. Connecticut* (1937), the justices decided that the Fourteenth Amendment required states to accept rights essential to a "scheme of ordered liberty." Rights received constitutional protection, Justice Benjamin Cardozo wrote for the majority, if their denial imposed "hardships so shocking that our polity will not endure it" or if the actions of government violated the "fundamental principles of liberty and justice which lie at the base of all our civil and political institutions."
>
> In criminal matters, the guarantee of fair trial alone was fundamental to liberty. States could employ widely different procedures without denying fair treatment. The fair trial test meant that the Court would decide case-by-case which rights of the accused enjoyed constitutional protection.

The case-by-case approach by the Supreme Court regarding the right to counsel was affirmed by the 1942 case *Betts v. Brady*. The case involved a state robbery prosecution of a farmhand with little education who was not provided a lawyer. The six-to-three majority opinion was written by Owen J. Roberts, who served as associate justice from 1930 to 1945 and was noted for his independence and his large number of written opinions. Roberts states that the right of the accused to a lawyer applies only to federal courts, and that such a right applies to state courts only in special circumstances, which he argues were not met in this case. *Betts v. Brady* set the standard for such cases involving the Sixth and Fourteenth Amendments for over twenty years, until it was overruled in 1963 in *Gideon v. Wainwright*.

The petitioner was indicted for robbery in the Circuit Court of Carroll County, Maryland. Due to lack of funds, he was unable to employ counsel, and so informed the judge at his arraignment. He requested that counsel be appointed for him. The judge advised him that this would not be done, as it was not the practice in Carroll County to appoint counsel for indigent defendants, save in prosecutions for murder and rape.

Without waiving his asserted right to counsel, the petitioner pleaded not guilty and elected to be tried without a jury. At his request witnesses were summoned in his behalf. He cross-examined the State's witnesses and examined his own. The latter gave testimony tending to establish an alibi. Although afforded the opportunity, he did not take the witness stand. The judge found him guilty and imposed a sentence of eight years. . . .

Was the petitioner's conviction and sentence a deprivation of his liberty without due process of law, in violation of the Fourteenth Amendment, because of the court's refusal to appoint counsel at his request?

Due Process and the Sixth Amendment

The Sixth Amendment of the national Constitution applies only to trials in federal courts. The due process clause of the Fourteenth Amendment does not incorporate, as such, the specific guarantees found in the Sixth Amendment, although a denial by a State of rights or privileges specifically embodied in that and others of the first eight amendments may, in certain circumstances, or in connection with other elements, operate, in a given case, to deprive a litigant of due process of law in violation of the Fourteenth. Due process of law is secured against invasion by the federal Government by the Fifth Amendment, and is safeguarded against state action in identical words by the Fourteenth. The phrase formulates a concept less rigid and more fluid than those envisaged in other specific and particular provisions of the Bill of Rights. Its application is less a matter of rule. Asserted denial is to be tested by an appraisal of the totality of facts in a given case. That which may, in one setting, constitute a denial of fundamental fairness, shocking to the universal sense of justice, may, in other circumstances, and in the light of other considerations, fall short of such denial. In the application of such a concept, there is always the danger of falling into the habit of formulating the guarantee into a set of hard and fast rules, the application of which in a given case may be to ignore the qualifying factors therein disclosed.

The petitioner, in this instance, asks us, in effect, to apply a rule in the enforcement of the due process clause. He says the rule to be deduced from our former decisions is that, in every case, whatever the circumstances, one charged with crime, who is unable to obtain counsel, must be furnished counsel by the State. Expressions in the opinions of this court lend color to the argument, but, as the petitioner admits, none of our decisions squarely adjudicates the question now presented.

In *Powell* v. *Alabama*, ignorant and friendless negro youths, strangers in the community, without friends or means to obtain counsel, were hurried to trial for a capital offense without effective appointment of counsel on whom the burden of preparation and trial would rest, and without adequate opportunity to consult even the counsel casually appointed to represent them. This occurred in a State whose statute law required the appointment of counsel for indigent defendants prosecuted for the offense charged. Thus the trial was conducted in disregard of every principle of fairness and in disregard of that which was declared by the law of the State a requisite of a fair trial. This court held the resulting convictions were without due process of law. It said that, in the light of all the facts, the failure of the trial court to afford the defendants reasonable time and opportunity to secure counsel was a clear denial of due process. The court stated further that "under the circumstances . . . the necessity of counsel was so vital and imperative that the failure of the trial court to make an effective appointment of counsel was likewise a denial of due process," but added: "Whether this would be so in other criminal prosecutions, or under other circumstances, we need not determine. All that it is necessary now to decide, as we do decide, is that, in a capital case, where the defendant is unable to employ counsel, and is incapable adequately of making his own defense because of ignorance, feeble-mindedness, illiteracy, or the like, it is the duty of the court, whether requested or not, to assign counsel for him as a necessary requisite of due process of law. . . ."

. . . The question we are now to decide is whether due process of law demands that in every criminal case, whatever the circumstances, a State must furnish counsel to an indigent defendant. Is the furnishing of counsel in all cases whatever dictated by natural, inherent, and fundamental principles of fairness? The answer to the question may be found in the common understanding of those who have lived under the Anglo-American system of law. By the Sixth Amendment the people ordained that, in all criminal prosecutions, the accused should "enjoy the right . . . to have the assistance of counsel for his defence." We have construed the provision to require appointment of counsel in all cases where a defendant is unable to procure the services of an attorney, and where the right has not been intentionally and competently waived. Though, as we have noted, the Amendment lays down no rule for the conduct of the States, the question recurs whether the constraint laid by the Amendment upon the national courts expresses a rule so fundamental and essential to a fair trial, and so, to due process of law, that it is made obligatory upon the States by the Fourteenth Amendment. Relevant data on the subject are afforded by constitutional and statutory provisions subsisting in the colonies and the States prior to the inclusion of the Bill of Rights in the national Constitution, and in the constitutional, legislative, and judicial history of the States to the present date. These constitute the most authoritative sources for ascertaining the considered judgment of the citizens of the States upon the question.

Examining State Constitutions

The Constitutions of the thirteen original States, as they were at the time of federal union, exhibit great diversity in respect of the right to have counsel in criminal cases. Rhode Island had no constitutional provision on the subject until 1843, North Carolina and South Carolina had none until 1868. Virginia has never had any. Maryland, in 1776, and New York, in 1777, adopted provisions to the effect that a defendant accused of crime should be "allowed" counsel. A constitutional mandate that the accused should have a right to be heard by himself and by his counsel was adopted by Pennsylvania in 1776, New Hampshire in 1774, by Delaware in 1782, and by Connecticut in 1818. In 1780 Massachusetts ordained that the defendant should have the right to be heard by himself or his counsel at his election. In 1798 Georgia provided that the accused might be heard by himself or counsel, or both. In 1776 New Jersey guaranteed the accused the same privileges of witnesses and counsel as their prosecutors "are or shall be entitled to."

The substance of these provisions of colonial and early state constitutions is explained by the contemporary common law. Originally, in England, a prisoner was not permitted to be heard by counsel upon the general issue of not guilty on any indictment for treason or felony. The practice of English judges, however, was to permit counsel to advise with a defendant as to the conduct of his case and to represent him in collateral matters and as respects questions of law arising upon the trial. In 1695 the rule was relaxed by statute to the extent of permitting one accused of treason the privilege of being heard by counsel. The rule forbidding the participation of counsel stood, however, as to indictments for felony, until 1836, when a statute accorded the right to defend by counsel against summary convictions and charges of felony. In misdemeanor cases and, after 1695, in prosecutions for treason, the rule was that the defense must be conducted either by the defendant in person or by counsel, but that both might not participate in the trial.

Palko v. Connecticut

The basis for Betts v. Brady *came six years earlier in* Palko v. Connecticut, *when the Court ruled that the Fourteenth Amendment made some of the provisions of the Bill of Rights binding on state governments, but only if they were the "essence of a scheme of ordered liberty." Freedom of speech and of the press were ruled essential, but the right to trial by jury was not. The Supreme Court would determine which rights were to be protected on a case-by-case basis. Chief Justice Benjamin Cardozo wrote the* Palko *opinion.*

The right to trial by jury and the immunity from prosecution except as the result of an indictment may have value and importance. Even so, they are not of the very essence of a scheme of ordered liberty. To abolish them is not to violate a "principle of justice so rooted in the traditions and conscience of our people as to be ranked as fundamental.". . . Few would be so narrow or provincial as to maintain that a fair and enlightened system of justice would be impossible without them. What is true of jury trials and indictments is true also, as the cases show, of the immunity from compulsory self-incrimination. . . . This too might be lost, and justice still be done. Indeed, today as in the past there are students of our penal system who look upon the immunity as a mischief rather than a benefit, and who would limit its scope or destroy it altogether. . . . The exclusion of these immunities and privileges from the privileges and immunities protected against the action of the states has not been arbitrary or casual. It has been dictated by a study and appreciation of the meaning, the essential implications, of liberty itself.

We reach a different plane of social and moral values when we pass to the privileges and immunities that have been taken over from the earlier articles of the federal Bill of Rights and brought within the Fourteenth Amendment by a process of absorption. These in their origin were effective against the federal government alone. If the Fourteenth Amendment has absorbed them, the process of absorption has had its source in the belief that neither liberty nor justice would exist if they were sacrificed. This is true, for illustration, of freedom of thought and speech.

In the light of this common law practice, it is evident that the constitutional provisions to the effect that a defendant should be "allowed" counsel or should have a right "to be heard by himself and his counsel," or that he might be heard by "either or both," at his election, were intended to do away with the rules which denied representation, in whole or in part, by counsel in criminal prosecutions, but were not aimed to compel the State to provide counsel for a defendant. At the least, such a construction by State courts and legislators can not be said to lack reasonable basis.

The statutes in force in the thirteen original States at the time of the adoption of the Bill of Rights are also illuminating. It is of interest that the matter of appointment of counsel for defendants, if dealt with at all, was dealt with by statute rather than by constitutional provision. The contemporary legislation exhibits great diversity of policy.

The constitutions of all the States, presently in force, save that of Virginia, contain provisions with respect to the assistance of counsel in criminal trials. Those of nine States may be said to embody a guarantee textually the same as that of the Sixth Amendment, or of like import. In the fundamental law of most States, however, the language used indicates only that a defendant is not to be denied the privilege of representation by counsel of his choice. . . .

This material demonstrates that, in the great majority of the States, it has been the considered judgment of the people, their representatives and their courts that appointment of counsel is not a fundamental right, essential to a fair trial. On the contrary, the matter has generally been deemed one of legislative policy. In the light of this evidence, we are unable to say that the concept of due process incorporated in the Fourteenth Amendment obligates the States, whatever may be their own views, to furnish counsel in every such case. Every court has power, if it deems proper, to appoint counsel where that course seems to be required in the interest of fairness.

The practice of the courts of Maryland gives point to the principle that the States should not be straight-jacketed in this respect, by a construction of the Fourteenth Amendment. . . . [I]n Maryland the usual practice is for the defendant to waive a trial by jury. This the petitioner did in the present case. Such trials . . . are much more informal than jury trials and it is obvious that the judge can much better control the course of the trial and is in a better position to see impartial justice done than when the formalities of a jury trial are involved. . . .

As we have said, the Fourteenth Amendment prohibits the conviction and incarceration of one whose trial is offensive to the common and fundamental ideas of fairness and right, and while want of counsel in a particular case may result in a conviction lacking in such fundamental fairness, we cannot say that the Amendment embodies an inexorable command that no trial for any offense, or in any court, can be fairly conducted and justice accorded a defendant who is not represented by counsel.

Viewpoint 4

"In our adversary system of criminal justice, any person haled into court, who is too poor to hire a lawyer, cannot be assured a fair trial unless counsel is provided for him."

Due Process Does Include the Right to a Lawyer at Public Expense

Hugo Black (1886-1971)

The famous case of *Gideon v. Wainwright* was the culmination of many years of debate within and outside the Supreme Court over whether the right to counsel in criminal cases protected in the Sixth Amendment should be applied to state as well as federal courts. While the Supreme Court ruled in the 1938 case *Johnson v. Herbst* that all indigent defendants have the right to be provided a defense lawyer in federal cases, it also ruled in the 1942 case *Betts v. Brady* that state courts only had to meet a standard of "fundamental fairness" that may not always require the provision of counsel.

One of the dissenters in *Betts v. Brady* was Justice Hugo Black, a former police court judge, prosecuting attorney, and U.S. senator. He wrote in dissent:

> The Sixth Amendment makes the right to counsel in criminal cases inviolable by the Federal Government. I believe the Fourteenth Amendment made the Sixth applicable to the states. But

From the majority opinion of the U.S. Supreme Court in *Gideon v. Wainwright*, 372 U.S. 335 (1963).

this view, although often urged in dissents, has never been accepted by a majority and is not accepted today.

For the next two decades the Supreme Court overturned some cases in which defendants lacked counsel, while letting others stand, depending on the "special circumstances" of the case. At the same time Justice Black tried to persuade his fellow justices that the Fourteenth Amendment's guarantee of "due process" meant, at the very least, that the procedural safeguards summarized in the Fifth through Eighth Amendments should be applied to state as well as federal courts, regardless of any "special circumstances."

With the appointments of Earl Warren in 1953, William J. Brennan in 1956, and Arthur J. Goldberg in 1962, Black's views concerning the Bill of Rights gained influence. While never endorsing Black's call for the "total incorporation" of the Bill of Rights into the Fourteenth Amendment guarantee of due process, the Supreme Court accelerated what had been a slow process of "selective incorporation" of specific guarantees of different amendments. Thus, in *Mapp v. Ohio* in 1961 the Court applied to the states the exclusionary rule (excluding police evidence gathered in violation of the Fourth Amendment). The following year in *Robinson v. California* the Eighth Amendment's prohibition against cruel and unusual punishment was also applied to the states.

In 1963 the question of a criminal defendant's right to counsel again faced the court. The case involved Clarence Earl Gideon, a resident of the state of Florida, one of the few states that did not routinely provide counsel for indigent defendants except in capital cases. Without a lawyer Gideon was convicted in 1961 of breaking and entering a poolroom. His handwritten petition for appeal reached the Supreme Court, and in 1963 in *Gideon v. Wainwright*, the Court ruled that a right to counsel was a "fundamental right" that applied to state as well as federal courts, and that the precedent set by *Betts v. Brady* should be overturned. Black, the dissenter in *Betts*, wrote the majority opinion for *Gideon*.

Petitioner was charged in a Florida state court with having broken and entered a poolroom with intent to commit a misdemeanor. This offense is a felony under Florida law. Appearing in court without funds and without a lawyer, petitioner asked the court to appoint counsel for him, whereupon the following colloquy took place:

"The Court: Mr. Gideon, I am sorry, but I cannot appoint Counsel to represent you in this case. Under the laws of the State of

Florida, the only time the Court can appoint Counsel to represent a defendant is when that person is charged with a capital offense. I am sorry, but I will have to deny your request to appoint Counsel to defend you in this case.

"The Defendant: The United States Supreme Court says I am entitled to be represented by Counsel."

Clarence Earl Gideon, an uneducated ex-convict, successfully appealed his conviction to the Supreme Court and in so doing changed how the Court interpreted a key provision of the Bill of Rights.

Put to trial before a jury, Gideon conducted his defense about as well as could be expected from a layman. He made an opening statement to the jury, cross-examined the State's witnesses, presented witnesses in his own defense, declined to testify himself, and made a short argument "emphasizing his innocence to the charge contained in the Information filed in this case." The jury returned a verdict of guilty, and petitioner was sentenced to serve five years in the state prison. . . . Since 1942, when *Betts v. Brady* was decided by a divided Court, the problem of a defendant's federal constitutional right to counsel in a state court has been a continuing source of controversy and litigation in both state and federal courts. To give this problem another review here, we granted certiorari. Since Gideon was proceeding in forma pauperis, we appointed counsel to represent him and requested both sides to discuss in their briefs and oral arguments the following: "Should this Court's holding in *Betts v. Brady* be reconsidered?"

The facts upon which Betts claimed that he had been unconstitutionally denied the right to have counsel appointed to assist him are strikingly like the facts upon which Gideon here bases his federal constitutional claim. Betts was indicted for robbery in a Maryland state court. On arraignment, he told the trial judge of his lack of funds to hire a lawyer and asked the court to appoint one for him. Betts was advised that it was not the practice in that county to appoint counsel for indigent defendants except in murder and rape cases. He then pleaded not guilty, had witnesses summoned, cross-examined the State's witnesses, examined his own, and chose not to testify himself. He was found guilty by the judge, sitting without a jury, and sentenced to eight years in prison. Like Gideon, Betts sought release by habeas corpus, alleging that he had been denied the right to assistance of counsel in violation of the Fourteenth Amendment. Betts was denied any relief, and on review this Court affirmed. It was held that a refusal to appoint counsel for an indigent defendant charged with a felony did not necessarily violate the Due Process Clause of the Fourteenth Amendment, which for reasons given the Court deemed to be the only applicable federal constitutional provision. The Court said:

> Asserted denial [of due process] is to be tested by an appraisal of the totality of facts in a given case. That which may, in one setting, constitute a denial of fundamental fairness, shocking to the universal sense of justice, may, in other circumstances, and in the light of other considerations, fall short of such denial.

Treating due process as "a concept less rigid and more fluid than those envisaged in other specific and particular provisions of the Bill of Rights," the Court held that refusal to appoint counsel under the particular facts and circumstances in the Betts Case was not so "offensive to the common and fundamental ideas of fairness" as to amount to a denial of due process. Since the facts and circumstances of the two cases are so nearly indistinguishable, we think the *Betts v. Brady* holding if left standing would require us to reject Gideon's claim that the Constitution guarantees him the assistance of counsel. Upon full reconsideration we conclude that *Betts v. Brady* should be overruled.

The Sixth Amendment

The Sixth Amendment provides, "In all criminal prosecutions, the accused shall enjoy the right . . . to have the Assistance of Counsel for his defense." We have construed this to mean that in federal courts counsel must be provided for defendants unable to employ counsel unless the right is competently and intelligently waived. Betts argued that this right is extended to indigent defendants in state courts by the Fourteenth Amendment. In response the Court stated that, while the Sixth Amendment laid down "no rule for the conduct of the States, the question recurs whether the constraint laid by the Amendment upon the national courts expresses a rule so fundamental and essential to a fair trial, and so, to due process of law, that it is made obligatory upon the States by the Fourteenth Amendment." In order to decide whether the Sixth Amendment's guarantee of counsel is of this fundamental nature, the Court in *Betts* set out and considered "[r]elevant data on the subject . . . afforded by constitutional and statutory provisions subsisting in the colonies and the States prior to the inclusion of the Bill of Rights in the national Constitution, and in the constitutional, legislative, and judicial history of the States to the present date." On the basis of this historical data the Court concluded that "appointment of counsel is not a fundamental right, essential to a fair trial." It was for this reason the *Betts* Court refused to accept the contention that the Sixth Amendment's guarantee of counsel for indigent federal defendants was extended to or, in the words of that Court, "made obligatory upon the States by the Fourteenth Amendment." Plainly, had the Court concluded that appointment of counsel for an indigent criminal defendant was "a fundamental right, essential to a fair trial," it would have held that the Fourteenth Amendment requires appointment of counsel in a state court, just as the Sixth Amendment requires in a federal court.

We think the Court in *Betts* had ample precedent for acknowledging that those guarantees of the Bill of Rights which are fundamental safeguards of liberty immune from federal abridgment are equally protected against state invasion by the Due Process Clause of the Fourteenth Amendment. This same principle was recognized, explained and applied in *Powell v. Alabama* (1932), a case upholding the right of counsel, where the Court held that despite sweeping language to the contrary in *Hurtado v. California* (1884), the Fourteenth Amendment "embraced" those "'fundamental principles of liberty and justice which lie at the base of all our civil and political institutions,'" even though they had been "specifically dealt with in another part of the federal Constitution." In many cases other than *Powell* and *Betts*, this Court has looked to the fundamental nature of original Bill of Rights guarantees to decide whether the Fourteenth Amendment makes them obligatory on the States. Explicitly recognized to be of this "fundamental nature" and therefore made immune from state invasion by the Fourteenth, or some part of it, are the First Amendment's freedoms of speech, press, religion, assembly, association, and petition for redress of grievances. For the same reason, though not always in precisely the same terminology, the Court has made obligatory on the States the Fifth Amendment's command that private properly shall not be taken for public use without just compensation, the Fourth Amendment's prohibition of unreasonable searches and seizures, and the Eighth's ban on cruel and unusual punishment. On the other hand, this Court in *Palko v. Connecticut* (1937), refused to hold that the Fourteenth Amendment made the double jeopardy provision of the Fifth Amendment obligatory on the States. In so refusing, however, the Court, speaking through Mr. Justice Cardozo, was careful to emphasize that "immunities that are valid as against the federal government by force of the specific pledges of particular amendments have been found to be implicit in the concept of ordered liberty, and thus, through the Fourteenth Amendment, become valid as against the states" and that guarantees "in their origin . . . effective against the federal government alone" had by prior cases "been taken over from the earlier articles of the federal Bill of Rights and brought within the Fourteenth Amendment by a process of absorption."

Fundamental Rights

We accept *Betts v. Brady*'s assumption, based as it was on our prior cases, that a provision of the Bill of Rights which is "fundamental and essential to a fair trial" is made obligatory upon the States by the Fourteenth Amendment. We think the Court in *Betts* was wrong, however, in concluding that the Sixth Amendment's guarantee of counsel is not one of these fundamental rights. Ten years before *Betts v. Brady*, this Court, after full consideration of all the historical data examined in *Betts*, had unequivocally declared that "the right to the aid of counsel is of this fundamental character." . . . While the Court at the close of its *Powell* opinion did by its language, as this Court frequently does, limit its holding to the particular facts and circumstances of that case, its conclusions about the fundamental nature of the right to counsel are unmistakable. Several years later, in 1936, the Court reemphasized what it had said about the fundamental nature of the right to counsel in this language:

> We concluded that certain fundamental rights, safeguarded by the first eight amendments against federal action, were also safeguarded against state action by the due process of law clause of the Fourteenth Amendment, and among them the fundamental right of the accused to the aid of counsel in a criminal prosecution. *Grosjean v. American Press Co.* (1936).

And again in 1938 this Court said:

> [The assistance of counsel] is one of the safeguards of the Sixth Amendment deemed necessary to insure fundamental human rights of life and liberty. . . . The Sixth Amendment stands as a constant admonition that if the constitutional safeguards it provides be lost, justice will not "still be done." *Johnson v. Zerbst* (1938). . . .

223

In light of these and many other prior decisions of this Court, it is not surprising that the *Betts* Court, when faced with the contention that "one charged with crime, who is unable to obtain counsel, must be furnished counsel by the State," conceded that "[e]xpressions in the opinions of this court lend color to the argument. . . ." The fact is that in deciding as it did—that "appointment of counsel is not a fundamental right, essential to a fair trial"—the Court in *Betts v. Brady* made an abrupt break with its own well-considered precedents. In returning to these old precedents, sounder we believe than the new, we but restore constitutional principles established to achieve a fair system of justice. Not only these precedents but also reason and reflection require us to recognize that in our adversary system of criminal justice, any person haled into court, who is too poor to hire a lawyer, cannot be assured a fair trial unless counsel is provided for him. This seems to us to be an obvious truth. Governments, both state and federal, quite properly spend vast sums of money to establish machinery to try defendants accused of crime. Lawyers to prosecute are everywhere deemed essential to protect the public's interest in an orderly society. Similarly, there are few defendants charged with crime, few indeed, who fail to hire the best lawyers they can get to prepare and present their defenses. That government hires lawyers to prosecute and defendants who have the money hire lawyers to defend are the strongest indications of the widespread belief that lawyers in criminal courts are necessities, not luxuries. The right of one charged with crime to counsel may not be deemed fundamental and essential to fair trials in some countries, but it is in ours. From the very beginning, our state and national constitutions and laws have laid great emphasis on procedural and substantive safeguards designed to assure fair trials before impartial tribunals in which every defendant stands equal before the law. This noble ideal cannot be realized if the poor man charged with crime has to face his accusers without a lawyer to assist him.

VIEWPOINT 5

"Specific guarantees in the Bill of Rights have penumbras . . . [that] create zones of privacy."

The Bill of Rights Implies a Right to Privacy

William O. Douglas (1898-1980) and Arthur Goldberg (1908-1990)

The Bill of Rights does not specifically mention a right to privacy. Does that mean such a right does not exist? Do the guarantees against deprivation of liberty "without due process of law" in the Fifth and Fourteenth Amendments suggest a right to privacy? The Supreme Court faced these questions in *Griswold v. Connecticut* in 1965, an important case that established and expanded a constitutional right to privacy that remains controversial to this day.

The case involved the arrest and conviction of Estelle Griswold and Charles Buxton, the executive director and medical director of the Planned Parenthood League of Connecticut, for violating an 1879 Connecticut law prohibiting the use of birth control or the assisting of anyone seeking contraception. Griswold and Buxton had publicized their lawbreaking and deliberately let themselves be arrested and convicted in the hopes of getting their convictions appealed to the Supreme Court to have the Court rule on what they believed to be an an unfair law. Almost four years after their arrest, they succeeded, and their case was heard before the Court in March 1965.

The Supreme Court ruled seven to two to overturn the convic-

From separate opinions comprising the majority opinion of the U.S. Supreme Court in *Griswold v. Connecticut*, 381 U.S. 479 (1965).

tions, and it established privacy as a constitutionally protected right. However, the seven justices in the majority differed in their reasoning, and four of them wrote separate opinions. The following two-part viewpoint is comprised of excerpts from two of these opinions. Part I is the opinion of the Court, written by William O. Douglas and signed by Douglas and three other justices. Douglas, who served as an associate justice from 1939 to 1975, was a noted advocate of civil liberties and defender of the Court's role in defining and protecting them. He argues that several of the amendments of the Bill of Rights, taken together, imply "zones of privacy." Part II is taken from a concurring opinion by Arthur Goldberg, an associate justice from 1962 to 1965 who later resigned to become U.S. ambassador to the United Nations. Goldberg's opinion, signed by himself, William Brennan, and Chief Justice Earl Warren, argues that the Ninth Amendment of the Bill of Rights "reveal[s] that the Framers of the Constitution believed that there are additional fundamental rights . . . which exist alongside those . . . specifically mentioned in the first eight constitutional amendments." Goldberg concludes that privacy is such a fundamental right and that its protection is included in the due process clause of the Fourteenth Amendment.

The Court's decision in *Griswold v. Connecticut* helped lay the foundation for its 1973 decision in *Roe v. Wade*, in which the constitutional right to privacy was held to include a woman's right to choose an abortion.

I

Coming to the merits, we are met with a wide range of questions that implicate the Due Process Clause of the Fourteenth Amendment. Overtones of some arguments suggest that *Lochner v. New York*, should be our guide. But we decline that invitation. . . . We do not sit as a super-legislature to determine the wisdom, need, and propriety of laws that touch economic problems, business affairs, or social conditions. This law, however, operates directly on an intimate relation of husband and wife and their physician's role in one aspect of that relation.

The association of people is not mentioned in the Constitution nor in the Bill of Rights. The right to educate a child in a school of the parents' choice—whether public or private or parochial—is also not mentioned. Nor is the right to study any particular subject or any foreign language. Yet the First Amendment has been construed to include certain of those rights.

By *Pierce* v. *Society of Sisters, supra,* the right to educate one's children as one chooses is made applicable to the States by the force of the First and Fourteenth Amendments. By *Meyer* v. *Nebraska* . . . the same dignity is given the right to study the German language in a private school. In other words, the State may not, consistently with the spirit of the First Amendment, contract the spectrum of available knowledge. The right of freedom of speech and press includes not only the right to utter or to print, but the right to distribute, the right to receive, the right to read . . . and freedom of inquiry, freedom of thought, and freedom to teach . . . —indeed the freedom of the entire university community. . . . Without those peripheral rights the specific rights would be less secure. . . .

Roe v. Wade

Some of the same arguments for privacy used by Justices William O. Douglas and Arthur Goldberg were echoed in the Court's 1973 Roe v. Wade *decision to legalize abortion, as this excerpt from Justice Harry A. Blackmun's opinion demonstrates.*

The Constitution does not explicitly mention any right of privacy. . . . [However,] the Court has recognized that a right of personal privacy, or a guarantee of certain areas or zones of privacy, does exist under the Constitution. In varying contexts, the Court or individual Justices have, indeed, found at least the roots of that right in the First Amendment . . . in the Fourth and Fifth Amendments . . . in the penumbras of the Bill of Rights . . . in the Ninth Amendment . . . or in the concept of liberty guaranteed by the first section of the Fourteenth Amendment. . . . These decisions make it clear that only personal rights that can be deemed "fundamental". . . are included in this guarantee of personal privacy. They also make it clear that the right has some extension to activities relating to marriage . . . procreation . . . contraception . . . family relationships . . . and child rearing and education. . . .

This right of privacy, whether it be founded in the Fourteenth Amendment's concept of personal liberty and restrictions upon state action, as we feel it is, or, as the District Court determined, in the Ninth Amendment's reservation of rights to the people, is broad enough to encompass a woman's decision whether or not to terminate her pregnancy.

In *NAACP* v. *Alabama* . . . we protected the "freedom to associate and privacy in one's associations," noting that freedom of association was a peripheral First Amendment right. Disclosure of membership lists of a constitutionally valid association, we held, was invalid "as entailing the likelihood of a substantial restraint upon the exercise by petitioner's members of their right to freedom of association." In other words, the First Amendment has a penumbra where privacy is protected from governmental intrusion. In like context, we have protected forms of "association" that are not political in the customary sense but pertain to the social, legal, and economic benefit of the members.

Those cases involved more than the "right of assembly"—a right that extends to all irrespective of their race or ideology. . . . The right of "association," like the right of belief (*Board of Education v. Barnette*), is more than the right to attend a meeting; it includes the right to express one's attitudes or philosophies by membership in a group or by affiliation with it or by other lawful means. Association in that context is a form of expression of opinion; and while it is not expressly included in the First Amendment its existence is necessary in making the express guarantees fully meaningful.

The foregoing cases suggest that specific guarantees in the Bill of Rights have penumbras, formed by emanations from those guarantees that help give them life and substance. . . . Various guarantees create zones of privacy. The right of association contained in the penumbra of the First Amendment is one, as we have seen. The Third Amendment in its prohibition against the quartering of soldiers "in any house" in time of peace without the consent of the owner is another facet of that privacy. The Fourth Amendment explicitly affirms the "right of the people to be secure in their persons, houses, papers, and effects, against unreasonable searches and seizures." The Fifth Amendment in its Self-Incrimination Clause enables the citizen to create a zone of privacy which government may not force him to surrender to his detriment. The Ninth Amendment provides: "The enumeration in the Constitution, of certain rights, shall not be construed to deny or disparage others retained by the people."

The Fourth and Fifth Amendments were described in *Boyd* v. *United States* . . . as protection against all governmental invasions "of the sanctity of a man's home and the privacies of life." We recently referred in *Mapp* v. *Ohio* . . . to the Fourth Amendment as creating a "right to privacy, no less important than any other right carefully and particularly reserved to the people.". . .

We have had many controversies over these penumbral rights of "privacy and repose." See, e.g., *Breard* v. *Alexandria* . . .; *Public Utilities Comm'n* v. *Pollak.* . . . These cases bear witness that the right of privacy which presses for recognition here is a legitimate one.

The present case, then, concerns a relationship lying within the zone of privacy created by several fundamental constitutional guarantees. And it concerns a law which, in forbidding the *use* of contraceptives rather than regulating their manufacture or sale, seeks to achieve its goals by means having a maximum destructive impact upon that relationship. Such a law cannot stand in light of the familiar principle, so often applied by this Court, that a "governmental purpose to control or prevent activities constitutionally subject to state regulation may not be achieved by means which sweep unnecessarily broadly and thereby invade the area of protected freedoms.". . . Would we allow the police to search the sacred precincts of marital bedrooms for telltale signs of the use of contraceptives? The very idea is repulsive to the notions of privacy surrounding the marriage relationship.

We deal with a right of privacy older than the Bill of Rights—older than our political parties, older than our school system. Marriage is a coming together for better or for worse, hopefully enduring, and intimate to the degree of being sacred. It is an association that promotes a way of life, not causes; a harmony in living, not political faiths; a bilateral loyalty, not commercial or social projects. Yet it is an association for as noble a purpose as any involved in our prior decisions.

II

I agree with the Court that Connecticut's birth-control law unconstitutionally intrudes upon the right of marital privacy, and I join in its opinion and judgment. Although I have not accepted the view that "due process" as used in the Fourteenth Amendment incorporates all of the first eight amendments, . . . I do agree that the concept of liberty protects those personal rights that are fundamental, and is not confined to the specific terms of the Bill of Rights. My conclusion that the concept of liberty is not so restricted and that it embraces the right of marital privacy though that right is not mentioned explicitly in the Constitution is supported both by numerous decisions of this Court, referred to in the Court's opinion, and by the language and history of the Ninth Amendment. In reaching the conclusion that the right of marital privacy is protected, as being within the protected penumbra of specific guarantees of the Bill of Rights, the Court refers to the Ninth Amendment. I add these words to emphasize the relevance of that Amendment to the Court's holding. . . .

The Court, in a series of decisions, has held that the Fourteenth Amendment absorbs and applies to the States those specifics of the first eight amendments which express fundamental personal rights. The language and history of the Ninth Amendment reveal that the Framers of the Constitution believed that there are additional fundamental rights, protected from governmental infringement, which exist alongside those fundamental rights specifically mentioned in the first eight constitutional amendments.

The Ninth Amendment reads, "The enumeration in the Constitution, of certain rights, shall not be construed to deny or disparage others retained by the people." The Amendment is almost entirely the work of James Madison. It was introduced in Congress by him and passed the House and Senate with little or no debate and virtually no change in language. It was proffered to quiet expressed fears that a bill of specifically enumerated rights could not be sufficiently broad to cover all essential rights and that the specific mention of certain rights would be interpreted as a denial that others were protected. . . .

The Right to Be Left Alone

In 1928 Justice Louis Brandeis, dissenting from a ruling that held that wiretapping was constitutional, was one of the earliest Supreme Court justices to explore the meaning of the right to privacy.

The makers of our Constitution undertook to secure conditions favorable to the pursuit of happiness. They recognized the significance of man's spiritual nature, of his feelings and of his intellect. They knew that only a part of the pain, pleasure and satisfactions of life are to be found in material things. They sought to protect Americans in their beliefs, their thoughts, their emotions and their sensations. They conferred, as against the government, the right to be let alone—the most comprehensive of rights and the right most valued by civilized men. To protect that right, every unjustifiable intrusion by the government upon the privacy of the individual, whatever the means employed, must be deemed a violation of the 4th Amendment.

While this Court has had little occasion to interpret the Ninth Amendment, "[i]t cannot be presumed that any clause in the Constitution is intended to be without effect." *Marbury* v. *Madison*. In interpreting the Constitution, "real effect should be given to all the words it uses." *Meyers* v. *United States*. The Ninth Amendment to the Constitution may be regarded by some as a recent discovery and may be forgotten by others, but since 1791 it has been a basic part of the Constitution which we are sworn to uphold. To hold that a right so basic and fundamental and so deep-rooted in our society as the right of privacy in marriage may be infringed because that right is not guaranteed in so many words by the first eight amendments to the Constitution is to ignore the Ninth Amendment and to give it no effect whatsoever. Moreover, a judicial construction that this fundamental right is not protected by the Constitution because it is not mentioned in explicit terms by one of the first eight amendments or elsewhere in the Constitution would violate the Ninth Amendment, which specifically states that "[t]he enumeration in the Constitution, of certain rights, shall not be *construed* to deny or disparage others retained by the people." (Emphasis added.)

. . . I do not take the position of my Brother Black . . . that the entire Bill of Rights is incorporated in the Fourteenth Amendment, and I do not mean to imply that the Ninth Amendment is applied against the States by the Fourteenth. Nor do I mean to state that the Ninth Amendment constitutes an independent source of rights protected from infringement by either the States or the Federal Government. Rather, the Ninth Amendment shows a belief of the Constitution's authors that fundamental rights exist that are not expressly enumerated in the first eight amendments and an intent that the list of rights included there not be deemed exhaustive. . . . The Ninth Amendment simply shows the intent of the Constitution's authors that other fundamental personal rights should not be denied such protection or disparaged in any other way simply because they are not specifically listed in the first eight constitutional amendments. I do not see how this broadens the authority of the Court; rather it serves to support what this Court has been doing in protecting fundamental rights.

Nor am I turning somersaults with history in arguing that the Ninth Amendment is relevant in a case dealing with a *State's* infringement of a fundamental right. While the Ninth Amendment—and indeed the entire Bill of Rights—originally concerned restrictions upon *federal* power, the subsequently enacted Fourteenth Amendment prohibits the States as well from abridging fundamental personal liberties. And, the Ninth Amendment, in indicating that not all such liberties are specifically mentioned in the first eight amendments, is surely relevant in showing the existence of other fundamental personal rights, now protected from state, as well as federal, infringement. In sum, the Ninth Amendment simply lends strong support to the view that the "liberty" protected by the Fifth and Fourteenth Amendments from infringement by the Federal Government or the States is not restricted to rights specifically mentioned in the first eight amendments. . . .

Although the Constitution does not speak in so many words of the right of privacy in marriage, I cannot believe that it offers these fundamental rights no protection. The fact that no particular provision of the Constitution explicitly forbids the State from disrupting the traditional relation of the family—a relation as old and as fundamental as our entire civilization—surely does not show that the Government was meant to have the power to do so. Rather, as the Ninth Amendment expressly recognizes, there are fundamental personal rights such as this one, which are protected from abridgment by the Government though not specifically mentioned in the Constitution.

VIEWPOINT 6

"I like my privacy as well as the next one, but I am nevertheless compelled to admit that government has a right to invade it unless prohibited by some specific constitutional provision."

The Bill of Rights Does Not Imply a Right to Privacy

Hugo Black (1886-1971)

Hugo Black was an associate justice of the Supreme Court from 1937 to 1971. He was noted as a strong supporter of the Bill of Rights and of civil liberties. His views often dissented from the judicial majority early in his career. But in the 1950s and 1960s he often sided with fellow justices William O. Douglas, Earl Warren, and other liberal justices in successfully overturning laws they believed were in violation of the Bill of Rights.

In the case *Griswold v. Connecticut*, Black once against found himself in the minority over interpreting the Constitution. The case involved the conviction of two Planned Parenthood officials for violating a Connecticut law against contraception. The Court ruled that the law violated the defendants' right to privacy, implied in the First, Fourth, Fifth, and Ninth Amendments of the Bill of Rights. In his dissenting opinion, Black strongly objects to this line of reasoning. He argues that the Supreme Court should not create rights that are not specifically mentioned in the Consti-

From Hugo Black's dissenting opinion in the U.S. Supreme Court decision in *Griswold v. Connecticut*, 381 U.S. 479 (1965).

tution. He criticizes Arthur Goldberg's use of the Ninth Amendment, saying that its intent was to restrict the powers of the federal government, not to enlarge the Supreme Court's power of striking down state laws.

The Court talks about a constitutional "right of privacy" as though there is some constitutional provision or provisions forbidding any law ever to be passed which might abridge the "privacy" of individuals. But there is not. There are, of course, guarantees in certain specific constitutional provisions which are designed in part to protect privacy at certain times and places with respect to certain activities. Such, for example, is the Fourth Amendment's guarantee against "unreasonable searches and seizures." But I think it belittles that Amendment to talk about it as though it protects nothing but "privacy." To treat it that way is to give it a niggardly interpretation, not the kind of liberal reading I think any Bill of Rights provision should be given. The average man would very likely not have his feelings soothed any more by having his property seized openly than by having it seized privately and by stealth. He simply wants his property left alone. And a person can be just as much, if not more, irritated, annoyed and injured by an unceremonious public arrest by a policeman as he is by a seizure in the privacy of his office or home.

One of the most effective ways of diluting or expanding a constitutionally guaranteed right is to substitute for the crucial word or words of a constitutional guarantee another word or words, more or less flexible and more or less restrictive in meaning. This fact is well illustrated by the use of the term "right of privacy" as a comprehensive substitute for the Fourth Amendment's guarantee against "unreasonable searches and seizures." "Privacy" is a broad, abstract and ambiguous concept which can easily be shrunken in meaning but which can also, on the other hand, easily be interpreted as a constitutional ban against many things other than searches and seizures. I have expressed the view many times that First Amendment freedoms, for example, have suffered from a failure of the courts to stick to the simple language of the First Amendment in construing it, instead of invoking multitudes of words substituted for those the Framers used. . . . For these reasons I get nowhere in this case by talk about a constitutional "right of privacy" as an emanation from one or more constitutional provisions. I like my privacy as well as the next one, but I am nevertheless compelled to admit that government has a

The Incorporation of the Bill of Rights

Hugo Black believed that the Due Process Clause of the Fourteenth Amendment applied, or incorporated, the Bill of Rights to state governments. Although the Supreme Court never accepted Black's theory of "total incorporation," it did over the years engage in "selective incorporation" of Bill of Rights provisions.

Amend.	Provision Incorporated	Supreme Court Case	Year
Fifth	Just Compensation Clause	*Chicago, Burlington & Quincy Railroad Co. v. Chicago*	1897
First	Freedom of speech	*Gitlow v. New York*	1925
First	Freedom of press	*Near v. Minnesota*	1931
Sixth	Right to counsel in capital felonies	*Powell v. Alabama*	1932
First	Freedom of assembly, petition	*DeJonge v. Oregon*	1937
First	Free Exercise Clause	*Cantwell v. Connecticut*	1940
First	Establishment Clause	*Everson v. Board of Education*	1947
Sixth	Right to public trial	*In re Oliver*	1948
Fourth	Protection from unreasonable searches, seizures	*Wolf v. Colorado*	1949
Fourth	Exclusionary rule	*Mapp v. Ohio*	1961
Eighth	Prohibition of cruel and unusual punishment	*Robinson v. California*	1962
Sixth	Right to counsel in noncapital felonies	*Gideon v. Wainwright*	1963
Fifth	Protection from self-incrimination	*Malloy v. Hogan*	1964
Sixth	Right to confront adverse witnesses	*Pointer v. Texas*	1965
Sixth	Right to an impartial jury	*Parker v. Gladden*	1966
Sixth	Right to speedy trial	*Klopfer v. N. Carolina*	1967
Sixth	Right to obtain favorable witnesses	*Washington v. Texas*	1967
Sixth	Right to trial by jury in nonpetty criminal cases	*Duncan v. Louisiana*	1968
Fifth	Prohibition of double jeopardy	*Benton v. Maryland*	1969
Sixth	Right to counsel in imprisonable misdemeanor cases	*Argersinger v. Hamlin*	1972

right to invade it unless prohibited by some specific constitutional provision. For these reasons I cannot agree with the Court's judgment and the reasons it gives for holding this Connecticut law unconstitutional. . . .

My Brother Goldberg has adopted the recent discovery that the Ninth Amendment as well as the Due Process Clause can be used by this Court as authority to strike down all state legislation which this Court thinks violates "fundamental principles of liberty and justice," or is contrary to the "traditions and [collective] conscience of our people." He also states, without proof satisfactory to me, that in making decisions on this basis judges will not consider "their personal and private notions." One may ask how they can avoid considering them. Our Court certainly has no machinery with which to take a Gallup Poll. And the scientific miracles of this age have not yet produced a gadget which the Court can use to determine what traditions are rooted in the "[collective] conscience of our people." Moreover, one would certainly have to look far beyond the language of the Ninth Amendment to find that the Framers vested in this Court any such awesome veto powers over lawmaking, either by the States or by the Congress. Nor does anything in the history of the Amendment offer any support for such a shocking doctrine. The whole history of the adoption of the Constitution and Bill of Rights points the other way, and the very material quoted by my Brother Goldberg shows that the Ninth Amendment was intended to protect against the idea that "by enumerating particular exceptions to the grant of power" to the Federal Government, "those rights which were not singled out, were intended to be assigned into the hands of the General Government [the United States], and were consequently insecure." That Amendment was passed, not to broaden the powers of this Court or any other department of "the General Government," but, as every student of history knows, to assure the people that the Constitution in all its provisions was intended to limit the Federal Government to the powers granted expressly or by necessary implication. If any broad, unlimited power to hold laws unconstitutional because they offend what this Court conceives to be the "[collective] conscience of our people" is vested in this Court by the Ninth Amendment, the Fourteenth Amendment, or any other provision of the Constitution, it was not given by the Framers, but rather has been bestowed on the Court by the Court. This fact is perhaps responsible for the peculiar phenomenon that for a period of a century and a half no serious suggestion was ever made that the Ninth Amendment, enacted to protect state powers against federal invasion, could be used as a weapon of federal power to prevent state legislatures from passing laws they consider appropriate to govern local affairs. Use of any such broad, unbounded judicial authority would make of this Court's members a day-to-day constitutional convention.

I repeat so as not to be misunderstood that this Court does have power, which it should exercise, to hold laws unconstitutional where they are forbidden by the Federal Constitution. My point is that there is no provision of the Constitution which either expressly or impliedly vests power in this Court to sit as a supervisory agency over acts of duly constituted legislative bodies and set aside their laws because of the Court's belief that the legislative policies adopted are unreasonable, unwise, arbitrary, capricious or irrational. The adoption of such a loose, flexible, uncontrolled standard for holding laws unconstitutional, if ever it is finally achieved, will amount to a great unconstitutional shift of power to the courts which I believe and am constrained to say will be bad for the courts and worse for the country. Subjecting federal and state laws to such an unrestrained and unrestrainable judicial control as to the wisdom of legislative enactments would, I fear, jeopardize the separation of governmental powers that the Framers set up and at the same time threaten to take away much of the power of States to govern themselves which the Constitution plainly intended them to have.

Changing the Constitution

I realize that many good and able men have eloquently spoken and written, sometimes in rhapsodical strains, about the duty of this Court to keep the Constitution in tune with the times. The idea is that the Constitution must be changed from time to time and that this Court is charged with a duty to make those changes. For myself, I must with all deference reject that philosophy. The Constitution makers knew the need for change and provided for it. Amendments suggested by the people's elected representatives can be submitted to the people or their elected agents for ratification. That method of change was good for our Fathers, and being somewhat old-fashioned I must add it is good enough for me. And so, I cannot rely on the Due Process Clause or the Ninth Amendment or any mysterious and uncertain natural law concept as a reason for striking down this state law. The Due Process Clause with an "arbitrary and capricious" or "shocking to the conscience" formula was liberally used by this Court to strike down economic legislation in the early decades of this century, threatening, many people thought, the tranquility and stability of the Nation. See, e.g., *Lochner* v. *New York*. . . . That formula, based on subjective considerations of "natural justice," is no less dangerous when used to enforce this Court's views about personal rights than those about economic rights. I had thought that we had laid that formula, as a means for striking down state legislation, to rest once and for all.

VIEWPOINT 7

"The [Supreme] Court has progressively handcuffed the police, turned trial judges into automatons, and blindfolded juries, all to the immense benefit of criminals."

Supreme Court Rulings Have Unfairly Hampered the Police

Eugene H. Methvin (1934-)

During the 1960s the Supreme Court under Chief Justice Earl Warren issued a controversial series of rulings that bound the states to follow the Bill of Rights in criminal procedures. Among the significant rulings was *Mapp v. Ohio*, in which the Court ruled in 1961 that state evidence seized in violation of the Fourth Amendment's prohibitions against "unreasonable searches and seizures" had to be excluded from criminal trials. Another controversial decision was *Miranda v. Arizona* (1966), in which the Court prohibited certain police practices as violating the Bill of Rights Fifth Amendment prohibition against self-incrimination.

These and other rulings unleashed a storm of criticism. The following viewpoint is taken from an article by Eugene H. Methvin, an editor of *Reader's Digest*. Methvin argues that the Supreme Court has greatly interfered with police work and has allowed guilty criminals to go free. He concludes that the Court has become absolutist in its rulings on the Bill of Rights with little regard for the consequences.

Eugene H. Methvin, "Let's Have Justice for Non-Criminals, Too!" Reprinted with permission from the December 1966 *Reader's Digest*. Copyright © 1966 by The Reader's Digest Assn., Inc.

In a Washington, D.C., courtroom, Federal Judge George L. Hart faced the jury and shook his finger angrily at 41-year-old James W. Killough, on trial before him for murder. "On three separate occasions this man voluntarily confessed foully killing his wife and throwing her body on a dump like a piece of garbage. He led police there. Yet the U.S. Court of Appeals has seen fit to throw the confessions out. Though it makes me almost physically ill, I must direct a verdict of acquittal. I feel I'm presiding not over a search for truth but over an impossible farce. We know the man is guilty, but we sit here blind, deaf and dumb, and we can't admit what we know. Tonight felons can sleep better."

An Impossible Farce

Thus, in a spectacle now being repeated across the nation, after confessing a murder the confessor walked free, a scoffing example of the "impossible farce" the Supreme Court has made of American justice. For, in a series of rulings over the past nine years, the Court has progressively handcuffed the police, turned trial judges into automatons, and blindfolded juries, all to the immense benefit of criminals.

Last June 13, 1966 the Court went further than ever before in a decision the New York *Times* called "an over-hasty trespass into the legislative area, . . . lacking either constitutional warrant or constructive effect." Chief Justice Earl Warren, in a razor-thin five-four decision, announced a new interpretation of the 175-year-old Fifth Amendment: now it requires that police, in questioning suspects, not only first warn them of their right to silence, but even furnish a lawyer and allow him to sit in on the interrogation if the suspect wishes. Moreover, if the suspect "indicates in any manner" that he does not want to answer questions, the police must stop.

Dissenting thunderously, Justice Byron R. White said the Court's ruling "has no significant support in the history or language of the Fifth Amendment" and "in some cases will return a killer, a rapist or other criminal to the streets to repeat his crime whenever it pleases him. As a consequence, there will not be a gain but a loss in human dignity."

Justice White's prediction was speedily verified. Consider these two cases.

• After a $10,000 fire almost killed a sleeping housewife and her three children, a Washington policeman answered a radio call. Two men walked up to him. "This is the guy who set the fire," said one. The policeman blinked, looked at the other and asked, "What have you got to say?" "I did it!" the man blurted. A painter who showed up for work drunk and was ordered off the job, he had returned at night to explode a Molotov-cocktail firebomb in the home.

At the arson trial, his lawyer argued that the mere presence of the uniformed policeman psychologically coerced him, thereby violating his Fifth Amendment privilege against self-incrimination. Incredibly, the judge excluded the confession from the jury. (However, in this case a conviction was obtained on other evidence.)

• A young probationer in Cleveland admitted killing another youth. But because police neglected to warn him of his rights, Judge Angelo J. Gagliardo had to let him go.

"There is no question in my mind that this is anything but a willful, deliberate act of murder without any justification," Judge Gagliardo fumed. "Someday members of the Supreme Court will engage themselves in the practical problems of life in a modern urban society, and deal with realities rather than theories that place individual rights far above the community."

Since Chief Justice Warren announced the new rules, Philadelphia police are finding that 56 percent of the suspects they arrest refuse to answer police questions. In Brooklyn, police find four times as many suspects as before—96 out of 239—arrested in homicide, robbery, felonious assault and rape cases are refusing to make statements. "Most of these men will walk the streets as free men," warns District Attorney Aaron E. Koota. "These vicious crimes may never be solved." Police in Boston, Washington, Cleveland, Los Angeles, San Francisco and Memphis report similar results, and the percentages can be expected to increase in every U.S. city.

Squeal-Room Tactics

The Supreme Court's foray into legislating rules for police conduct springs from one of the oldest riddles of American criminal justice: How can we ensure that police obey the rules protecting individual liberties, yet have enough freedom themselves to protect society against criminals?

The Constitution offers no solutions. When the Bill of Rights was written, the United States had only four million citizens and was 95-percent rural; the largest city, New York, had only 33,000 people; there was no such thing as police. Magistrates questioned defendants—vigorously—and their statements or refusals could be laid before a trial jury.

As police evolved, city by city, the chief demand was that they catch criminals, and few questioned how. With no authoritative guidance, police did the best they could—and often that was horrendous. In 1931 a Presidential commission documented shocking "lawlessness in law enforcement," including the use of third-degree interrogations in at least two thirds of America's cities. Cleveland police, for example, would beat prisoners from behind (so they couldn't be identified in court), over kidneys, and in the soft hollows above the hips, using a sausage-shape sandbag made of silk to avoid leaving telltale bruises.

The Supreme Court waited five years for state legislatures and courts to start cleaning up this sordid mess. Then came a murder conviction, duly approved by Mississippi's supreme court—a case in which a deputy sheriff had hanged a Negro suspect by his neck to a tree and whipped him until he confessed. The deputy unblushingly admitted he had beaten the man, "but not too much for a nigger." The Supreme Court reversed the conviction, using the Fourteenth Amendment's "due process" clause to limit state law-enforcement officers for the first time in history.

An Absolutist Court

In undertaking to police the police, basically a legislative and executive function, the Supreme Court until recently operated under Justice Cardozo's wise injunction: "Justice, though due to the accused, is due to the accuser also. The concept of fairness must not be strained till it is narrowed to a filament. We are to keep the balance true."

Now, as Dean Erwin Griswold of the Harvard Law School points out, the Court has become "absolutist." It is pursuing defensible doctrines beyond the realm of rationality and common sense. Such extremism has spread like moral rot throughout federal and state appellate courts until, as the then Attorney General Nicholas Katzenbach protested: "The judges have left the public behind, and even among judges the margins of consensus have been passed."

Take, for example, the crucial problem of search and seizure. "It must be remembered that what the Constitution forbids is not all searches and seizures, but unreasonable searches and seizures," says Justice Potter Stewart. But judges are handing down increasingly unreasonable decrees on what constitutes reasonable police conduct. Consider:

• In Tucson a policeman followed a suspected stolen car. The driver parked and went into a college fraternity house. The officer crawled under the car, looked at the transmission serial number and, sure enough, it matched one on the list of stolen property.

• In Washington, police had a tip that a known prostitute had illegal dope. They went to her rooming house, knocked on the door, then started inside to find her room. At that moment she dashed past them and dropped a small package into a garbage can under the front porch. The officers looked in the garbage can and found a package of narcotics.

In each of these cases, hair-splitting judges ruled the searches "unreasonable," dismissed the evidence and turned the defendants loose upon the community, as a "lesson" to police.

Yet the reasonable citizen is likely to agree with Federal Judge Warren Burger's acid dissent in the garbage-can case: The police would have been derelict in their duty if they had *not* done precisely what they did. Judge Burger declared, "I can not find a constitutional right to privacy in the garbage pail of a rooming house." He denounced the "unfortunate trend of judicial decisions which stretch and strain to give the guilty not the same but vastly more protection than the law-abiding citizen."

The Meaning of Mallory. Until 1957 non-coercive police interrogations were taken for granted. Then came the Mallory case. After police questioning and a lie-detector test, Andrew Mallory, a Washington, D.C., handyman, confessed to raping a woman in the apartment house where he lived. But the Supreme Court freed Mallory by—in effect—writing a new rule for federal law-enforcement officers. The Court said taking Mallory to the police station for questioning represented an "unnecessary delay" in presenting him before an arraigning magistrate, and his confession therefore could not be used in evidence.

The net results? Thirty-three months after Mallory's release he attacked another woman in a Philadelphia apartment. This time he got a 10-to-20-year sentence. His Philadelphia victim was, as one Justice Department lawyer told me sardonically, "deprived of her constitutional right to equal protection of the laws by the Supreme Court, without due process of law."

Unnecessary delay in Mallory's case meant seven and a half hours. In 1962 the courts said "three hours" was unreasonable; in 1964, 30 minutes; in 1965 *five* minutes.

Since the *Mallory* decision applied only to federal officers, federally ruled Washington, D.C., was the only city affected. But there the impact was devastating. In the five years before *Mallory*, with crime rising nationally, Washington's police had reduced serious crimes 37 percent. But thereafter the rate began to climb sharply, and in nine years it has gone up 124 percent. Holdups, purse-snatchings and muggings, down a third before *Mallory*, skyrocketed 305 percent—five times the national increase. Worse, the rate of police success in solving crimes has been cut in half, to an all-time low.

Like Mallory himself, both his victims were Negroes from underprivileged backgrounds. A survey of slum dwellers in Harlem and Watts (Los Angeles) found that the problem worrying most families was "crime in the streets" and "the need for more police protection"—not "policy brutality." In a similar poll in Washington, D.C., 1500 people were asked to name the two or three biggest problems "something should be done about." More than half singled out crime and law enforcement.

Chief Justice Earl Warren, a former attorney general from California, presided over the Supreme Court from 1953 to 1969. He was the focus of criticism from many political leaders who charged that Supreme Court rulings on the criminal justice system enabled criminals to go free.

True Confessions. Other American cities can expect similar results now that the Supreme Court is undertaking detailed supervision of their police in questioning suspects. Consider two recent decisions:

• In Tacoma, Wash., shortly after a filling-station holdup, police in a squad car saw a likely-looking suspect walking through a suburban neighborhood. They drove up alongside and asked him what he was doing. "Going home," he said. As the officers followed him slowly, he turned in at a house, walked up to the door—and found it locked. At that, he came back to the parked police car and said, "Okay, you got me! Let's go." On the drive to the police station, he pointed out the filling station. Before locking him up for the night, the officers questioned him for 30 minutes, and he confessed again. Next morning he made a third oral confession and asked to call his wife. "Let's get this in writing first," the police said. Taken to a prosecutor's office, he confessed a fourth time and signed a transcript.

No easily led youngster, the man had previously been convicted of housebreaking, robbery, jailbreak, car theft and other crimes. He made no claim of abuse or prolonged questioning. Yet the Supreme Court ruled that the refusal to let him call his wife meant that the signed transcript "cannot be said to be the voluntary product of a free and unconstrained will."

• A wave of brutal street crimes erupted in a Los Angeles low-income area. Women—Negroes, Mexican and Japanese—were being knocked down from behind in the dark, horribly beaten and robbed. One elderly Negro woman was kicked to death. Police had not the slightest clue until a check from one victim's purse was cashed under a forged signature. They traced the passer, Roy Allen Stewart, and found his residence to be a veritable Fagin's nest lined with empty purses, wallets and other stolen property. Stewart, his wife and three others in the house were arrested. But which, if any, had committed the street crimes?

Under California law the police had five days before they were required to produce the suspect before a magistrate for arraignment. They questioned Stewart eight times, for a total of two hours and 46 minutes, and on the day of arraignment he confessed robbing and kicking the woman who died. At his trial he made not the slightest claim that police had abused him or denied any right to see anyone—lawyer, family or bondsman. Yet Stewart's was one of the four convictions based on confessions historically admitted as voluntary and reliable that the Supreme Court reversed in June's landmark decision.

Such monstrous miscarriages of justice result directly from the Supreme Court's practice of excluding evidence not because it is unreliable but because the judges may disagree with police conduct in gathering it. They hand police a complex set of "interpretations" that, says California Chief Justice Roger Traynor, "dot just enough t's to cross the eyes." In the quiet of their chambers they cannot themselves agree on just what the law prescribes, yet they demand absolute perfection of the policeman who must make a snap judgment in the heat of conflict and danger. An American Bar Association committee long ago protested that the rigid exclusionary rule "warps the conduct of a criminal trial from the main issues which determine guilt or innocence" and turns it into "an inquiry into the misconduct of police after the crime itself."

British courts have found a middle way. They have given police a set of "Judges' Rules" to follow in interrogations: They must warn the suspect only of his right to silence; he may consult a lawyer, but the lawyer is not allowed to be present during questioning. If, however, police for some reason depart from these rules, judges are not automatically bound to exclude whatever evidence might result. The trial judge inquires into all the circumstances. Was the police infraction a mere questionable judgment, or a willful disregard of settled standards? The judge is then free to decide which in this case is more important: to protect the public from such police conduct, or from the criminal.

Thus the power to exclude valid evidence is a seldom-used club, hanging on the courtroom wall as a reminder, not a bludgeon used indiscriminately against the police even when the real victim is the law-abiding public. A similar process could be applied to police searches and seizures of physical evidence.

Says Chief Judge Edward Lumbard of the U.S. Court of Appeals for the Second Circuit: "The British are much better at these commonsense compromises. We ride logic to hell."

Supreme Court Extremism

Congress has the clear duty and power to curb the Supreme Court's extremism; Article III of the Constitution lays on the legislators the responsibility to make "exceptions and regulations" for the Court's appellate jurisdiction. Thus, declare the classic essays in *The Federalist*, Congress "would certainly have full power to provide that in appeals to the Supreme Court there should be no re-examination of facts where they had been tried by juries." Or it clearly could permit the jury to decide finally whether a confession is voluntary within the Fifth Amendment's terms. What could be a more democratic way of enforcing standards upon police and safeguarding individual rights?

Moreover, state legislatures have a heavy duty to provide safeguards against "squeal room" secrecy and the occasional instances of police abuse. "It's time the American people tell policemen how they want the law enforced, and back them to the hilt in doing it," says former New York City Police Commissioner Michael J. Murphy. "We want and need legislative guidelines. Virtually every policeman in America wants to obey the Constitution—if somebody will only tell him what it says."

One fact is clear: Police must be allowed a fair opportunity to do their job. To police its 198 million people the United States has 397,000 state and local law-enforcement officers. Only 70,000 are on duty on any 4 p.m.-to-midnight shift. With 7600 serious crimes reported every day (on the average), and untold thousands more unreported, police already have to pick and choose which they will investigate. Says Quinn Tamm, executive director of the International Association of Chiefs of Police, "It would be grand if the officer could play Sherlock Holmes and contemplate all aspects of a case for hours on end. But he has 15 cases, and, in the real world, many of them simply cannot be solved without questioning." Even vast increases in police manpower and scientific techniques will not prevent a substantial loss in law-enforcement effectiveness. Some form of interrogation is necessary.

The American Law Institute, representing 1800 law professors, judges, prosecuting and defense attorneys, is working on a Model Code that provides police authority to stop and frisk citizens on the streets in suspicious circumstances, question them for 20 minutes without formal arrest, and question them at the police station up to four hours. They must warn the subject of his rights, and tape-record the station-house sessions so judges and jurors can be sure what goes on. On their own, New Orleans police have even installed a television-tape device so they can later *show* courts the whole interrogation process.

Find Out the Truth

The Supreme Court today is rewriting the Bill of Rights. Dominating this process are five Justices who apparently prefer turning patently guilty criminals loose if the slightest flyspeck can be found on police conduct. But, as Brooklyn's erudite prosecutor William I. Siegel reminded them, "No human institution is perfect, and we cannot require from a prosecutorial apparatus a level of perfection not found anywhere else in human affairs. 'Ideal' is by definition unobtainable. The true function of a court is to find out where the truth lies." Even Chief Justice Warren has recognized that the Court is ill-fitted to "police the police" on a case-by-case basis, and has urged legislative action.

A wholesale revision of state and federal laws is urgent. British practice suggests one form of compromise that would be more workable than the Supreme Court's absolutist doctrine. If nothing is done, we will live under a system prescribed not by elected representatives but by a committee of five lawyers sitting in a far-away marble palace and unaccountable to anyone at the ballot box for the results of their legislating.

So extreme have the present Court rulings become that Federal Appeals Judge Wilbur K. Miller spoke for millions when he protested in Washington's Killough murder, "Nice people have some rights, too!"

VIEWPOINT 8

"The Bill of Rights was specifically designed to put 'handcuffs' on the government in its dealings with its citizens."

Supreme Court Rulings Have Made the Police Follow the Bill of Rights

William H. Dempsey Jr. (1930-)

During the 1960s the Supreme Court under Chief Justice Earl Warren used the Fourteenth Amendment's due process clause to dramatically change America's criminal justice system. Historian David J. Bodenhamer writes in *Crucible of Liberty:*

> Commentators aptly termed it a "due-process revolution." In decision after decision, the justices overturned long-standing precedents by declaring that the various provisions of the Fourth, Fifth and Sixth Amendments applied to state law enforcement practices. For the first time in history, the rights of the accused became truly national. The guarantee of due process for criminal defendants no longer depended upon accidents of geography.

Many people were sharply critical of these Supreme Court rulings, arguing that the Supreme Court was usurping legislative power and impairing the ability of the police and the courts to

William H. Dempsey Jr., "Is It Wrong to Handcuff the Police?" *The Catholic World*, February 1967. Reprinted with the permission of *The Catholic World*.

prosecute criminals. In the following viewpoint, taken from an article written in 1967, William H. Dempsey Jr. defends rulings of the Supreme Court that extend Bill of Rights protections to state criminal defendants. Dempsey asserts that the function of the Bill of Rights is to restrict the government when it invades a person's liberties, and that the Warren Court rulings have extended the Bill of Rights to the poor and underprivileged. At the time of the article's publication Dempsey was a practicing attorney in Washington, D.C.

On October 5, 1953, President Eisenhower appointed Earl Warren Chief Justice of the United States. This selection of the extraordinarily popular governor was not controversial. It seemed likely that he would be a middle-of-the-roader who might use his political skills to keep the Court in tune with dominant public opinion.

Thirteen years later, Warren is variously pilloried as an archenemy of the people and praised as one of the greatest Chief Justices since John Marshall, and the "Warren Court" has become the most controversial bench since the "Nine Old Men" were thwarting President Roosevelt's efforts to deal with the Great Depression.

It all began on May 17, 1954, when the Chief Justice, for a unanimous Court, handed down probably the most important decision in the country's history—*Brown* v. *Board of Education*, the desegregation case. There the Court required us finally to begin redeeming the promise made to the Negro in the Civil War. The effort is painful, and the Court has been bitterly assailed for forcing us to make it.

But if the *Brown* decision were the Warren Court's only departure from precedent, it is unlikely that any serious attack upon the Court could have been long sustained. A series of decisions before *Brown* had undermined the old "separate but equal" doctrine, so that, while *Brown* was the final and decisive step, it was hardly unexpected. More importantly, the harsh injustice of the country's treatment of the Negro was perfectly evident, so that the *Brown* decision carried the authority of high moral principle that could not for long be denied.

Judicial Innovation

It is now clear, of course, that *Brown* signaled only the beginning of a remarkable period of judicial innovation. However, for some time after *Brown* the course the Warren Court would chart was uncertain. Shortly after *Brown*, the Court dealt with the first wave of cases generated by the McCarthy-inspired legislative investigations of Communists past and present, real and alleged. When the Court sharply limited those investigations, the reaction was just as abusive, and possibly more broadly based, than that which followed *Brown*. However, the Court retreated in its next group of Communist-investigation decisions, leaving the law cloudy and the critics confused.

"What's so great about due process? Due process got me ten years."

This sort of ambiguity in the Court's attitude toward politically sensitive questions was due primarily to Justice Frankfurter, whose vote was frequently decisive in a narrowly divided Court. While Frankfurter sometimes expressed personal sympathy with the liberal approach of the Chief Justice and Justices Black, Douglas, and Brennan, he believed that the Court should pay great deference to the Congress and to the states. Consequently, more often than not he struck a cautious—some would say a timid—note in the name of what he termed "judicial restraint."

In 1962, however, Frankfurter was replaced by Arthur Goldberg, who in turn has been replaced by Abe Fortas. The impact of this shift in *dramatis personae* has been enormous. Building on some scattered prior decisions, the Court has in the past few years imposed important new limitations upon federal and state governments respecting such matters as reapportionment of legislatures, the relationship between government and religion, and law enforcement.

Criminal Justice Controversy

Of these recent decisions, none have been more controversial than those dealing with criminal law. In one speech and article after another, law enforcement officers have complained bitterly that they have been "handcuffed" by the Court, and they have been seconded by a battery of journalists and lawyers. While the Court has also had its defenders, the drumbeat of criticism, against the background of mounting concern over "crime in the streets," has generated a wave of antagonism toward the Court.

To be sure, the Court has been at the center of maelstroms before during its long history and has often emerged with enhanced stature. Still, if the current criticism of the Court is well founded, Justice Frankfurter's fears for the Court may yet be realized. The question, then, is: "Who is right, the critics or the Court?"

If the controversy could be resolved by answering the question whether the Court has "handcuffed" the police, cloture on the debate would be quite in order. There is no doubt that this is precisely what the Court has done. That is to say, there is no doubt that the Court has made more difficult the policeman's job of putting criminals in jail.

But framing the question in such terms is just a debater's trick. It scores points with the audience, but does not represent a genuine effort to appraise the Court's decisions.

The fact is that the Bill of Rights was specifically designed to put "handcuffs" on the government in its dealings with its citizens. Thus, although the legislature may rightly conclude that domestic peace would best be secured by stilling a dissenting political or religious minority, the First Amendment says "Thou Shalt Not." And although the police may believe that dragnet arrests and indiscriminate searches would make law enforcement more efficient—a belief that is surely well founded, as the experience of Nazi Germany demonstrates—the Fourth Amendment bars the way.

Thus the question is not whether the police have been "handcuffed," but to what purpose and to what extent. While the answer in large measure turns upon an analysis of the relevant constitutional provisions, this is not as arcane a subject as some would have it appear. Consider the principal decisions:

In 1961, the Court ruled in *Mapp* v. *Ohio* that evidence seized by the police in violation of the search and seizure provisions of the Fourth Amendment may not be used in state criminal prosecutions. It could be, and has been, argued—as it is most artfully put—that just because the constable blunders the criminal should not go free.

While that argument has an appealing ring, it was ultimately rejected by the Court because experience demonstrated that the police could not be deterred from violating the Constitution except by removing the incentive—that is, except by preventing convictions based on illegally secured evidence.

While as a matter of abstract logic the decision in *Mapp* could have gone either way, surely the Court's view was best designed to secure to the public the safeguards of the Fourth Amendment. There was compelling evidence that, in those states permitting the use at trial of illegally obtained evidence, the police had blatantly ignored the strictures of the Constitution.

If the police themselves, or state or local legislative units, had enforced sanctions against these police transgressions, *Mapp* might never have been decided. But who ever heard of a policeman being fired or demoted because he conducted an illegal search or seizure? And since the victims of this sort of police illegality are almost invariably the hapless poor, private lawsuits against offending police were virtually nonexistent. Enforcement of the Fourth Amendment fell to the Court by default. . . .

Next, in 1963 the Court, in *Gideon* v. *Wainwright*, ruled that the states are obliged to provide attorneys to defend all indigents charged with felonies. The Sixth Amendment secures the right of counsel in criminal cases, and in 1938 the Court ruled that this provision means, not merely that a rich person may have a lawyer defend him, but also that the federal government must provide counsel to the poor person. In *Gideon* (which was argued by then Mr., now Mr. Justice, Fortas), the Court extended this same principle to the states by virtue of the "fundamental fairness" doctrine of the Fourteenth Amendment.

The reasonableness of this decision hardly seems open to question. Anyone should realize that requiring a layman to defend himself against a criminal charge is like requiring him to take out his own appendix. So the aftermath of *Gideon* dramatically demonstrated, for on a new trial, this time with the aid of counsel, Gideon himself was acquitted.

Once again, the impact of this decision on law enforcement will probably be minimal. The federal government has survived since 1938 under the *Gideon* right-to-counsel rule, and in *Gideon* some

22 states urged the Court to apply the same rule to the states. This widespread governmental support for the *Gideon* principle suggests that the picture of a cagey lawyer securing acquittal of a guilty defendant by a masterful stratagem is, by and large, the product of TV scenario writers, not of the courtroom.

In a related series of cases, the Court has made other efforts to

---

Depriving Defendants of Their Rights

In the 1966 case Miranda v. Arizona, *the Supreme Court ruled that the Bill of Rights meant that criminal suspects under police interrogation should be provided counsel. Writing for the Court, Chief Justice Earl Warren argued that past examples of police misconduct necessitated the decision.*

The constitutional issue we decided in each of these cases is the admissibility of statements obtained from a defendant questioned while in custody and deprived of his freedom of action. In each, the defendant was questioned by police officers, detectives, or a prosecuting attorney in a room in which he was cut off from the outside world. In none of these cases was the defendant given a full and effective warning of his rights at the outset of the interrogation process. In all the cases, the questioning elicited oral admissions, and in three of them, signed statements as well which were admitted at their trials. They all thus share salient features—incommunicado interrogation of individuals in a police-dominated atmosphere, resulting in self-incriminating statements without full warning of constitutional rights.

An understanding of the nature and setting of this in-custody interrogation is essential to our decisions today. The difficulty in depicting what transpires at such interrogations stems from the fact that in this country they have largely taken place incommunicado. From extensive factual studies undertaken in the early 1930s, including the famous Wickersham Report to Congress by a Presidential Commission, it is clear that police violence and the "third degree" flourished at that time. In a series of cases decided by this Court long after these studies, the police resorted to physical brutality—beating, hanging, whipping—and to sustained and protracted questioning incommunicado in order to extort confessions. The 1961 Commission on Civil Rights found much evidence to indicate that "some policemen still resort to physical force to obtain confessions." . . . The use of physical brutality and violence is not, unfortunately, relegated to the past or to any part of the country. . . .

The examples given above are undoubtedly the exception now, but they are sufficiently widespread to be the object of concern. Unless a proper limitation upon custodial interrogation is achieved—there can be no assurance that practices of this nature will be eradicated in the foreseeable future.

keep the true balance between the rich and poor by requiring the states to provide counsel for indigents on appeal as well as at trial, and to provide a transcript of the trial so that the right to appeal might be meaningful. The justifications for the decisions, as well as their probable impact on law enforcement, are of the same order as *Gideon's*.

The Court's most recent important criminal law decision, *Miranda v. Arizona*, is the most controversial and the most difficult. There the Court, in a 5-4 decision, determined that no conviction based upon a confession would be sustained where the defendant had not been warned that he had the right to remain silent, that anything he said could be used against him, that he had the right to speak with counsel before speaking to the police, and that if he could not afford a lawyer one would be provided for him.

The Court based *Miranda* upon the Fifth Amendment, which prescribes that no one may be compelled to incriminate himself in a criminal case. In principle, the decision seems unexceptionable. A confession is obviously "incriminating," so that the question is whether a confession obtained through police interrogation is "compelled" within the meaning of the Fifth Amendment where the accused is not advised of his rights and does not have the chance to consult counsel. Certainly there must be grave doubt whether such a confession is truly voluntary rather than compelled.

Moreover, since a person who is arrested *does* have the right not to confess and the right to talk to a lawyer, it is hard to see how anyone could reasonably object because the Court insists that a person be told that he has those rights.

In addition, in *Miranda* as in *Mapp*, the Court was troubled by the continuing failure of the police to police themselves. The 1931 disclosure by the Wickersham Report of widespread police brutality, coupled with the repeated judicial injunctions against such practices, should have led to their elimination long ago. Yet cases still arise all too frequently in which the police have literally beaten confessions out of the accused.

The Court was also influenced by the fact that, although police have probably abandoned the crudest methods of coercion, the more sophisticated techniques of psychological pressures have come into widespread use. . . .

The dissenting Justices in *Miranda* thought that instances of physical or psychological coercion could be dealt with on a case-by-case basis without the imposition upon the police of any inflexible rules. But assuming that this is so—and the disheartening experience under this traditional approach suggests that it is not—it does not explain why there should be any criticism of the Court's effort to make doubly sure that the Fifth Amendment is not breached.

There is, of course, an explanation. It emerges clearly from the dissenting opinions as well as from other attacks upon *Miranda*. It is that we cannot really afford to apply the Bill of Rights in full measure.

To be sure, if a wealthy person is arrested he is bound to call his lawyer right away, and there is nothing that can be done about that. But the vast majority of criminal defendants are poor and have no lawyer to call, and they must not be permitted to see one before they confess lest our system of law enforcement collapse. So reads the indictment of *Miranda* in what is doubtless its least attractive, but also its only plausible, form.

The plea to that indictment must at this moment be the Scotch verdict "not proven."

Some scattered post-*Miranda* returns suggest that those who claim that the psychological urge of a guilty person to confess is almost overwhelming may be correct, so that warning him of his legal rights may have little impact. But the data is too slim for judgment. . . .

The Plight of the Poor

Miranda, together with the *Mapp* enforcement of the search and seizure amendment and the *Gideon* enforcement of the right to counsel amendment, are in a most important sense emanations of our growing moral sensitivity to the plight of our poor and our oppressed. The civil rights movement and the war on poverty have brought to general attention what should have been obvious: the poor—who are also generally the Negro—have been severely put upon by our society for a long time, and one instrument of their degradation has been their treatment by the police. It is hardly any wonder that crime is a prominent dividend of our sins of injustice and want of charity.

As the Warren Court in *Brown* took the lead in desegregation— to the everlasting shame of the Executive and the Congress—so too in *Miranda* it has taken the lead in insuring to the poor the rights that we recognize as a matter of course for the rich.

In taking this step, the Court has staked its fortune upon our capacity to live up to our own ideals. Perhaps our society has become so complex and our ills so grave that we cannot.

Or perhaps, by encouraging the police to accommodate themselves to the new standards and by sacrificing so that they can be given the financial resources necessary to effective law enforcement, we can. The Court has taken a generous, rather than a mean, view of our capacities and our goodwill. We may pray that the Court is right.

Chapter 6

Historians Debate the Supreme Court's Impact on the Bill of Rights

Chapter Preface

The Bill of Rights was born in political controversy, debate, and ultimate compromise between supporters and defenders of America's Constitution. Of relatively minor practical significance in the first century of its existence, its second century was marked by greater recognition—and controversy—as America struggled to apply its fundamental principles to constantly changing situations. Today the Bill of Rights remains the object of both celebration and dispute. Historian Raymond Arsenault writes in *Crucible of Liberty*:

> Two centuries after the ratification of the first ten amendments, the Bill of Rights remains a subject of controversy and compelling interest for millions of Americans. Historical experience tells us that the reinterpretation of rights and liberties is an inescapable part of American life. It also tells us that in a complex nation such as the United States, judicial review seldom results in consensus. Indeed, the most divisive domestic controversies of our time . . . have revolved around conflicting interpretations of one or more of the first ten amendments. Abortion, women's rights, gun control, capital punishment, the rights of criminal defendants and prison inmates, the protection of privacy, mandatory drug testing, the burning of flags and draft cards, radical political dissent and academic freedom, affirmative action and racial equality, prayer in schools and crèches in public parks, pornography and obscenity, government censorship and freedom of the press—all of these important issues require an ongoing consideration of the contemporary meaning and implications of the Bill of Rights.

In attempting to understand and apply the Bill of Rights, many Supreme Court justices, judges, political leaders, legal philosophers, and others have looked at its history. They have tried to determine what the people who wrote and ratified the Bill of Rights meant by its various provisions. Some legal commentators, such as former federal judge Robert Bork and historian Gary L. McDowell, have argued that the "original intent" of the writers of the Bill of Rights should be the primary guide to applying the Bill of Rights today. They have criticized many rulings of the Supreme Court justices for substituting their own opinions as to what the Bill of Rights should mean.

The "original intent" approach of interpreting the Bill of Rights has been sharply criticized by many, including former Supreme Court justice Thurgood Marshall and historian Kermit L. Hall.

They argue that it is by evolving public understandings and Supreme Court interpretations that the Bill of Rights remains a "living document" that continues to be relevant to Americans today.

In studying the Bill of Rights, it is important to note that while Supreme Court justices have the official responsibility of interpreting it, it is ordinary Americans such as Jacob Abrams, Fred Korematsu, and Clarence Earl Gideon who are ultimately responsible for bringing the cases to the Supreme Court that have changed constitutional law, and that it is ordinary Americans who by their beliefs and actions with others finally determine whether the Bill of Rights is a truly living document. Judge Learned Hand, who served fifty years on the federal bench, wrote that ultimately, "Liberty lies in the hearts of men and women. When it dies there, no constitution, no law, no court can save it. No constitution, no law, no court can even do much to help it."

VIEWPOINT 1

"The textual provisions for rights in . . . the Bill of Rights are relatively few in number and are rather precisely crafted. To fit ever more innovative claims of rights within those original provisions requires more than a little stretching of the text."

The Supreme Court Has Distorted the Meaning of the Bill of Rights

Gary L. McDowell (1949-)

Gary L. McDowell, a scholar at the Institute of the United States at London University in England, has written and edited numerous books on the Constitution, including *Taking the Constitution Seriously: Essays on the Constitution and Constitutional Law* and *Curbing the Courts: The Constitution and the Limits of Judicial Power.* In addition, he has written numerous papers and articles on American constitutional law.

In the following viewpoint, McDowell examines how the public's concept of rights in general and the Bill of Rights in particular has changed in the two centuries since the Bill of Rights' ratification in 1791. He argues that the founders of America who created the Constitution and the Bill of Rights sought to create a system of limited government which the people would consent to obey in

Excerpted from Gary L. MacDowell, "The Explosion and Erosion of Rights." In *The Bill of Rights in Modern America: After Two Hundred Years,* edited by David J. Bodenhamer and James W. Ely Jr. Bloomington: Indiana University Press, 1993. Copyright © 1993 by Indiana University Press. Reprinted with permission.

order to create a viable community. The ten amendments that form the Bill of Rights, which McDowell states "are relatively few in number and are rather precisely crafted," were meant to refine the Constitution and its careful balancing between individual rights, community rights, and powers of government. Rights, he argues, were "originally seen as a matter of community judgment as to what the limits of governmental power ought to be."

Today's role of the Supreme Court as the ultimate arbiter of whether state and federal laws violate individual rights is a significant and relatively recent change in the nation's understanding of the Bill of Rights, according to McDowell. He finds several things disturbing about this change. He argues that the Supreme Court has taken it upon itself to define and decide which rights are fundamental and worthy of constitutional protection, often going beyond the written provisions of the Bill of Rights. Thus the text of the Bill of Rights becomes less important than what federal judges interpret or consider to be fundamental rights. Instead of limiting government, the new understanding of the Bill of Rights has greatly increased the scope and power of the federal judicial branch, a development McDowell argues is ultimately threatening to freedom. In addition, he argues that the American devotion to rights has caused political leaders to couch their arguments and goals in "the rhetorical garb of rights" when not strictly appropriate. Such measures, he asserts, cheapen and thus endanger the whole concept of human rights.

McDowell concludes that Americans must closely examine the history of the Bill of Rights in order to appreciate the original intent and understanding of the framers of the Constitution. Such understanding, he argues, would help Americans fully understand the roots of individual rights in America and prevent their erosion.

The history of America is, by and large, the history of the idea of individual liberty and rights. As a nation we were, as Abraham Lincoln reminded his morally torn generation, "conceived in liberty and dedicated to the proposition that all men are created equal." When Thomas Jefferson and the other patriots of 1776 declared their independence from England and proclaimed their rightful place among the powers of the Earth, they believed that the rightness of their cause impelled them to the separation—an act never before undertaken as a moral matter. To that generation, there was no doubt that men are created equal; that they are endowed by their Creator with certain inalienable rights; and that governments, to be legitimate, must derive their just powers from the consent of the governed. The laws of nature and of nature's God demanded nothing less. . . .

During the twentieth century this American devotion to rights has grown even stronger. Especially since World War II there has been an ever-increasing public consciousness about rights and liberties. And with that has come a subtle transformation in the way we think about rights.

Rights have come to be associated in the public mind almost exclusively with the courts of law and with the Supreme Court of the United States in particular. Where earlier generations thought rights were to be protected by the constitutional system as a whole—including the states in their sovereign capacities—we have come to think of rights primarily as the result of judicial review at the national level. Sooner or later, it seems, every political question is reduced to a question of rights, and the definition of those rights left to the courts.

As a result, ours is the age of rights—or at the very least, the age of rights rhetoric. Nothing dresses up a political cause like the rhetorical garb of rights; and neither the political Right nor the political Left is able to resist the seductive allure the rhetoric of rights presents. Thus the contemporary debate over the nature and extent of rights exposes at once what is best and worst in American politics and, thereby, in American law.

We see our best side—what Abraham Lincoln once called "the better angels of our nature"—in the continuing commitment to the notion that all are created equal and are endowed by their Creator with certain inalienable rights. On the whole, we continue to believe, as did Jefferson and the others of his age, that governments are instituted in order to secure those rights that nature gives but leaves insecure. Our noblest impulse moves us to seek ways to render those abstract philosophic principles into concrete political reality.

But this worthy side cannot conceal what all too often is really going on. For the very power of fundamental principles to inspire carries with it a terrible temptation. If one can couch policy preferences in the evocative and provocative language of civil rights, those preferences will have a far greater chance of success in the political battles that must be fought. It is simply unseemly to argue against, or even to appear to argue against, what is proffered as a further step toward the American goal of securing rights for all.

The problem is that such temptation is not without its costs: it cheapens the very idea of rights. Calling an ordinary policy preference a fundamental right does not, because it cannot, make that preference a right in any meaningful, philosophical sense. It only confounds the idea of rights with the power of clever rhetoric.

There is yet a deeper problem: the new logic of rights wreaks havoc on the idea of a written constitution. By and large, the textual provisions for rights in the original Constitution and in the Bill of Rights are relatively few in number and are rather precisely crafted. To fit ever more innovative claims of rights within those original provisions requires more than a little stretching of the text. Take, for example, the question of whether a person has the "right" to burn the American flag.

Burning the Flag

The First Amendment is splendidly unambiguous on the protection it affords free speech: "Congress shall make no law abridging the freedom of speech." But what about the states? What if a person chooses to express his political views not in words but in actions—as one Joey Johnson did when he burned the flag outside the Republican National Convention in 1984. Does the First Amendment cover such circumstances? The Supreme Court in *Texas* v. *Johnson* (1989) ruled that it did indeed. But the Court could not base its decision on the text of the First Amendment; nor could it base it on the original intentions of those who framed and ratified that amendment. Rather the Court had to rest its decision only on prior decisions of its own, decisions that had departed in very serious—and arguably illegitimate—ways from text and original intention.

To reach its decision in *Texas* v. *Johnson*, the Court had to accept its prior holdings that the First Amendment applies not just to Congress but to the states; this was achieved by the doctrine that the due process clause of the Fourteenth Amendment "incorporates" certain provisions of the Bill of Rights and obliges the states to be bound by them. Second, burning the flag may be many things, but strictly speaking, it is not speech. Thus the Court had to point to yet another earlier decision wherein a majority of the justices had agreed that there is, within the protections afforded speech by the First Amendment, a special category called "symbolic speech." Protests such as flag burning, the Court held, are properly understood as symbolic speech.

However one might view the results reached in the *Texas* v. *Johnson* case, this much is indisputable: the holding had nothing to do with the original understanding of the First Amendment. It could only be reached by a Court willing to stretch the document to fit a new situation that was looked down upon by a majority of the Court as it is presently constituted. The "right" thus protected depended not upon the Bill of Rights in any strict sense, but only upon how the Court has been persuaded to view the Bill of Rights.

The claim raised in *Texas* v. *Johnson* at least began by raising the question of what the text of the First Amendment means. In yet another world of rights, special protections as fundamental rights are claimed for an assortment of human endeavors, even though they are founded on no explicit provision of the Constitution or any of its amendments. Rather, these claims rest on the assumption that there is an "unwritten constitution" of unenumerated rights that both antedates and transcends the written Constitution and all of its amendments. By this logic, the textual constitution contains metaphysical portals such as the due process clause and the Ninth Amendment through which judges may import new rights that are not mentioned in the existing texts. This jurisprudential view was granted the legitimating imprimatur of the Supreme Court in the 1965 birth control case of *Griswold* v. *Connecticut*. The impact has been profound. Indeed, *Griswold* has ceased to be merely a case in constitutional law and has become a metaphor for the new politics of rights.

The Court in *Griswold* declared unconstitutional a Connecticut law restricting the use of contraceptives even by married couples in the privacy of their own home. The majority held that, despite the Constitution's failure to mention it explicitly, the document contained an implicit "right to privacy." It emerged, said Justice William O. Douglas, as a penumbra formed by emanations of particular rights that were explicit—rights such as being free from unreasonable searches and seizures in one's home. Thus this unenumerated right, once discerned and decreed by the Court, became equal in power to those rights that are enumerated.

By definition, such a broad and unenumerated right must depend for its form on judicial decree. What is included and excluded by the right to privacy must remain a matter of judicial discretion on a case-by-case basis. This is why Judge Robert Bork has called this right "the loose canon of constitutional law." Its lines and limits depend not upon any clear textual provision but only upon judicial predilection. This judicially created right is best known as the foundation for *Roe* v. *Wade* (1973) and the idea of a woman's right to have an abortion. But it is far more than simply that. It is simply pregnant with possibilities for new rights.

There are new notions of privacy that go far beyond the questions of contraception and abortion in *Griswold* and *Roe*. . . .

Articles defending the private use of hard-core pornography (and thus, by extension, its production and availability), arguing for the abolition of laws prohibiting incest, and urging freedom for drug use as a matter of "psychic freedom" have begun to appear with regularity in the major law reviews. The authors are not a group of fringe theorists; they constitute the new "mainstream" of legal education. . . .

Before *Griswold* enshrined the idea of a fundamental right to privacy it was understood that in such areas in which the Constitution was silent, the power to deal with those issues touching privacy resided with the states where the opinions of the people as to what was moral or immoral, acceptable or unacceptable, would fashion laws reflective of the moral sense of the community. After *Griswold* such laws cannot reflect the moral sense of the community unless the judge or justice in question happens to agree.

Weakening the Constitution

Lawrence J. Block and David B. Rivkin Jr., lawyers who worked for the Department of Justice under President George Bush, write in a Winter 1990 issue of Policy Review *that expansive Supreme Court rulings have harmed the cause of civil rights by weakening the Constitution.*

Ironically, the courts—the branch of government popularly identified with the protection of rights—have also played a role in weakening the Constitution's system for protecting liberty. By all too frequently acting as Platonic guardians—enforcing not the language of the statutes or the Constitution to decide cases and controversies brought before them, but rather imposing their own subjective moral values in the process of creating new "rights" not found in the Constitution—the courts have abridged the right of the people to decide basic moral and policy questions. By acting as "super-legislatures," courts have too often imposed the will of a tiny elite on the vast majority and, in the process, skewed the balance wheel of constitutional machinery.

The judicial arbitrariness inherent in the idea of a fundamental right to privacy is what raises serious questions about its legitimacy—and, by extension, about the legitimacy of the whole notion of unenumerated rights for which privacy stands. The public morality of the community is supplanted by the private morality of the judge. By the logic of *Griswold* and its constitutional progeny, the individual becomes everything, the community nothing. And thereby an older and more stable understanding of rights is abandoned. To understand where we are, it is helpful to remember where we began.

To those who framed and ratified the Constitution and the Bill of Rights the primary concern was not simply rights in an abstract and absolute sense. For that generation, rights were properly understood only within the context of a scheme of government that served to define and protect those rights. While they surely appreciated and accepted the idea that there were rights bestowed upon mankind by nature and nature's God, they also knew that without governments being instituted among men, those rights nature gave were left in a most precarious position. . . .

By the device of a written constitution duly ratified by those to live under it, the consent of the governed would be given concrete expression. Such a written constitution, said Alexander Hamilton, would be seen by all, and especially the judges, as "a fundamental law." The Constitution was to be understood as embodying "the intention of the people"; as such it would serve as the basic check against the pretensions of power. It was to be preferred to the "intentions of [the people's] agents" of any branch of the government.

The Constitution reflected the structure of the government to which the people consented; further, and perhaps more important, it reflected the wishes of the people as to the lines and limits of the powers granted to the government. In particular, as Hamilton noted, a "limited constitution . . . [is] one which contains certain specified exceptions to the legislative authority; such for instance as that it shall pass no bills of attainder, no *ex post facto* laws, and the like." As a result of such "specified exceptions," Hamilton could argue that "the constitution is itself in every rational sense, and to every useful purpose, a BILL OF RIGHTS."

Thus were rights originally seen as a matter of community judgment as to what the limits to governmental power ought to be. Within the text of the Constitution itself the framers, as Hamilton indicated, put things off limits. They undertook to protect rights precisely, by clear and common definitions of what was, and what was not, to be tolerated. When the demand for a Bill of Rights led to the first ten amendments to the original Constitution, they opted again for precision. In particular, they added the Bill of Rights at the behest of the Anti-Federalists, who feared that an overreaching national government would in time "devour" the states. Thus there was no ambiguity as to the applicability of the Bill of Rights: it did not extend as a restriction on the powers of the several states.

This issue, which in fact lies at the heart of the rise of the privacy metaphor and the decline of community, was first addressed by Chief Justice John Marshall in his last constitutional decision, *Barron* v. *Baltimore* (1833), in which it was argued that the Fifth Amendment was a brake not merely on national power but on the powers of states and localities as well. In dismissing this argument, Marshall went to the very heart of the notion of constitutionalism that informed the American founding. . . .

Implicit in Marshall's opinion in *Barron* are two fundamental principles. First, rights are rights by virtue of having been given certain concrete expression in a constitutional text. . . . They are not natural but civil in their origin and practical extent. While there may arguably be a constellation of natural rights or common law rights, they do not become constitutional rights until explicitly adopted in the manner prescribed by the Constitution itself.

Marshall's second point is equally significant: rights are fashioned as restraints on government antecedent to the government itself. Thus they are not subject to creation or recreation by the powers of that government. The courts are no more empowered to exercise their will independent of the people in their original collective capacity than is the legislature or the executive. The opinions of the judges stand in the same relation as the laws of the legislature to the original will and consent of the people. Neither is superior to the other nor to the people themselves. Indeed, as Hamilton said, "the power of the people is superior to both."

This view of rights generally held sway until the middle of the nineteenth century. . . .

In 1857 the first fissure in this foundation appeared. It came in the opinion of Chief Justice Roger B. Taney in the slavery case *Dred Scott* v. *Sandford*, a case aptly described at one level as a "self-inflicted wound." In seeking to calm the political waters so roiled by slavery, Taney set out to deny that Congress had the power to prohibit slavery in the territories lining up to enter the Union. In the end, of course, he decreed that the Missouri Compromise was unconstitutional; it was the first time since *Marbury* v. *Madison* (1803) that the Court had struck down a federal law by judicial review.

Unenumerated Rights

In the course of his opinion, however, Taney did more than merely declare an act of Congress invalid; he introduced into a seemingly ordinary, if vexatious, case a truly revolutionary principle. "[A]n act of Congress," the Chief Justice wrote, "which deprives a citizen of the United States of his liberty or property in a particular Territory of the United States, and who has committed no offence against the laws, could hardly be dignified with the name of due process of law." By linking the idea of vested interests to the due process clause of the Fifth Amendment, and using it to protect the property of slaveholders—in this case, Dred Scott—Taney imported into the Constitution the notion that rights were protected even though unenumerated. In the name of protecting the citizens such as John Sandford from the zeal of government, Taney radically expanded the objects to which the judicial power was originally thought to extend. . . .

But ultimately it was not *Dred Scott* that would most contribute to the demise of community and the transformation of the meaning of rights under the Constitution: that distinction, ironically, was reserved for that device meant to rid the republic of the more noxious elements of *Dred Scott*, the Fourteenth Amendment ratified in 1868.

The Fourteenth Amendment sought to clear the constitutional waters muddied by *Dred Scott* by guaranteeing each citizen that the privileges and immunities of their national citizenship would not be abridged by any state; that they would not be deprived of "life, liberty, or property without due process of law"; and that no state would be able to "deny to any person within its jurisdiction the equal protection of the laws." (The Thirteenth Amendment, of course, had laid the foundation: it had prohibited slavery and involuntary servitude.) . . .

Within a very short time the Fourteenth Amendment would be put to uses never imagined by those who framed and ratified it—and not uses for which it had been intended. While the Court would deny the applicability of the amendment to racial discrimination in *The Civil Rights Cases* (1883) and *Plessy* v. *Ferguson* (1896), the justices would infuse it with new meaning by its creation of the idea of "liberty of contract," a doctrine whereby the Court stretched the meaning of "liberty" in the due process clauses of both the Fifth and the Fourteenth Amendments to protect economic interests against governmental regulation.

This reached its high-water mark in *Lochner* v. *New York* (1905), when the Court struck down New York law that regulated (in the name of health and safety) the hours bakers could work. . . .

Lochner and its descendants would rule the juridical roost until 1937 when the Court, bearing the marks of Franklin D. Roosevelt's appointments, handed down its decision in *West Coast Hotel* v. *Parrish* allowing a state wage law to stand. . . . Yet all was not well: while the Court gave with one hand, it took away with the other. That same year the Court handed down one of its truly landmark cases, *Palko* v. *Connecticut*, in which the justices sought to defend the idea that the Fourteenth Amendment "incorporated" at least certain if not all of the provisions of the Bill of Rights.

Palko was not the first time the Court had argued that a particular limitation in the Bill of Rights applied with equal force to the states. That honor goes to *Gitlow* v. *New York* (1925), a First Amendment case. In *Gitlow*, the Court had not bothered to defend its radical move by anything approaching a reasoned argument; the majority simply asserted that the First Amendment applied to the states. And between 1925 and 1937 the Court had "incorporated" yet other provisions of the first ten amendments. But in *Palko* the Court sought finally to offer a defense of its encroaching power.

The essence of the *Palko* decision by Justice Benjamin Cardozo lies in his notion that not all rights are equal; some few are properly deemed "superior," he argued, in that they are distinguished from those without which "justice . . . would not perish." Certain rights, Cardozo went on, are "implicit in the concept of ordered liberty [and] so rooted in the traditions and conscience of our people as to be ranked fundamental." While procedural rights such as the prohibition against "double jeopardy" (the issue in *Palko*) were not to be held as fundamental, such rights as the "freedom of thought and speech" were. The reason, Justice Cardozo concluded, is that they form the "matrix, the indispensable condition of nearly every other form of freedom."

Incorporating the Bill of Rights

The significance of *Palko* for understanding our current confusions over the nature and extent of rights can be reduced to Cardozo's two essential premises. First, incorporation of the rights spelled out in the Bill of Rights was not to be wholesale but rather on a case-by-case basis. Second, and most important, because all rights are not equal in their applicability, it is up to the Court—or, in truth, to a majority of the justices—to determine on that case-by-case basis which rights are superior or fundamental and which are not. The implication of the opinion in *Palko* was stunning: rights depend only upon the Court not only for their application but for their definition. . . .

There is a paradox to the legacy spawned by these early cases. As their underlying logic has been allowed to expand in case after case, two seemingly contradictory principles have emerged as dominant. On the one hand, rights have come to be seen as increasingly absolute; on the other, rights are seen as amorphous and ill-defined things, dependent on judicial definition. Taken together, these two strands of legal logic have formed the fabric of contemporary judicial activism, what has aptly been labeled government by judiciary.

This new thinking about the nature and extent of rights was not limited simply to applying the Bill of Rights. For some, as Justice William O. Douglas once put it, the Bill of Rights was not enough. There was a need to free judges from the misconception, in this view, that the only rights to be enforced in the courts were rights to be found in the Constitution and its subsequent amendments. There, it was argued, a universe of rights was simply waiting to be divined and decreed by the courts; these were "unwritten but still binding principles of higher law." Appropriately, it was Justice Douglas who took the lead in creating the doctrine of unenumerated rights that finally captured a majority of the Court in *Griswold* v. *Connecticut*.

As he famously put it: "specific guarantees in the Bill of Rights have penumbras, formed by emanations from those guarantees that help give them life and substance. . . . Various guarantees create zones of privacy. . . . The present case, then, concerns a relationship lying within the zone of privacy created by several

266

fundamental constitutional guarantees." Douglas reached his conclusion by reasoning from particular rights to a general spirit. Those who framed and ratified the Bill of Rights itself had reasoned from a general principle to specifics they thought worthy of special treatment by singling them out for special and explicit protection. Douglas thus left the reasoning characteristic of the judge and engaged in the reasoning of a framer.

This was precisely the point of Justice Hugo Black's spirited dissent. Black did not disagree because he thought the law in question prudent or appropriate as a matter of policy; indeed, he dissented precisely because he thought it was none of the Court's business whether the law was wise or not. The power of the Court to weigh constitutionality did not extend that far. What Douglas had undertaken to do in the majority opinion, Black said, was to "keep the Constitution in tune with the times." And that the Court did not have the power to do; that was left to the cumbersome but safe process of formal amendment. . . .

As the nation celebrates in earnest the [1991] bicentennial of the Bill of Rights, it is a good time to pause and think about precisely what rights are—and what rights are not.

Modern constitutionalism contains at its core a philosophic paradox: a stable political order depends upon the successful reconciliation of the undeniable fact of men's individuality and natural independence with their absolute need for community and rule in light of the common good. The only means likely to transform radically isolated individuals into citizens is a system of majority rule in a constitutional order derived from the consent of the governed.

The framers understood very well the dangers posed to individual liberty by majority rule; indeed, the Constitution was framed expressly to deal with the problem of majority tyranny. However, the framers did not abandon the idea of majority rule but only strove to reconcile, as James Madison said, the "rights of individuals" and "the permanent and aggregate interests of the community." This the framers sought to do by so contriving the interior structure of the Constitution that its balanced and checked institutions would combine "the requisite stability and energy in government, with the inviolable attention due to liberty, and to the republican form."

In the framers' view, rights were too important to leave dependent upon any institution of government; no governmental power could ever be so trusted. The contemporary view of rights forgets that judicial power exercised by the Supreme Court is still governmental power and hence not to be trusted to create new rights as the ideological mood may strike a majority of justices. The true roots of our rights are worth remembering if our rights are to be truly preserved.

VIEWPOINT 2

"In the hands of the federal judiciary, the Bill of Rights has developed as a living organism."

The Supreme Court Has Strengthened the Bill of Rights

Kermit L. Hall (1944-)

Kermit L. Hall is dean of the Henry Kendall College of Arts and Sciences and professor of history and law at the University of Tulsa, Oklahoma. He is the author of numerous essays and articles. His books include *The Oxford Companion to the Supreme Court*, *By and for the People: Constitutional Rights in American History*, and *The Magic Mirror: Law in American History*.

In the following viewpoint, he examines the creation and evolution of the Bill of Rights and its role in American history. In doing so he defends the role of the Supreme Court against criticism that it has distorted the original intent and meaning of the Bill of Rights. Hall argues that changing conceptions and interpretations are a necessary part of the American system of government, and that, indeed, change was part of the original intent of the nation's founders. American society has changed much over the past two centuries, Hall writes, and it is up to the Supreme Court to adapt the Bill of Rights to today's realities while maintaining the sometimes delicate balance between individual rights and the rights of the community.

Excerpted from Kermit L. Hall, "The Bill of Rights, Liberty, and Original Intent." Edited with permission of The Free Press, a division of Macmillan, Inc., from *Crucible of Liberty: Two Hundred Years of the Bill of Rights*, edited by Raymond Arsenault. Copyright © 1991 by Raymond Arsenault.

Any consideration of rights in American history begins with the simple observation that we are deeply conflicted about them. Survey after survey has disclosed as much. Asked, for example, if an individual has a right to see or show a pornographic movie, or to send or receive lewd materials through the mails, a majority of Americans respond negatively. Time and again, when offered a choice between liberty and community control, many Americans select the latter. Yet these same respondents routinely insist—and insist in overwhelming numbers—that, of the Constitution's provisions, the Bill of Rights is sacred. For example, recent efforts to amend the federal Constitution through a national convention have foundered because so many Americans worry that its delegates just might tamper with the Constitution's first ten amendments. We love to hate, it would seem, those provisions of our fundamental law that we most cherish.

Liberty and the Social Order

This tension is readily explained. Liberty is not an absolute; indeed, granting total freedom to any individual could theoretically result in the restriction of freedom for everyone else. Social control is essential if rights are to have meaning. The far more difficult issue is how liberty is distributed within the social order, and in what institutions we lodge responsibility for this task. This concern about the distribution of rights forms the very fabric of American legal culture. . . .

Today, two centuries after the ratification of the Bill of Rights, we are being treated to the odd spectacle of public officials arguing about how best the Supreme Court can balance rights with community control amidst massive social change. Former Attorney General Edwin Meese and Chief Justice William Rehnquist, on the one hand, and [the late] Justice Thurgood Marshall and recently retired Justice William J. Brennan, on the other, have exchanged bitter comments about the devotion of the Court to the framers' wishes when interpreting the Bill of Rights. Meese complains that, with the chief justiceship of Earl Warren in the 1950s and 60s, the Court became little more than a continuing constitutional convention, in which the justices rewrote our fundamental law to suit their own prejudices and redistributed rights in a way that favored minorities. The Court, they charge, has become an *imperial judiciary* awash in its own personal excesses and locked in a kind of rapturous fit of liberalism and welfare statism in which the rights of minorities have taken precedence over the rights of the majority, and in which reverse discrimination has replaced just plain old discrimination. If, the argument runs, the justices only heeded the wishes—the intentions—of the framers, the present mess—in which we find the courts supposedly subverting community control and unfairly redistributing rights—would cease.

Of course, liberals have praised the Court's sensitivity to contemporary demands for social justice through law. Former Justice Brennan and Justice Marshall have ridiculed Meese and other conservative commentators for their commitment to the doctrine of original intent. . . . More generally, liberals insist that, given the heavy emphasis in American politics on majority will, the judiciary is the only institution capable of making more equal in law those who are less equal in life.

This debate took a dramatic turn with the failed nomination of Judge Robert Bork to the Supreme Court. Bork's Senate confirmation proceedings revealed the profoundly different visions that public leaders hold about how best to interpret what Justice Robert H. Jackson once aptly described as the "majestic generalities" of the Bill of Rights. These same proceedings also raised the perennial question of whether there are liberties protected by the Bill of Rights that are not explicitly provided for in the first ten amendments. For example, even though the Constitution nowhere mentions it, is there a right of privacy? Can the universe of liberties expand beyond those enumerated in the Bill of Rights? If so, what branch of government is to determine what they are and how they are to be distributed? Courts and judges? Legislatures and legislators? Or, should such changes come only through the amending process?

Changes in American Society

These questions have special urgency today because of the startling social and cultural changes that have generated them. It is self-evident that the Constitution and American society have changed enormously since 1791. Just in this century, for example, great changes can be discerned in patterns of parental authority; in attitudes toward treason, patriotism, and national defense; and in the rights of women, ethnic and racial minorities, students, and various other categories of persons previously at the bottom of the social pecking order. . . . Changes in the field of law enforcement have been important as well. The right to be apprised of one's legal rights and to be represented by attorneys has become part of the Fifth and Sixth Amendments. Courts are far more likely to question the use of evidence under the Fourth Amendment than was true even forty years ago. Groups that were once silenced or unorganized—the aged, homosexuals, prisoners, and the physically and mentally handicapped—have entered the constitutional arena demanding a share of the national wealth and fuller protection for their rights.

At no time in our own history have law and the courts figured so prominently in at once responding to social demands and nationalizing rights. We have come to rely on the law and judges in ways that would truly astound our forebears. We hear today of a litigation explosion, of "hyperlexis," of excessive law, of everyone suing everyone else. . . .

Digesting all these social changes, while attempting to balance freedom and control, renders us a bit schizophrenic. We are at once proud of the gifts of freedom in a bountiful land, yet deeply introspective. Some of us brood about our rights in an indeterminate future in which community control is threatened and in which the only constant is change. Are we moving fast enough to fulfill the promise of the Bill of Rights, of equality before the law? Or have we broken from what Thomas Jefferson called the great promise of the Bill of Rights—that it would provide "equal rights for all, special privileges for none"? Does freedom of religion still have meaning in a country in which one million churches dot the landscape, but only one-third of the population regularly attends church? Aren't we only inviting anarchy by coddling smut peddlers and drug dealers when we clothe them with rights? Some see in this resort to constitutional protections the evidence not only of a collapse of community authority but of moral authority generally. Others argue that, over the long haul, fidelity to the Bill of Rights will save us from ourselves.

Change and Judicial Review

The simple truth of the matter is that we live in a constitutional system that forces us repeatedly to reexamine the Bill of Rights in the light of social change. One of the simple lessons of the anniversary just beginning is that the Bill of Rights as it is, is always becoming—and so too is American society. . . .

There are many reasons for this peculiar turn to the relationship between rights and social change in our culture, but the most important, and most controversial, is judicial review. This is the practice by which judges—unelected judges in the case of the Supreme Court—review the merits of state and federal legislative enactments in the light of the Bill of Rights. This process has emerged as the chief means by which the federal Bill of Rights has been adapted to social change, making it an instrument of social reform and reconstruction.

There are two points to make about this development. First, judicial review has been important historically to the Bill of Rights because the United States does not have a *social constitution*, as many Third World countries do. What distinguished the social constitutions of such nations as the Philippines, Nigeria, and

Brazil, are the extensive commitments of governments to guarantee economic rights, equality for different ethnic groups, and the rights of the urban poor. These lengthy documents make the allocation of rights *explicit*. The problem with such social constitutions is that if the explicit promises go unfilled, the people lose faith in the constitution itself. The American scheme is different, because it has come to leave to courts the task of giving substance to, and adapting to, those "majestic generalities" of the Bill of Rights.

Second, while judicial review has many virtues, it has also stirred great concern about the power of unelected judges to readjust the balance between liberty and community control. A poll published in the *New York Times* indicated the depth of public concern about the Court and its powers. That poll revealed that Americans revere the Bill of Rights, but that they are deeply troubled by what seems to be the unaccountable nature of the Supreme Court. More than 60 percent of the respondents concluded that the present system of tenure during good behavior should be changed to make the justices less independent. The polling data revealed, as well, that the decisions in matters of school prayer, busing to achieve racial balance, and abortion have promoted social division and even outright hostility to the Supreme Court.

Much of this hostility stems not just from political differences about the appropriateness of judges mandating a redistribution of rights, but also from concerns about who is benefiting as a result. The doctrine of original intent has appeal because it promises to limit judicial discretion while promoting stability amid unrelenting social change. Its proponents insist that by invoking it we can link the present to a seemingly stable and secure past, while simultaneously restoring genuine liberty by reemphasizing community control.

Yet even the most casual reading of the history used by judges ought to give us pause. . . .

Bluntly put, the idea of original intention as a way of understanding our rights carries with it problematical methodological assumptions, and the potential to abuse the past; as a result, it raises profound ethical problems. As Justice Oliver Wendell Holmes, Jr., observed at the beginning of this century: historical continuity in the law is "not a duty, it is only a necessity." We root answers to contemporary disputes about rights in historical terms because our legal culture, with its common law roots and its emphasis on precedent, requires as much. But we should, at the same time, be alert to the limits of doing so.

What ought to make us worry about the doctrine of original intention is the realization that the Supreme Court is the only institution in our national experience that has the power to *declare* history: that is, to articulate some understanding of the past and then compel the rest of society to conform its behavior based on that understanding. No Ministry of State Security, no Thought Police, has ever succeeded in establishing such authority. This power exists irrespective of the degree to which judicial perceptions of the past conform to reality or even to a consensus of trained historians. Even where the Court's history is at odds with the past, that judicial history, as absorbed into a decision, and then into a doctrine, becomes the progenitor of a rule of law. So without belaboring Justice Robert H. Jackson's concession that "judges are often not thorough or objective historians," it is worth reiterating that judicial history has had an impact on the evolution of our rights in the form of constitutional doctrines that govern us all.

Broadening the Bill of Rights

Alexander Wohl, a clerk for a federal appeals court judge, wrote in the August 1991 issue of the ABA Journal *that the changing interpretation of the Bill of Rights has enabled it to better protect the rights of all Americans.*

The founders of this nation were devoted to the idea of liberty. It was, however, a liberty we might not recognize today. Individual freedoms of expression were virtually nonexistent. Women, members of minority religions and, most prominently, black Americans were denied many if not all of the rights "guaranteed" to the rest of society.
Our celebration of the Bill of Rights should be tempered by this knowledge. But we may hope that the broadening interpretation of the Bill has meant a corresponding betterment for the citizenry.

The selective use of historical facts and interpretations, while doubtless suitable to writing a legal brief, is often disastrous in judicial opinions. Moreover, this use of history has often been undertaken to break precedent and enable a justice to get around established law. The famous *Dred Scott* case of 1857, which involved the Fifth Amendment to the Constitution, found Chief Justice Roger B. Taney declaring that, as a matter of history, persons of African-American descent had no rights that white persons were bound to respect. Since, Taney concluded, the framers had not intended for African-Americans to be covered by the Bill of Rights, then there was no way they could share in those rights—ever. . . .

Examining the Past

The past, unfortunately, reveals itself only ambiguously, and, once we recognize as much, there are real questions to be asked about whether sound public policy can actually rest on judicial interpretation rooted in original intentions. A few examples drawn from our early history will underscore how difficult it can be to apply the past to the present.

Proponents of original intent argue that judicial power is legitimate only as long as it remains faithful to the wishes of the framers of the Bill of Rights. Unfortunately, the framers' intentions are insufficiently clear on a number of important matters.

Take, for example, the seemingly simple question of what were the origins of the Bill of Rights. There is no doubt that its framers believed that the power of government was and would continue to be a constant threat to individual liberty. They drew this lesson from several sources rather than from just one, including the Magna Carta of 1215, subsequent English constitutional history leading up to and then flowing from the Glorious Revolution of 1689, and the common law tradition. But the American framers of the Bill of Rights had more immediate experience to draw on, including lessons from establishing their own colonial governments, of protecting their rights within the empire, and of fighting, winning, and then securing a revolution. But which of these sources most influenced the framers of the Bill of Rights?

One way of answering this question is to ask another question: was a bill of rights necessary in the first place? The framers of the Constitution in 1787 did not think so. They worried incessantly about protecting liberty from encroaching governmental power, but most of them concluded that a separate bill of rights was unnecessary. James Madison, the single most influential person at the Philadelphia convention, argued that since the Constitution was one of strictly enumerated powers, the federal government was prevented from passing legislation that would trample individual rights. Madison was hardly alone; for most delegates to the Philadelphia convention agreed that a bill of rights was unnecessary. It became essential only when its absence complicated significantly the process of ratifying the Constitution. Within hours of the delegates' signing the Constitution, George Mason, of Madison's Virginia, published a pamphlet, the central theme of which was that the absence of a "declaration of rights" made the Constitution unacceptable. Without limitations, Mason believed, the federal government would infringe the basic rights of the citizenry. Because the laws of the general government, according to Mason, would be paramount to the laws and constitutions of the states, state bills of rights would provide no protection at all against that central government.

The Anti-Federalist opponents of the Constitution repeated these arguments in the state ratification debates over the next ten months. While the federal convention had withheld from the ratifying conventions the power to propose amendments, the delegates in the states nonetheless adopted the tactic of offering "recommendatory amendments."

Madison was impressed by the strength of demands in his home state for the addition of a bill of rights, which was the one issue that seemed to coalesce the Constitution's various opponents. Virginia and New York both voted to ratify the Constitution, but they did so with the proviso that the first Congress would consider the addition of a bill of rights. The Federalists in general, and Madison in particular, gained ratification by promising to address the issue of a bill of rights in the first Congress. Thus, Madison, who originally discounted the necessity of such a bill, quickly grasped how essential it was in order to preserve his handiwork in Philadelphia. At the same time, Anti-Federalist critics reversed field. They now worried that its adoption would secure the strong central government that they did not want.

The point is not to accuse Madison—or the Anti-Federalists, for that matter—of being unprincipled. Instead, it is to affirm that compromise and political sagacity, as much as constitutional principles, shaped the framers' original reasons for adopting the Bill of Rights. Was the Bill of Rights necessary? Yes, but for reasons entirely different from those that the proponents of original intent would have us believe.

No Single Source

In discerning the original intentions of the framers, we need some idea of where they turned for authority. One of the most important problems presented by the doctrine of original intention is the matter of whose intentions we are speaking of: Madison's, as the chief architect? Or the intentions of the members of the conference committee that redrafted Madison's work? Or the intentions of the state legislatures that ratified only ten of the twelve amendments sent to them?

Madison borrowed conspicuously from several sources, and often what is most revealing is what he ignored. Of the twenty-six rights ultimately declared in the Bill of Rights, only four—due process, illegal seizures, fines, and jury trials—can be traced to the Magna Carta. While many present-day commentators point to our English inheritance of liberty, that connection was in fact quite weak.

Nor did Madison give much heed to the ninety-seven "recommendatory" amendments proposed by the ratifying conventions. His draft included only 17 percent of the rights they urged upon him. He purposefully ignored most of the proposed amendments because they seriously constrained the power of the new central government, something that even Madison, for all of his states' rights sympathies, could not tolerate.

Where, then, did Madison turn? Existing state bills of rights were certainly an important source. More than 60 percent of the rights proclaimed in Madison's draft were taken from these documents, and if one adds those rights that were ultimately put in the Bill of Rights—that is, the additions made to Madison's initial nine-amendment proposal—then more than 75 percent were from the state bills of rights.

The most comprehensive body of authority for Madison, however, actually predated the Revolution itself. This important source consisted of the various charters, compacts, and governing documents drawn up by the colonists themselves in the century and a half before the Revolution. Everything that was included in Madison's draft, in the revised draft of the conference committee, and in the federal Bill of Rights had previously been treated in these precursor documents such as the Mayflower Compact, the Massachusetts Charter of Liberties, and the Fundamental Orders of Connecticut. In short, the federal Bill of Rights summed up and encapsulated what colonial Americans had already taken to be their rights. There is, in fact, no single source to which we can turn today to discern these rights authoritatively. Instead, there are many sources.

Yet even if we know in a general way where these rights came from, we do not know what, in most instances, their framers and ratifiers actually thought they meant. The framers' own words are of little help. Proponents of an originalist reading of the Bill of Rights suggest that we can know, but such is certainly not the case. The problem with the originalists' position is that there is so little evidence left behind about what actually was said, let alone intended. The 1789 debates in Congress are sketchy, the discussions in the conference committee that revised Madison's proposed amendments are even sketchier, and the debates over ratification in the states are essentially nonexistent. We search, in vain, to find out exactly what the framers and ratifiers meant with regard to "free speech," the right to "bear arms," or "cruel and unusual punishment." Most often the evidence suggests that these Bill of Rights provisions were cast broadly not because a consensus existed over their precise meaning, but for just the opposite reason. There was sufficient disagreement about them that a consensus could be achieved only by stating them as majestic generalities. To have done otherwise would have threatened the fragile consensus upon which the new Constitution and government rested.

Furthermore, these very same pressures meant that all sides recognized that the rights listed in the Bill of Rights were not meant to be exhaustive. That is why Madison, Congress, and the states agreed to the Ninth and Tenth Amendments, which, while guaranteeing no specific rights, as did the first eight amendments, did outline divisions of powers within the Constitution. Both of these amendments were critical to fashioning written guarantees that would protect individual rights against encroachment by the national government. Their inclusion is particularly instructive because both of them affirm that the entire thrust of the Bill of Rights was not to list rights but instead to set broad substantive and procedural guarantees designed to bridle government. Indeed, the proponents of original intent misapprehend what the framers of the Bill of Rights did. The Bill of Rights was really not a catalog of rights; instead, it was a "bill of restraints," one that told the government where it could not encroach.

The Bill of Rights and the States

There remain, of course, the final issues of who was to interpret the Bill of Rights and against whom was it to apply—the nation or the states? These issues are at the heart of the contemporary criticism of the High Court and judicial review, since critics charge that the justices have usurped power that the framers never intended them to exercise, and that they have meddled in local and state affairs to a degree that would have horrified the framers. Once again, we have to be impressed by the ambiguity of the record.

The creation of an independent federal judiciary with status co-equal to that of the other branches was one of the important innovations of the federal Constitution. It was also a source of great concern among proponents of states' rights, who feared that the federal government would become, through the courts, an engine to oppress them. We know, however, that Madison shared none of this uncertainty when it came to the role of the federal judiciary in implementing the Bill of Rights. He advanced the key argument that the reason to adopt the Bill of Rights was that it offered additional *legal* protection against excessive legislative power. Since these guarantees would go into the Constitution, Madison insisted that "independent tribunals of justice will consider themselves in a peculiar manner the guardians of those rights." Madison intended that the newly created federal courts would be a countermajoritarian legal force to protect individual rights against the excesses of the political and popularly elected branches. He also expected that, as agents of the law, judges would give an impartial, lawful interpretation to rights that would bind the public in a way the political branches could never do.

We also know that, at least in its most important provisions, Madison expected that the Bill of Rights would be applied against the states and not just against the national government.

Madison's original draft included exactly such a provision.

But once again what Madison wanted was not what others agreed to. The Congressional conference committee that reviewed Madison's draft struck the state action provision from the Bill of Rights, making it apply only against the national government. Even after this action, considerable difference of opinion persisted over whether federal judges could invoke the Bill of Rights against state legislation, and whether state judges could invoke its terms against legislatures in their own states. As early as 1810, Chancellor James Kent of New York relied on the Fifth Amendment provision against the taking of property without just compensation to strike down an act of the New York state assembly. Moreover, throughout the pre-Civil War period all but the most extreme abolitionists argued not only that the framers had intended the Bill of Rights to apply against the states but that it could be used as a basis upon which to eradicate the peculiar institution of slavery. Chief Justice John Marshall in 1833 became so worried about the consequences to the Union of this antislavery vision of the Bill of Rights that in *Barron* v. *Baltimore* he rendered his famous opinion that the Bill of Rights applied only to the nation and not to the states. Yet, thirty-five years later, when the Reconstruction Congress debated the Fourteenth Amendment's due process, equal protection, and privileges and immunities clauses, several moderate and radical Republicans argued that the Bill of Rights had *always* applied to the states. Conservative Democrats were equally emphatic that it had not, and that by passing the Fourteenth Amendment it would not. There is, in sum, no clear answer to either the question of whether the framers of the Bill of Rights originally intended that it apply to the states or whether the framers of the Fourteenth Amendment meant to do so.

Today, of course, most of the Bill of Rights has been incorporated through the Fourteenth Amendment and applies against the states. The most controversial High Court decisions of this century—involving free speech and the press, separation of church and state, and the rights of the accused—have resulted from justices broadly construing the meaning of the Bill of Rights, often doing so, somewhat ironically for proponents of original intent, with a strong reliance on historical arguments.

What the framers of the Bill of Rights did was to put forth certain broad *concepts*—there could be no cruel and unusual punishment, there had to be due process—but they did not attempt to put forth *conceptions* (what exactly cruel and unusual punishment was, what a denial of due process precisely amounted to). Instead, they left to the judiciary the task of defining those notions, and of conceptualizing them. In essence, the history of the creation of the Bill of Rights leads us to one clear conclusion—the framers adopted broadly stated limitations on government, leaving to courts and judges the task of giving precise meaning to these majestic generalities.

This excursion into the historical meaning, scope, and interpretation of the Bill of Rights ought to give us pause in resorting to a doctrine of original intention. The current prophets of this doctrine argue that judicial power is only legitimate so long as it remains faithful to principles embraced by the framers. Unfortunately, the framers held often contradictory views and, as a result, the thin surviving historical record is marked by ambiguity, not clarity.

But does this conclusion mean that the framers themselves had no sense of original intent on matters of rights? Simply put, did the framers believe that what they did was going to bind future generations? The answer to that question is certainly, *yes*. These men had fought a revolution, seen the blood of friends and brothers shed, and passionately believed in what they were doing. As the words of the Constitution indicate, they meant to create a more perfect Union that was intended to endure for the ages. They did invoke the concept of original intent, but it differed significantly from that espoused by modern critics, such as Judge Bork and Attorney General Meese, of judicially protected constitutional rights. As James Madison observed in 1796: "Whatever veneration might be entertained for the body of men who formed our Constitution, the sense of that body could never be regarded as the oracular guide in expounding the Constitution."

Flexible Language

Of course, as citizens of a nation blessed with a written constitution, Americans must be bound by its words, must presume that those words have meaning, and must understand that meaning in light of how those words were used by their authors and by subsequent generations. But the Bill of Rights does not, like a cookbook, specify which ingredients, combined in what orders and amounts, will yield "liberty." Even more important, this character of the Bill of Rights was no accident, as we have seen. On many crucial questions, its framers, in order to establish a nation, selected language flexible enough to anticipate social, economic, and political crises. That is what Chief Justice John Marshall meant when he wrote that the Constitution was intended to "endure for ages to come and adapt to the various crises of human affairs."

That, in sum, was the framers' original "original intent." They expected Americans pragmatically, through the legal process, to fit the Bill of Rights to changing exigencies, but to do so in ways that would preserve the Union, sustain broad principles of human worth, maintain skepticism about government's power, and leave sufficient room for the community control that all of the framers knew was essential to true liberty. . . .

The federal judiciary is not an imperial force and the law explosion is not a catastrophe. The federal courts remain the branch with the least discretionary power and the one best suited to balancing freedom and community control while doing what the political branches—because they are political branches—cannot do: protect the rights of minorities from majority tyranny. In the circumstances of contemporary society, in which racial and gender equality are professed to a degree unknown to the framers, any other approach seems unsound. The great problem with the concept of original intent is not that it lacks validity, but that it lacks the importance with which it has been so solemnly invested. The notion that we can return to a simpler past and purer time, of less law and government, is illusory. . . .

Moreover, we should recognize that even amid the rights explosion of this century, liberty and community control remain unbalanced and justice remains unevenly distributed throughout the social order. The social categories of class, race, ethnicity, and gender continue to have powerful influence in shaping the distribution of rights. We know that white middle-class Americans are far more likely to benefit from the recent expansion of the right to counsel and Miranda warnings than are persons of color at the lower end of the social spectrum. In the case of the death penalty, the evidence is overwhelming that, despite the cruel and unusual punishment clause of the Eighth Amendment, African-Americans—especially lower class African-Americans that kill white persons—are far more likely to die at the hands of the state than are white offenders.

Yet even as we recognize these limitations, we can take comfort in the fact that the history of the Bill of Rights does teach us an important lesson—a lesson quite different from that of original intent. In the hands of the federal judiciary, the Bill of Rights has developed as a living organism. Justice Thurgood Marshall rightly says that "the true miracle was not the birth of the Bill of Rights, but its life, a life nurtured through two turbulent centuries of our own making, and a life embodying much good fortune that was not." It is fitting, therefore, to . . . "commemorate the suffering, struggle, and sacrifice that has triumphed over much of what was wrong with the original Bill of Rights, and observe the anniversary with hopes not realized and promises not fulfilled." Yet it is precisely those hopes . . . that sustain the importance of the Bill of Rights.

For Discussion

Chapter One

1. What examples of protections from different states' bills of rights does Brutus cite as being fundamental to the preservation of liberty? How many of these examples ultimately made it into the Bill of Rights?

2. What does Alexander Hamilton mean when he states that the original Constitution in its entirety is a bill of rights? Do you agree or disagree?

3. How well do you believe Thomas Jefferson responded to James Madison's objections to adding a bill of rights? Are there additional points you would have included? Possible rejoinders Madison could have made?

4. Both James Madison and Thomas Jefferson made predictions as to the effect of a bill of rights on America. Who do you believe was more prescient? Why?

Chapter Two

1. What causes the differences in George Hay's and the Fifth Congress's interpretations of the First Amendment? Which interpretation do you support? Why or why not?

2. What parallels exist between Theodore Schroeder's views on the Bill of Rights and James Madison's views on "parchment barriers" expressed more than a century earlier?

3. Critics have accused Oliver Wendell Holmes of being inconsistent in his reasoning in the *Schenck* and *Abrams* cases. Do the cases mark a changing of mind? Explain.

4. How would you compare the opinions of Theodore Schroeder and John H. Wigmore on the general state of free speech in the United States? Do the two men have different ideas on what free speech means? Explain.

5. Why is free speech important, according to Louis Brandeis? Are his views and reasoning significantly different from those of Edward T. Sanford? Of Oliver Wendell Holmes? Explain.

Chapter Three

1. List five reasons James Madison opposed religious taxes in 1785. Which reasons do you believe have the most relevance today?

2. The Presbytery of Hanover supported religious freedom and opposed an established church, but they concluded that religious taxes may be consistent with those beliefs. Do you agree or disagree? Are similar arguments being made today?

3. Why do you suppose Hugo Black paid close attention to a 1785 Virginia debate in determining a 1947 Supreme Court case?

4. Do you think the flag salute cases of the 1940s relate primarily to free speech or freedom of religion? Explain your answer.

5. In 1992 the Supreme Court ruled in *Lee v. Weisman* that prayers by officials or teachers in high school graduation ceremonies violate the Bill of Rights. Some argue that prayers would be acceptable if they were planned and said by students rather than public officials or clergy. What do you think? What do you think Hugo Black and Strom Thurmond would say?

6. Do you believe that the free exercise and establishment clauses of the First Amendment in regard to religion are in conflict? Why or why not?

Chapter Four

1. What reasons does Abraham Lincoln give for restricting civil liberties during the Civil War? Does Justice David Davis directly address any of Lincoln's points?

2. What factors external to the specific cases do you believe might have influenced Supreme Court rulings concerning Japanese internment? Do you believe the decisions justifying internments were mistaken? Why or why not?

3. Many people in the 1950s argued that since the goal of the Communist party was to create a totalitarian government with no freedom, giving communists freedom to speak, assemble, and distribute newspapers was pointless and potentially dangerous. Should free speech be granted to people who advocate the abolition of freedom? How does William O. Douglas respond to this question?

4. How does the Supreme Court decision in *Dennis v. United States* compare with the decisions discussed in Chapter Two? How do you think Oliver Wendell Holmes, applying the "clear and present danger" test, would have decided? Explain your answer.

Chapter Five

1. Synopsize the views of Supreme Court justices Stanley Matthews, John Marshall Harlan, Hugo Black, and William O. Douglas concerning the due process clause and the Bill of

Rights. Which comes closest to your own opinion? Explain.

2. The Supreme Court has ruled over the years that certain parts of the Bill of Rights were essential to "fundamental fairness" and hence should be applied to state governments under the Fourteenth Amendment. If you had to select the clauses and parts of the Bill of Rights that are descriptive of truly fundamental rights, which would you include? Which would you leave out? Explain your reasons.

3. Does Hugo Black demonstrate a consistent judicial philosophy in his rulings as excerpted in this and other chapters? How would you describe his philosophy?

4. Both William O. Douglas and Arthur Goldberg argue that a right to privacy exists, but they give different arguments to support that right. How does their reasoning about the Ninth Amendment and other parts of the Bill of Rights compare? Do you believe the Bill of Rights includes a right to privacy? Why or why not?

5. How would you summarize the fundamental difference of opinion between Eugene H. Methvin and William H. Dempsey Jr. concerning the Bill of Rights?

Chapter Six

1. Gary L. McDowell suggests in his viewpoint that the Supreme Court stretched the Bill of Rights beyond all recognition when it ruled in 1989 that state laws prohibiting the burning of the American flag were unconstitutional. What arguments does he use to support his assertion? Do you agree or disagree with him? Why?

2. What social and other conditions have changed in America in the two hundred years since the Bill of Rights was ratified, according to Kermit L. Hall? Can you think of any others?

3. Which viewpoints in the book do you believe Gary L. McDowell would find himself most in agreement with? Which would Kermit L. Hall agree with? Explain.

General

1. Do you believe Supreme Court justices should pay primary attention to the original intent of the writers of the Bill of Rights in deciding cases? Why or why not?

2. Do the viewpoints in this book make you feel more or less secure about your civil liberties being protected by the Bill of Rights? Why?

Chronology

1641	The Massachusetts General Court drafts the New England Body of Liberties, which is the first general statement of American liberties in colonial history, and which includes a right of petition and a statement of due process.
1663	Rhode Island becomes the first colony to grant religious freedom.
1689	The year of the Glorious Revolution in England, which culminates with a bill of rights declaring as unconstitutional the suspension of acts of Parliament, the levying of taxes without the consent of Parliament, the maintenance of a standing army in peacetime, the denial of the right of petition, and the infliction of cruel and unusual punishment.
1708	Connecticut passes the first dissenter statute in the colonies by granting "full liberty of worship" to Anglicans and Baptists, while still requiring the payment of town taxes for the benefit of Congregational churches only.
1765	The Stamp Act Congress calls for trial by jury, the right of petition, and the "full and free enjoyment of the rights and liberties" of American colonists.
1771	Fifty Baptists are jailed in Virginia for preaching a gospel contrary to the Anglican Book of Common Prayer.
1772	Colonists issue complaints against the writs of assistance, which were general search warrants leaving "our houses and even our bed chambers exposed to be ransacked."
1773	James Madison begins to investigate the question of religious tolerance even before he meets Thomas Jefferson.
1774	Eighteen Baptists are jailed in Massachusetts for their refusal to pay taxes to support the Congregational minister in the town of Warwick.

1776	Virginia becomes the first state to adopt a bill of rights when its Declaration of Rights passes the House of Burgesses.
	New Jersey provides that no one should "ever be obliged to pay tithes or taxes for the purpose of building any church or for the maintenance of any minister."
1776-1780	Seven additional states adopt bills of rights as part of their new state constitutions.
1777	Thomas Jefferson drafts a bill for religious freedom in Virginia, which states that "no man shall be forced to frequent or support any religious worship, place, or ministry whatsoever."
1778	The citizens of Massachusetts reject their new constitution because it does not include a bill of rights.
	The citizens of North Carolina insist that a bill of rights is more basic than its constitution and a necessary preface to any constitution.
1781	The Articles of Confederation are ratified without a single article to assure American citizens of basic personal freedoms, the assumption being that it was the role of the states to protect their citizens in this critical area.
1784	Thomas Jefferson writes *Notes on Virginia*, in which he argues for the exclusion of aliens from Virginia.
1785	The Virginia House of Burgesses passes Jefferson's bill for religious freedom without a "general assessment" that would require that taxes be raised and designated for religious purposes.
1787	The Constitutional Convention in Philadelphia drafts a new Constitution and submits it for state ratification. A resolution by George Mason and Elbridge Gerry proposing the inclusion of a bill of rights is rejected by convention delegates, including James Madison.
	The first federal bill of rights is included in the Northwest Ordinance. It includes a guarantee of freedom of religion, the right to trial by jury, habeas corpus and reasonable bail, and a ban on cruel and unusual punishments.
1788	The states hold special conventions to vote whether to ratify the Constitution. Opponents, such as Patrick Henry of Virginia, argue against ratification because

there is no bill of rights, the absence of which constitutes a "betrayal of the revolution."

Eleven of the thirteen states ratify the Constitution;
several states, including Massachusetts, Virginia, and
New York, propose constitutional amendments to
form a bill of rights.

Madison contributes to the Federalist Papers, among
them Federalist No. 10, in which he discusses the "latent causes of faction," the first of which is a "zeal for
different opinions concerning religion."

1789   James Madison opens debate in the first Congress by
proposing an amendment forbidding the establishment of "any national religion" or the infringement
of the "full and equal rights of conscience."

Congress agrees on twelve proposed amendments to
the Constitution. President George Washington sends
them to the states for ratification. New Jersey is the
first state to ratify ten of the twelve amendments: the
Bill of Rights.

1790   Congress sends out twelve amendments for ratification as the Bill of Rights. Two are eventually rejected:
a call for a fixed schedule for apportioning House
seats and a ban on House and Senate members from
altering their salaries "until an election of representatives shall have intervened."

1791   The Bill of Rights is ratified in the form of the first ten
amendments to the Constitution.

1798   Congress enacts the Alien and Sedition Acts to
counter pro-French feeling in the United States, restricting freedom of speech and press in the process.

1799   Thomas Jefferson and James Madison write the Kentucky and Virginia resolutions in opposition to what
they perceive as the coercive power of the federal
government expressed in the Alien and Sedition
Acts.

1802   The Anglican church is finally disestablished in the
state of Virginia.

1803   *Marbury v. Madison* establishes the principle of judicial review.

1804   President Thomas Jefferson pardons those convicted
under the Sedition Act of 1798.

1809-1817   At various points in his presidency James Madison
reveals his commitment to the complete separation of

church and state by opposing such measures as the appointment of chaplains and the granting of tax exemptions to "houses of worship," as well as by vetoing a bill to grant a charter of incorporation to the Anglican church in Washington, D.C., and by objecting to presidential proclamations of days of thanksgiving.

1833   Massachusetts becomes the last state to end its establishment of religion.

The Supreme Court rules unanimously that the Bill of Rights does not apply to state governments (*Barron v. Baltimore*).

1836   Congress adopts a "gag rule," which blocks discussion of antislavery petitions in that body.

1857   The Supreme Court upholds the right to one's property to the extent of forbidding the federal government to enact laws blocking the spread of slavery into the territories (*Dred Scott v. Sandford*).

1863   President Abraham Lincoln moves to suspend the writ of habeas corpus.

1866   The Supreme Court rebukes President Lincoln and affirms the primacy of the Constitution by holding that military courts may not be used to try civilians and that the necessity for imposing martial law "must be actual and present."

1868   The Fourteenth Amendment, guaranteeing equal protection under the law, is ratified.

1873   In the first judicial test of the Fourteenth Amendment, the *Slaughterhouse* cases, the Supreme Court narrowly interprets the amendment, arguing that its privileges, immunities, and equal protection clauses do not incorporate the Bill of Rights's guarantees to the states.

Congress passes the Comstock laws, named after crusader Anthony Comstock. The laws include birth control information within the definition of obscene material that is barred from federal mails.

1884   The Supreme Court decrees that the due process clause of the Fourteenth Amendment does not require state governments to provide the accused with the protections of the Fifth Amendment (*Hurtado v. California*).

1897   The Supreme Court rules that an ordinance restricting meetings on Boston Common is "no more an infringement" of the right of public assembly than is a person's refusing to grant the use of his house for the same reason (*Davis v. Massachusetts*).

1897 The Supreme Court rules for the first time that a clause in the Bill of Rights (the just compensation clause of the Fifth Amendment) applies to state governments via the due process clause of the Fourteenth Amendment (*Chicago, Burlington, & Quincy Railroad Company v. Chicago*).

1903 Congress passes the Anarchist Exclusion Act in the aftermath of the assassination of President William McKinley by a self-proclaimed anarchist.

1914 The Supreme Court formulates the exclusionary rule, providing that evidence collected by the government in violation of the Fourth Amendment's prohibition of "unlawful search and seizure" is inadmissible in a federal court. State courts are unaffected (*Weeks v. United States*).

1917 Congress passes the Espionage Act at the request of the Wilson administration, making it a crime to "willfully obstruct the recruiting or enlistment service of the United States."

The postmaster general notifies all postmasters to "keep a close eye" on all publications that might "embarrass or hamper the government in conducting the war."

The Civil Liberties Bureau, a forerunner of the American Civil Liberties Union (ACLU), is created to oppose the Espionage Act.

1918 Congress passes the Sedition Act in a sweeping attack on free speech during wartime.

1919 The Supreme Court upholds the constitutionality of the Espionage Act by upholding the conviction of socialist Charles Schenck for mailing antiwar and anti-draft pamphlets to draft-age men (*Schenck v. United States*).

The Supreme Court upholds the constitutionality of the Sedition Act by upholding the conviction of defendants who distributed leaflets opposing American intervention in the Russian civil war. Justice Holmes dissents and his statement of the "clear and present danger" test signals a coming change in the Court's thinking (*Abrams v. United States*).

1919-1920	The "Red scare" is underway as alien radicals are rounded up and summarily deported from the United States.
1920	The American Civil Liberties Union is founded under the leadership of Roger Baldwin.
1923	The president of the American Federation of Labor, Samuel Gompers, attacks the ACLU for supporting "revolutionary organizations," and the head of the United Mine Workers, John L. Lewis, charges that the ACLU is "communistic."
	The Supreme Court strikes down a Nebraska law that prohibited teaching in any language other than English (*Meyer v. Nebraska*).
1925	The trial of biology teacher John Scopes dramatizes the issue of academic freedom, although Scopes is convicted of violating Tennessee law by teaching the theory of evolution in his classroom.
	The Supreme Court affirms the conviction of Benjamin Gitlow, who was a founding member of the American Communist party, by declaring that his revolutionary pamphlet *The Left-Wing Manifesto* is not constitutionally protected speech. But the court goes on to rule that freedom of speech and the press are among those personal rights and liberties protected by the due process clause of the Fourteenth Amendment from abridgement or impairment by the states (*Gitlow v. New York*).
1926	H. L. Mencken is arrested in Boston for selling copies of his *American Mercury*, which the Boston Watch and Ward Society had declared obscene.
1928	The Supreme Court upholds a New York law banning the use of masks in Ku Klux Klan parades as a form of intimidation (*Bryant v. Zimmerman*).
	In a wiretapping case, Justice Louis Brandeis's dissenting opinion argues that the "right to be left alone is the most comprehensive of rights" adhering to American citizenship (*Olmstead v. United States*).
1929	The ACLU announces that it is "wholly opposed to any censorship whatever of films accompanied by speech."
1931	The Supreme Court rules that a California law banning the wearing of a red flag by a Communist party member was "vague and indefinite" and "repugnant

to the guarantee of liberty contained in the Fourteenth Amendment" (*Stromberg v. California*).

The Supreme Court holds that the First Amendment protects the press against prior restraint in a case involving an anti-Catholic, anti-Semitic, antiblack scandal sheet in Minnesota (*Near v. Minnesota*).

1931-1936 Twenty-one states and the District of Columbia pass laws requiring teachers to take loyalty oaths.

1933 President Franklin Roosevelt pardons the remaining World War I era victims of the Espionage and Sedition Acts.

1934 Communists disrupt a Socialist party rally in Madison Square Garden in New York City, thereby prompting some members of the ACLU to expel communists from that organization.

1937 The Supreme Court overturns the conviction of a Communist party organizer in Oregon for organizing a meeting in support of a longshoreman's strike on the grounds that "peaceable assembly for lawful discussion cannot be made a crime" (*DeJonge v. Oregon*).

The Supreme Court rules that the Constitution contains a hierarchy of rights, at the top of which are freedoms of speech and the press, which represent the "indispensable condition of nearly every other form of freedom" (*Palko v. Connecticut*).

1938 The April 11, 1938, issue of *Life* magazine is banned across the country because it published thirty-five pictures from a public health film, *The Birth of a Baby*.

The House of Representatives creates the House Un-American Activities Committee (HUAC) to investigate subversion within the United States.

1939 The states of Virginia, Massachusetts, Connecticut, and Georgia, none of which ratified the original Bill of Rights, finally do so on the 150th anniversary of the Constitution.

Attorney General Frank Murphy creates the Civil Liberties Unit, a forerunner of the Civil Rights Division of the Justice Department.

The American Library Association adopts the Library Bill of Rights, which stands in opposition to all forms of censorship and calls on libraries to select books without reference to the author's race, nationality, or political or religious views.

1940	Congress passes the Smith Act, or the Alien Registration Act, making it illegal to "advocate, abet, advise, or teach the duty, necessity, desirability, or propriety of overthrowing or destroying any government in the United States by force or violence."
	Ten states move to ban the Communist party from state ballots.
	In a case involving the right of a member of the Jehovah's Witnesses to proselytize in a Catholic neighborhood, the Supreme Court rules that religious belief is entitled to protection under the First Amendment. It also holds that the Fourteenth Amendment renders the state legislatures as "incompetent as Congress" to make any laws respecting "an establishment of religion" (*Cantwell v. Connecticut*).
	Elizabeth Gurley Flynn is purged from the board of the ACLU because of her membership in the Communist party.
1941	Within two weeks of the bombing of Pearl Harbor, Congress authorizes the president to create the Office of Censorship.
1942	The Smith Act is put to use as the Justice Department indicts twenty-nine Minneapolis teamsters who belonged to the Trotskyist Socialist Workers party.
	Some 120,000 Japanese-Americans are interned in concentration camps in one of the most blatant examples of wholesale violations of civil liberties in American history.
1943	The Supreme Court upholds the conviction of a Japanese-American for violating a curfew order, concluding that the power to wage war means the "power to wage war successfully" (*Hirabayashi v. United States*).
	The Supreme Court rules that a requirement to salute the flag is a violation of the free speech provision of the First Amendment (*West Virginia State Board of Education v. Barnette*).
1947	The Supreme Court unanimously invalidates the use of racially restrictive covenants in the sale of private housing (*Shelley v. Kraemer*).
	On National Bill of Rights Day Attorney General Tom C. Clark urges his fellow Americans to "ferret out those who cloak themselves under the Bill of Rights

and who would undermine our form of government."

President Harry S Truman issues Executive Order 9835, which creates the first Federal Loyalty Program.

Attorney General Tom C. Clark makes public the first official government list of subversive organizations operating in the United States.

HUAC captures headlines for the first time in many years with its investigation of communist influence in Hollywood.

1948   Twelve top leaders of the Communist party are indicted under the Smith Act.

1950   Congress passes the McCarran Act over President Truman's veto, requiring communists and "communist-action" organizations to register with the newly created Subversive Activities Control Board and to disclose their officers, finances, and membership.

Singer-actor and left-wing activist Paul Robeson is asked to surrender his passport on the grounds that one does not have a constitutional right to a passport, thereby effectively denying the already blacklisted Robeson an opportunity to make a living.

1951   The Supreme Court upholds the constitutionality of the Smith Act (*Dennis v. United States*).

1952   The Supreme Court rules that New York students may be released from public school classes to attend religious instruction of their choice (*Zorach v. Clausen*).

1954   Congress passes the Immunity Act, which allows federal prosecutors and congressional investigators to compel testimony from witnesses by conferring them with immunity from prosecution.

1957   The Supreme Court begins to restrict the Smith Act by overturning the convictions of a second tier of Communist party members. The Court amends the "clear and present danger" test, ruling that proof of advocacy of some specific criminal action is necessary for criminal prosecution (*Yates v. United States*).

The Supreme Court unanimously strikes down a Michigan law forbidding the sale to the general public of material "containing obscene language [tending] to incite minors to violence or depraved acts"

(*Butler v. Michigan*).

1958 The Supreme Court upholds the right of the National Association for the Advancement of Colored People (NAACP) to keep secret its membership lists, stating that to demand otherwise would be to restrain freedom of association (*NAACP v. Alabama*).

1959 The Supreme Court seems to move away from its 1957 Smith Act stance by upholding the conviction of a college professor who refused to answer HUAC questions on the basis of the First Amendment (*Barenblatt v. United States*).

1961 The Supreme Court rejects First Amendment claims of those who refuse to answer questions from HUAC (*Wilkinson v. United States*).

The Supreme Court incorporates the Fourth Amendment into the due process clause of the Fourteenth Amendment in ruling that evidence seized in violation of the Fourth Amendment cannot be used against a suspect (*Mapp v. Ohio*).

1962 The Supreme Court holds that even a nondenominational prayer in a public school is a religious activity "wholly inconsistent" with the First Amendment (*Engel v. Vitale*).

1963 The Supreme Court establishes the primary effect test for government aid to religion. If either the purpose or primary effect is to advance religion, then the "enactment exceeds the scope of the legislative powers" (*Sherbert v. Verner*).

The Supreme Court rules that an indigent defendant has a right to counsel (*Gideon v. Wainwright*).

1964 The Supreme Court overturns a libel suit against the *New York Times*, holding that under the First Amendment, "debate on public issues should be uninhibited, robust, and wide open" (*New York Times Company v. Sullivan*).

The Supreme Court rules that right to counsel under the Sixth Amendment begins when a suspect is in custody and when questioning becomes accusatory (*Escobedo v. Illinois*).

1965 In overturning a Connecticut law banning the sale and distribution of contraceptive devices, the Supreme Court cites a right to privacy that is implied, but not explicitly stated, in the Bill of Rights

(*Griswold v. Connecticut*).

1966 The Supreme Court rules that a suspect in custody not only has a right to counsel, but also a more basic right not to be self-incriminating (*Miranda v. Arizona*).

The Supreme Court orders the seating of Georgia state legislator Julian Bond, who had been denied his seat because of his antiwar views (*Bond v. Floyd*).

1967 The Supreme Court upholds the conviction of an antiwar protester who burned his draft card in a public demonstration on the steps of the South Boston courthouse (*United States v. O'Brien*).

1968 The Supreme Court refuses to strike down a New York program of lending state-owned textbooks without charge to church-related private schools (*Board of Education v. Allen*).

1969 The Supreme Court upholds the right of a junior high school student to wear a black armband in protest against the war in Vietnam (*Tinker v. Des Moines Independent School District*).

In *Brandenburg v. Ohio*, a case involving the Ku Klux Klan, the Supreme Court rules that radical political speech, including speech that advocates violence, is protected by the First Amendment, unless such speech is "directed to inciting or producing imminent lawless action" and is likely to do so.

1970 The Supreme Court holds that tax exemptions granted to church properties do not constitute a violation of the establishment clause of the First Amendment (*Walz v. Tax Commission*).

Congress passes the Fair Credit Reporting Act, which requires private credit bureaus to disclose to individuals all information contained in their files.

1971 The Supreme Court permits the continued publication of the *Pentagon Papers*, holding that the dominant purpose of the First Amendment is to "prohibit the widespread practice of governmental suppression of embarrassing information" (*New York Times Company v. United States*).

1972 The Supreme Court holds that an Amish parent can disobey a valid law of the state of Wisconsin by not having a school-age child attend school (*Wisconsin v. Yoder*).

1973 The Supreme Court extends the right of privacy to include a woman's right to have an abortion under protection of the Fourteenth Amendment (*Roe v. Wade*).

1974   The official list of subversive organizations is withdrawn.

The Federal Privacy Act is passed, restricting disclosure of information from government files without the permission of the individual in question.

1976   The Supreme Court rules that restrictions on campaign spending by a politician on his or her own behalf constitute an infringement on freedom of speech (*Buckley v. Valeo*).

1977   The village of Skokie, Illinois, tries to ban a Nazi demonstration, thereby provoking a divisive battle within the ACLU over the lengths to which freedom of assembly might be taken.

1981   The Supreme Court declares unconstitutional an Arkansas law requiring balanced treatment of evolution and creationism in schools on the grounds that it violates the establishment clause of the First Amendment (*McLean v. Arkansas Board of Education*).

1983   Feminists enter the censorship debate by arguing that restrictions on pornography ought to be permitted because such literature discriminates against women.

1984   The Supreme Court holds that a crèche on public property does not violate the establishment clause of the First Amendment (*Lynch v. Donnelly*).

1987   The Supreme Court invalidates a Louisiana law that requires the teaching of scientific creationism (*Edwards v. Aquillard*).

1988   Congress seeks to atone for the World War II internment of Japanese-Americans by issuing an official apology and authorizing $20,000 in reparations to each surviving victim.

1989   In *Texas v. Johnson* the Supreme Court rules that burning the American flag is a form of symbolic speech protected under the First Amendment.

1989-1991   The bicentennial of the debate over and ratification of the Bill of Rights occasions a larger national debate over the state of civil liberties in a free society.

Annotated Bibliography

Ellen Alderman and Caroline Kennedy, *In Our Defense: The Bill of Rights in Action*. New York: William Morrow, 1991. A history of the Bill of Rights, featuring interviews and profiles of people who have brought important cases to the Supreme Court.

Raymond Arsenault, ed., *Crucible of Liberty: Two Hundred Years of the Bill of Rights*. New York: Free Press, 1991. An anthology of essays by historians, examining the evolution of the Bill of Rights.

Rosalyn Fraad Baxandall, *Works on Fire: The Life and Writings of Elizabeth Gurley Flynn*. New Brunswick, NJ: Rutgers University Press, 1987. A study of a leading radical of the 1930s who was purged by the American Civil Liberties Union because of her membership in the Communist party.

Walter Berns, *The First Amendment and the Future of American Democracy*. Washington, DC: Regnery, Gateway, 1985. A conservative critique of what the author regards as the excesses of First Amendment protection in twentieth-century America.

Alexander Bickel, *The Least Dangerous Branch*. New York: Bobbs-Merrill, 1962. A constitutional history of the political role of the Supreme Court and the use of judicial review.

Alexander Bickel and Benno Schmidt, *The Judiciary and Responsible Government*. New York: Macmillan, 1984. A constitutional lawyer's history of the White Court during the Progressive Era.

Richard Bingham, *Civil Liberties and Nazis*. New York: Praeger, 1985. An examination of the free speech issues involved when the American Nazi party tried to parade in the heavily Jewish suburb of Skokie, Illinois.

David Bodenhamer, *Fair Trial*. New York: Oxford University Press, 1992. A history of the rights of the accused in America from colonial times to the 1980s, including analyses of the Bill of Rights and the Fourteenth Amendment.

David Bodenhamer and James Ely Jr., eds., *The Bill of Rights in Modern America*. Bloomington: Indiana University Press, 1993. A series of essays on current interpretations of the Bill of Rights as it has been applied in this century.

Lee Bollinger, *The Tolerant Society*. New York: Oxford University Press,

1986. A history that argues for tolerating the most extreme speech, not necessarily because truth will eventually prevail, but because there is no absolute truth.

Paul Boyer, *Purity in Print*. New York: Scribner's, 1968. A history of literary censorship during the 1920s when freedom of expression was seriously testing its still unsteady wings.

Irving Brant, *James Madison: Father of the Constitution, 1787-1800*. Indianapolis: Bobbs-Merrill, 1950. The volume in a multivolume biography of Madison that deals with Madison's role in the creation of the Bill of Rights.

William Brennan, *The Bill of Rights and the States*. Santa Barbara, CA: Center for the Study of Democratic Institutions, 1961. A study of the evolution of the Supreme Court's application of the Bill of Rights to the states, written by a leading member of the Warren court.

Thomas J. Burke Jr., ed., *Man and State: Religion, Society, and the Constitution*. Hillsdale, MI: Hillsdale College Press, 1988. A collection of essays by historians and legal commentators arguing that the writers of the Bill of Rights wanted America to be rooted in Christian values and did not intend a strict separation of religion and government.

James MacGregor Burns and Stewart Burns, *A People's Charter: The Pursuit of Rights in America*. New York: Knopf, 1991. A history of America, focusing on its people's desire and struggle for rights, including the Federalist–anti-Federalist controversy that resulted in the Bill of Rights and subsequent labor, women's rights, civil rights, and other movements that sought to expand the Bill of Rights.

David Caute, *The Great Fear*. New York: Simon and Schuster, 1978. A history of cold war era anticommunism and the drive for enforced conformity, written from the perspective of a critic on the left.

Zechariah Chafee, *Free Speech in the United States*. Cambridge, MA: Harvard University Press, 1941. A classic history of free speech cases in the federal court system during the first four decades of the twentieth century.

Lawrence Chamberlain, *Loyalty and Legislative Action*. Ithaca, NY: Cornell University Press, 1951. A study of the investigations of the New York state legislature into allegedly subversive activities between World War I and the early cold war period.

Victor Cline, ed., *Where Do You Draw the Line?* Provo, UT: Brigham Young Press, 1974. A collection of essays written by those who favor some form of censorship of mass media material considered harmful to children.

Harry Clor, *Obscenity and Public Morality*. Chicago: University of Chicago Press, 1969. Both an analysis and a defense of the role of censorship in a pluralistic society.

Henry Steele Commager, *Majority Rule and Minority Rights*. New York: Oxford University Press, 1943. A thoroughly Jeffersonian statement for the acceptance of majoritarian principles as expressed through the democratic process.

Thomas Curry, *The First Freedoms*. New York: Oxford University Press, 1986. A history of church-state relations in the colonial period, culminating with the passage of the Bill of Rights.

Irving Dilliard, ed., *One Man's Stand for Freedom: Mr. Justice Black and the Bill of Rights*. New York: Knopf, 1963. A short biography and collection of Supreme Court opinions by Associate Justice Hugo Black, one of the most influential interpreters of the Bill of Rights to sit on the Supreme Court.

Frank Donner, *The Age of Surveillance*. New York: Knopf, 1980. A critical history of federal government surveillance from the Red scare of 1919-1920 through the Hoover years and Watergate.

Norman Dorsen, *Our Endangered Rights*. New York: Pantheon, 1972. A ringing defense of civil liberties written by a leader of the American Civil Liberties Union.

William O. Douglas, *The Court Years, 1939-1975*. New York: Random House, 1980. The autobiography of a Supreme Court justice and his role in expanding First Amendment rights during his long tenure.

Richard Drinnon, *Rebel in Paradise*. Chicago: University of Chicago Press, 1961. A biography of American radical Emma Goldman, who was deported during the Red scare of 1919-1920.

Gerald Dunne, *Hugo Black and the Judicial Revolution*. New York: Simon and Schuster, 1977. An essentially sympathetic biography of the Supreme Court justice who was a purist of the First Amendment.

Thomas Emerson, *The System of Freedom of Expression*. New York: Vintage, 1970. A discussion of challenges from the left and right in First Amendment cases involving the press, privacy, obscenity, libel, and academic freedom.

Morris Ernst, *The Best Is Yet . . . .* New York: Harper Brothers, 1945. The autobiography of a leading member of the American Civil Liberties Union and one who did not believe that the protections of civil liberties in the United States ought to be extended to communists, who by definition did not believe in the principle of civil liberties.

Felix Frankfurter, *Felix Frankfurter Reminisces*. New York: Doubleday, 1962. The autobiography of a justice whose lot it was to stand against Black and Douglas, who were both absolutists on the question of the First Amendment.

Fred Friendly, *Minnesota Rag*. New York: Random House, 1981. A history that culminates in the Supreme Court case of *Near v. Minnesota*, in which the Court significantly strengthened the freedom of the press.

Todd Gitlin, *The Sixties*. New York: Bantam, 1987. A history of what the author calls "years of hope, days of rage," written by a member of the radical group Students for a Democratic Society, and chronicling government violations of civil liberties during this turbulent decade.

Ira Glasser, *Visions of Liberty: The Bill of Rights for All Americans*. New York: Arcade Publishing, 1991. A general history that focuses on important twentieth-century Supreme Court rulings that have expanded the scope of the Bill of Rights. Written by the executive director of the American Civil Liberties Union.

Mary Ann Glendon, *Rights Talk: The Impoverishment of Political Discourse*. New York: Free Press, 1991. A Harvard law professor argues for a renewed emphasis on community and responsibility instead of continued focus on individual rights.

Walter Goodman, *The Committee*. New York: Farrar, Straus, and Giroux, 1968. A contemporary history of the House Un-American Activities Committee and its investigations into possible communist infiltration of American institutions.

Rosalie Gordon, *Nine Men Against America*. New York: Adair and Company, 1958. A highly critical history of the Supreme Court and what the author regards as the Court's attack on American liberties.

Arthur Garfield Hays, *Let Freedom Ring*. New York: Liveright, 1937.A first-hand account of important American Civil Liberties Union cases, written by a leading attorney for that organization.

Eugene Hickok, *The Bill of Rights: Original Meaning and Current Understanding*. Charlottesville: University of Virginia Press, 1991. An attempt to look at the issue of original intent in the light of recent interpretations and implementations of the Bill of Rights.

Robert Highsaw, *Edward Douglas White: Defender of the Conservative Faith*. Baton Rouge: Louisiana State University Press, 1981. A biography and examination of the constitutional philosophy of the conservative chief justice who held that post from 1910 through the Red scare years.

H. N. Hirsch, *The Enigma of Felix Frankfurter*. New York: Basic Books, 1981. A biography of the Supreme Court justice who was regarded as a liberal when appointed to the Court, but who did not take expected liberal positions on freedom of speech, press, and religion issues.

Peter Iron, *The Courage of Their Convictions*. New York: Free Press, 1988. Sixteen case studies of plaintiffs who took their convictions in civil liberties cases all the way to the Supreme Court.

Joan Jensen, *The Price of Vigilance*. Chicago: Rand McNally, 1968. A history of the free-lance vigilantism of the American Protective League and its violations of civil liberties between 1917 and 1919.

Donald Johnson, *The Challenge to American Freedoms*. Lexington: University of Kentucky Press, 1983. A history of the founding and early years of the American Civil Liberties Union, which was born in the antiradical hysteria of World War I.

Harry Kalven, *A Worthy Tradition*. New York: Harper and Row, 1988. A legal and intellectual history of the development of free speech doctrine from the 1790s through the Warren court.

David Kennedy, *Over Here: The First World War and American Society*. New York: Oxford University Press, 1980. A general social history of the home front during World War I, the occasion for wholesale violations of civil liberties.

Samuel Konefsky, *The Legacy of Holmes and Brandeis*. New York: Macmillan, 1956. A comparative study of the constitutional philosophies of the two justices whose dissenting opinions in the 1920s helped prepare the way for subsequent protections of civil liberties.

Milton Konvitz, *First Amendment Freedoms*. Ithaca, NY: Cornell University Press, 1963. An inclusive history of the various freedoms and their uneven protection throughout American history.

Milton Konvitz, ed., *Aspects of Liberty*. Ithaca, NY: Cornell University Press, 1958. A general history of the fundamental freedoms of religion, press, speech, assembly, and petition.

Stanley Kutler, *The American Inquisition*. New York: Hill and Wang, 1982. A series of essays dealing with specific cold war-related cases of violations of civil liberties by the U.S. government in its hunt for subversives.

Corliss Lamont, *Freedom Is as Freedom Does*. New York: Horizon, 1956. Part memoir and part tract, this volume is written from the perspective of the persecuted left and calls for freedom of expression even as it questions free expression for those on the right.

Peggy Lamson, *Roger Baldwin: Founder of the ACLU*. Boston: Houghton Mifflin, 1976. More an annotated interview with, than a biography of, the man who more than any other single individual was responsible for the founding of the ACLU.

Edward Larson, *Trial and Error*. New York: Oxford University Press, 1985. A recent history of the Scopes trial, including the debate about academic freedom and creationism through current cases.

James E. Leahy, *The First Amendment, 1791-1991*. Jefferson, NC: McFarland and Company, 1991. An examination of historical issues surrounding the First Amendment and its protection of freedoms of speech, press, religion, and association over its first two centuries.

Leonard Levy, *Jefferson and Civil Liberties: The Darker Side*. Cambridge, MA: Harvard University Press, 1963. A critical history of Thomas Jefferson, the libertarian who on occasion, as president, departed from his libertarian principles.

Leonard Levy, *Legacy of Suppression: Freedom of Speech and Press in Early American History*. Cambridge, MA: Belknap Press, 1960. A history of the difficulties in bringing the Bill of Rights to life in the early national period.

Anthony Lewis, *Gideon's Trumpet*. New York: Random House, 1964. A contemporary history of the Supreme Court case *Gideon v. Wainright*, which secured the right of counsel for indigents.

Anthony Lewis, *Make No Law*. New York: Random House, 1991. A history of the landmark Supreme Court case *New York Times Company v. Sullivan*, and its implications for a free press.

Dumas Malone, *Jefferson and the Ordeal of Liberty*. Boston: Little, Brown, 1962. The third volume in Malone's magisterial biography of Jefferson, the focus of which is the libertarian Jefferson of the post-revolutionary era.

Alpheus T. Mason, *Brandeis: A Free Man's Life*. New York: Viking, 1946. The first major biography of this important Supreme Court justice, based largely on materials provided by Brandeis himself.

Henry Mayer, *Son of Thunder*. New York: Watts, 1986. The most recent comprehensive biography of Patrick Henry, who was at the forefront of the demand for the inclusion of a Bill of Rights in the Constitution.

Alexander Meiklejohn, *Free Speech and Its Relation to Self-Government*. New York: Harper and Row, 1948. Originally University of Chicago lectures, this volume attacks not only government violations of free speech, but also communists and fascists who used free speech for their own purposes without believing in its principles.

Walter Metzger, *Academic Freedom in the Age of the University*. New York: Columbia University Press, 1961. A history of the problems and possibilities of free speech in the classroom in the first half of the twentieth century.

John C. Miller, *Crisis in Freedom*. Boston: Little, Brown, 1951. A general history of the Alien and Sedition Acts passed during the Federalist era.

William Miller, *The First Liberty*. New York: Knopf, 1986. A history of the colonial and revolutionary background to freedom of religion.

Charles Morgan, *One Man, One Voice*. New York: Holt, Rinehart, and Winston, 1979. A highly opinionated but very readable memoir written by a veteran member of the ACLU and a key civil rights lawyer of the 1960s.

Richard Morgan, *Disabling America: The "Rights" Industry in Our Time*. New York: Basic Books, 1984. A conservative criticism of recent civil liberties litigation in the United States.

Samuel Eliot Morison, Frederick Merk, and Frank Freidel, *Dissent in Three American Wars*. Cambridge, MA: Harvard University Press, 1970. A brief analysis of antiwar protest and freedom of speech in the War of 1812, the Mexican War, and the Spanish-American War.

Paul Murphy, *The Constitution in Crisis Times, 1918-1969*. New York: Harper and Row, 1971. A general history of this half-century in the life of the Constitution, written for the authority and the general reader alike.

Paul Murphy, *The Meaning of Freedom of Speech*. Westport, CT: Greenwood Press, 1972. A history of an increasing commitment to First Amendment freedoms and a decreasing concern for property rights, from Woodrow Wilson through Franklin Roosevelt.

Paul Murphy, *World War I and the Origins of Civil Liberties*. New York: Norton, 1979. Historical sketch of government machinery (intellectual or otherwise) for suppression of dissent during and after World War I.

Victor Navasky, *Naming Names*. New York: Viking, 1980. A history of government agencies, especially the House Un-American Activities Committee, and their efforts to root out communism by forcing former communists or fellow travelers to testify against their one-time comrades.

Russell Nye, *Fettered Freedom*. East Lansing: Michigan State University Press, 1949. A history of the slave issue and freedom of speech for pre-Civil War abolitionists.

William O'Neill, *The Last Romantic: A Life of Max Eastman*. New York: Oxford University Press, 1978. A biography of one of the most important World War I dissenters.

H. C. Peterson and Gilbert Fite, *Opponents of War*. Madison: University of Wisconsin Press, 1957. An account of civil liberties violations resulting from the crusade and accompanying hysteria surrounding the American entry into World War I.

Leo Pfeffer, *Church, State, and Freedom*. Boston: Beacon Press, 1967. A constitutional history of church-state relations, written from the perspective of one who believes in a high wall of separation between the two.

Richard Polenberg, *Fighting Faiths*. New York: Viking, 1987. A fascinating history of the Abrams case, which produced the Holmes dissent and the doctrine of clear and present danger.

Richard Gid Powers, *Secrecy and Power*. New York: Free Press, 1987. A critical but fair-minded biography of J. Edgar Hoover and his role in promoting the FBI, sometimes at the expense of American civil liberties.

William Preston, *Aliens and Dissenters*. Cambridge, MA: Harvard University Press, 1963. A history of federal government restraints on radicals, dissenters, and aliens from the McKinley assassination through the 1920s.

Richard Randall, *Censorship of the Movies*. Madison: University of Wisconsin Press, 1968. Path-breaking study of the history of film censorship from the early efforts at self-censorship in the 1920s through the openness of the 1960s.

Alan Reitman, ed., *The Pulse of Freedom*. New York: Norton, 1975. A collection of highly descriptive but occasionally highly polemical essays concerning American liberties from the 1920s through the 1970s, commemorating the first fifty years of the American Civil Liberties Union.

Charles Rembar, *The End of Obscenity*. New York: Random House, 1968. A history of censorship issues during the rebellious and experimental 1960s and an argument against censorship, given the difficulty in defining obscenity.

Fred Rodell, *Nine Men*. New York: Random House, 1955. A political rather than constitutional history of the Supreme Court from 1790 to the middle of the twentieth century.

Robert Rutland, *James Madison: Founding Father*. New York: Macmillan, 1987. The most recent single-volume biography of the acknowledged father of the Bill of Rights.

Robert Rutland, *The Ordeal of the Constitution*. Norman: University of Oklahoma Press, 1966. A study of the role of the anti-Federalists in the battle for ratification of the Constitution and their insistence on the inclusion of a Bill of Rights.

Nick Salvatore, *Eugene V. Debs: Citizen and Socialist*. Urbana: University of Illinois Press, 1982. A biography of the leading American socialist of the early part of the twentieth century and his clashes with authority over freedom of speech and assembly issues.

Ellen Schrecker, *No Ivory Tower*. New York: Oxford University Press, 1986. A critical history of the impact of McCarthyism on American higher education.

Theodore Schroeder, *Free Speech for Radicals*, New York: Burt Franklin, 1969. A collection of speeches and articles of an important free speech activist that were originally published in 1916.

Bernard Schwartz, *The Bill of Rights: A Documentary History*. New York: Chelsea House, 1971. Reprints primary sources for the background to and debates over the Bill of Rights.

Bernard Schwartz, *The Great Rights of Man*. New York: Oxford University Press, 1980. A history of the Bill of Rights from its background through its creation and evolution.

Bernard Schwartz, *Super Chief*. New York: New York University Press, 1987. An essentially sympathetic biography of Earl Warren and a history of the Warren court.

James Simon, *Independent Journey: The Life of William O. Douglas*. New York: Harper and Row, 1980. An essentially sympathetic biography of one of the leading absolutists on First Amendment issues in the history of the Supreme Court.

Donald Smith, *Zechariah Chafee, Jr.: Defender of Liberty and Law*. Cambridge, MA: Harvard University Press, 1986. A biography of the leading constitutional scholar on First Amendment issues during the years between the world wars.

James Morton Smith, *Freedom's Fetters*. Ithaca, NY: Cornell University Press, 1956. A history of the Alien and Sedition Acts and their impact on the early development of civil liberties in the United States.

Rodney A. Smolla, *Free Speech in an Open Society*. New York: Knopf, 1992. An examination of free speech and First Amendment controversies in American society and history, generally criticizing those who would limit free speech.

Frank Sorauf, *The Wall of Separation*. Princeton, NJ: Princeton University Press, 1976. A well-crafted study of sixty-seven cases bearing on the critical subject of church-state relations. Suggests that the religious preference of judges is a significant factor in how they decide these cases.

Anson P. Stokes and Leo Pfeffer, *Church and State in the United States*. New York: Harper and Row, 1950. A general overview of church-state relations with an emphasis on constitutional and social history.

Philipa Strum, *Louis D. Brandeis: Justice for the People*. New York: Cambridge University Press, 1984. A largely sympathetic political and intellectual biography of a legal theorist and political activist, both on and off the Supreme Court.

John M. Swomley, *Religious Liberty and the Secular State*. Buffalo, NY: Prometheus Books, 1987. The chairperson of the American Civil Liberties Union subcommittee on church-state relations argues that the U.S. Constitution and the Bill of Rights were intended to create a strict separation of church and state and that government should neither aid nor impede religion.

Athan Theoharis, *Spying on Americans*. Philadelphia: Temple University Press, 1978. A history of political surveillance in the United States from the early years of the FBI through the Watergate era.

Helen E. Veit, Kenneth R. Bowling, and Charlene Bangs Bickford, eds., *Creating the Bill of Rights: The Documentary Record from the First Federal Congress*. Baltimore, MD: Johns Hopkins University Press. A collection of congressional debate excerpts, private correspondence, and other primary source materials that focus on the first Federal Congress of 1789-1790, which created the Bill of Rights as we know it.

Samuel Walker, *In Defense of American Liberties*. New York: Oxford University Press, 1990. A sympathetic general history of the American Civil Liberties Union with an emphasis on its role in important Supreme Court cases and its internal disputes over such divisive issues as the civil liberties of communists during the cold war.

Samuel Walker, *Popular Justice: A History of American Criminal Justice*. New York: Oxford University Press, 1980. A history of the criminal justice system from the colonial period to the late twentieth century, which argues that popular control of the system is responsible for both its strengths and weaknesses.

Earl Warren, *The Memoirs of Earl Warren*. New York: Doubleday, 1977. An autobiography dealing with the thoughts and maneuverings of the chief justice who presided over the Court during its years of expanding First Amendment freedoms.

Leon Whipple, *The Story of Civil Liberty in the United States*. New York: Vanguard Press, 1927. A history of important civil liberties cases from 1776 to 1917, with an emphasis on the lack of tolerance for minority views.

John W. Whitehead, *The Rights of Religious Persons in Public Education*. Wheaton, IL: Crossway Books, 1991. A case made for greater accommodation for religious students, teachers, and practices in American public schools, with a critical analysis of Supreme Court rulings on the separation of church and state.

Bob Woodward, *The Brethren*. New York: Simon and Schuster, 1979. An outsider's rare glimpse at the inner workings and political dealings of the Supreme Court.

Melvyn Zarr, *The Bill of Rights and the Police*. Dobbs Ferry, NY: Oceana Publications, 1970. A history of the ongoing conflict between law enforcement agencies and the ten amendments, which are sometimes seen to be on a collision course with the work of those agencies.

Index